BARBECUE LOVER'S
THE CAROLINAS

Restaurants, Markets, Recipes & Traditions

Robert F. Moss

Globe Pequot

GUILFORD, CONNECTICUT

For Bobby

Globe
Pequot

An imprint of Rowman & Littlefield

Distributed by NATIONAL BOOK NETWORK

Copyright © 2015 by Rowman & Littlefield

All photos by the author unless otherwise noted.

Maps: Alena Joy Pearce © Rowman & Littlefield

British Library Cataloguing in Publication Information Available

Library of Congress Cataloging-in-Publication Data
Moss, Robert F.
Barbecue lover's the Carolinas : restaurants, markets, recipes & traditions / Robert F. Moss.
pages cm
Includes bibliographical references and index.
ISBN 978-0-7627-9198-9 (paperback : alkaline paper) — ISBN 978-1-4930-1601-3 (electronic)
1. Barbecuing—North Carolina—Guidebooks. 2. Barbecuing—South Carolina—Guidebooks. 3. Restaurants—North Carolina—Guidebooks. 4. Restaurants—South Carolina—Guidebooks. 5. Markets—North Carolina—Guidebooks. 6. Markets—South Carolina—Guidebooks. I. Title.
TX840.B3M68 2015
641.7'609756—dc23

2015008981

∞ The paper used in this publication meets the minimum requirements of American National Standard for Information Sciences—Permanence of Paper for Printed Library Materials, ANSI/NISO Z39.48-1992.

All the information in this guidebook is subject to change. We recommend that you call ahead to obtain current information before traveling.

CONTENTS

ABOUT THE AUTHOR

Robert F. Moss is a food writer and culinary historian living in Charleston, South Carolina. He is the Contributing Barbecue Editor for *Southern Living*, the Southern Food Correspondent for *Serious Eats*, and a frequent contributor to the *Charleston City Paper*. His work has also appeared in publications such as *Garden & Gun*, the *Los Angeles Times*, the *Charlotte Observer*, and *Early American Life*. Robert is the author of *Barbecue: The History of an American Institution* (2010), the first full-length history of barbecue in the United States, and *Going Lardcore: Adventures in New Southern Dining* (2012), a collection of essays about dining in the modern South. A native of Greenville, South Carolina, Robert attended Furman University and received a Ph.D. in English from the University of South Carolina.

ACKNOWLEDGMENTS

This book wouldn't be possible without the contributions of many barbecue lovers in the Carolinas and beyond. John Shelton Reed, William McKinney, and Jeff Allen helped me track down worthy restaurants to include in the guide, and Jeff introduced me to the fine art of cinderblock pit construction and all-night whole hog cookery. Many thanks as well go to Rodney Scott of Scott's Bar-B-Que in Hemingway, South Carolina, for sharing so many tips and insights and so much fantastic barbecue over the past few years.

Robert Donovan, Denny Culbert, Nicholas McWhirter, and Jonathan Boncek contributed splendid photographs for the book. A special thanks to all the pitmasters who took the time to talk with me about their craft, particularly Samuel Jones of Skylight Inn, Chip Stamey of Stamey's, and Aaron Siegel of Fiery Ron's Home Team BBQ, and to barbecue evangelists Lake High and Jim Early for their guidance, recipes, and enduring passion for traditional barbecue.

I still owe my agent, David Hale Smith, a trip to Scott's for helping get this thing off the ground. Tracee Williams and Lynn Zelem at Globe Pequot took a raw manuscript and transformed it into a finished book.

Most of all, I have to thank my wife, Jennifer, and my two sons, Bobby and Charlie, who accompanied me on multiple "barbecue tours" across the Carolinas. It wouldn't have been nearly as much fun without you guys along.

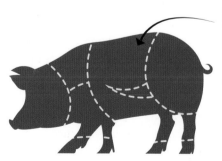

FRESH
BEST IN TOWN!

INTRODUCTION

To outsiders, many aspects of barbecue in the Carolinas seem odd. For starters, there's our obsession with pork. Send a Carolinian up to a buffet with instructions to bring you back some barbecue, and it's pretty certain what you'll get. That buffet may be brimming with baby back ribs, chicken quarters, and maybe even sliced brisket, all of which have been slow cooked on a hickory-fired pit, but the plate that comes back to you will invariably be piled high with pork.

This is not to say that no one in the Carolinas ever eats brisket, but only a handful of restaurants in the region actually cook it well. Barbecued chicken is a Carolina menu staple, almost as omnipresent as pig, but it will always be called just that: "barbecued chicken." The phrase *pork barbecue* sounds acceptable if somewhat redundant to Carolinian ears, but you'll never hear the term *chicken barbecue*. It just sounds wrong. *Barbecue*, used as a noun, means pork, though you can use it as a verb to mean any of the lesser meats cooked via barbecue techniques.

There's not a single restaurant in this guide that does not serve pork (be it pulled, chopped, sliced, or all of the above). But that's not the only distinctive characteristic to barbecue in the Carolinas. There are also our unique barbecue stews—Brunswick in North Carolina, hash and rice in South Carolina. The Brunswick variety is well known in Virginia and Georgia as well (in fact, it originated in Virginia—see "The Origin of Brunswick Stew" sidebar, in the Whole Hogs & Vinegar Sauce chapter), but hash—a rich, viscous concoction created to use up all the parts of the pig that you couldn't barbecue—is something almost unheard of beyond the Palmetto State. The sauces in the Carolinas are distinctive, too. There's the fiery, fundamental vinegar-and-pepper sauce of Eastern North Carolina and the Pee Dee region of South Carolina, the light vinegar-and-tomato based "dip" universal in the Piedmont of North Carolina, and the tangy, sweet, and bright-yellow mustard-based sauce that so baffles newcomers to the Midlands of South Carolina.

Each region has its own signature side dishes, too. You'll find boiled potatoes and corn sticks in Eastern North Carolina, red slaw and hush puppies in the Piedmont, and big fluffy onion rings in and around Charleston. Unique to the lower portions of South Carolina is the presence of rice at barbecue restaurants, which is fitting because, during the 18th and 19th centuries, rice formed the foundation of the state's economy. These days, the region may import long-grained rice from Louisiana or overseas, but its residents still tap into dining customs established centuries ago, and rice lives on in the form of hash and rice as well as pilau and chicken bog.

Barbecue in North Carolina is often discussed as if it stands alone, separately, from what's found in South Carolina. Most commentators note that the Tar Heel State has two dominant styles, Eastern and Piedmont, and partisans wrangle passionately over which is best. Meanwhile, South Carolina is typically said to have four distinct barbecue styles, defined primarily by the sauce used to dress the meat once it's cooked. But, if you expand your purview to the Carolinas as a whole, you realize that the dotted line on the map that zigzags from Sunset Beach all the way west to the Chattooga River really doesn't mean that much. The mode of cooking that originated in the Piedmont of North Carolina—pork shoulders roasted over hickory coals in closed brick pits and dressed with a light tomato-and-vinegar sauce—long ago snuck over the state line into the Upstate counties of South Carolina. A different barbecue tradition—whole hogs cooked on open pits and basted with a fiery pepper-laced vinegar sauce—is practiced in very much the same manner in the Pee Dee section of South Carolina as it is in the eastern part of the Tar Heel State. The distinctive Midlands South Carolina style, with its yellow mustard sauce and mysterious hash and rice, has made its way down to the coast around Charleston, while the counties along the Savannah River in South Carolina sometimes use a thick, red tomato-based barbecue sauce that is more akin to what's found on the Georgia side of the river than it is in the rest of the Carolinas. Once you get up into the mountainous regions of the two states, all bets are off.

This rich diversity of styles and techniques is well worth exploring and celebrating. There's something elemental and ancient about meat cooked over wood fires, and eating barbecue establishes a direct connection to the past. In this world of fast food and convenience meals—dinners bolted while standing up in the kitchen or zooming down the highway at breakneck speed—barbecue is one of the few things that is still laborious and slow. It makes us pause just long enough to enjoy our time together with family and friends. And, more than anything else, it's really delicious.

Barbecue has long been an essential thread in the social fabric of the Carolinas. Since the colonial era, communities throughout both states have come together over barbecue to celebrate important events, pass the hat for charitable causes, and decide who to elect to high office. It still plays that role today. In fact, when it comes to the history of American barbecue, the Carolinas are special. I have no desire to cast aspersions on Texas barbecue, but right-minded people agree that much of what passes for barbecue in the Lone Star State is little more than smoked meat—cheap, undesirable cuts cooked

How Do You Spell Barbecue?

It's safe to say that Carolinians can't agree on much of anything when it comes to barbecue, including the proper way to spell the word. Back in the 19th century, it was common to see it written as *barbacue* or *barbicu*, or in even weirder ways, but most of those variants eventually faded from use. In the Carolinas, and in the US at large, we have finally settled on two primary spellings for the word: *barbecue* and *barbeque*, at least when we have the time to spell the whole thing out.

The 20th century saw the rise of abbreviated versions, and they grew more compact over time. The spelling *Bar-B-Q* started popping up in newspapers in the 1920s, mostly in ads for barbecue restaurants. By 1926, companies were offering to sell outdoor electric *Bar-B-Q* signs for restaurants, which saved proprietors three expensive letters, and the usage soon because a standard commercial shorthand for an old favorite food. In *The American Language* (1936), H. L. Mencken included the term alongside *While-U-Wait* and *Q-Room* (for a billiard hall) as "familiar signs" of the day.

The even more efficient "BBQ" arrived on the scene later. It's not found in books or newspapers before 1940s, but after World War II it started to be used as a sort of shorthand to save a few pennies in classified ads, much like FROG ("finished room over garage") or OBO ("or best offer"). The faux acronym is one of the few terms in common use that's fully capitalized like an acronym but whose letters don't stand for separate words, and it really took off in the 1960s, appearing in advertisements of all kinds. By the late 1960s, products such as BBQ Turkey Roll and Lays BBQ potato chips were being offered for sale in trade journals and print ads.

In this book, we spell it *barbecue*, but we aren't dogmatic about it. Feel free to put the *q* in *barbeque* if it suits your fancy, or if you're into the whole brevity thing, go with *Bar-B-Q* or even *BBQ*. We'll all know what you're talking about.

over indirect heat in high-tech, new-fangled offset smokers. I suppose it's possible for someone to enjoy eating "barbecue" made in such a fashion, though it doesn't seem likely. It also doesn't matter much that the earliest historical references to barbecue explicitly discuss whole animals (most commonly, whole hogs) cooked over a bed of coals—that is, low and slow over direct heat—and not packer-trimmed cuts basking in smoke inside an enclosed metal chamber. I won't even mention the fact that the basic vinegar-and-pepper sauce still used today in many parts of the Carolinas is virtually indistinguishable from the basting liquid described in countless descriptions of 19th-century barbecues. There's no point in trying to reason with Texans.

But, I will say this: The Carolinas have the oldest continuous barbecue tradition to be found anywhere in the US. This book is meant to help the barbecue lover explore all facets of that long tradition and, in the process, enjoy some of the best barbecue the two states have to offer. It subdivides the Carolinas into four distinct barbecue regions, mapping out what is special and notable about each and then providing a guide to some of its most notable and representative restaurants. Along the way, it shares the stories, personalities, events, and signature dishes that make barbecue in the Carolinas such a rich and enjoyable experience.

For each restaurant included, the guide provides the basic details, like the address, phone number, and, for those that have such newfangled things, website URLs. It also documents a few of the key pieces of information about each restaurant, like when it opened and the cooking methods used. These techniques include the type of pit—open or closed, brick or metal—along with the type of fuel used and the cuts of meat cooked, for these factors help determine the qualities of the barbecue that winds up on your plate.

I will openly admit that this guide is biased toward restaurants that cook the old-fashioned way over oak or hickory coals instead of using electric or gas-fired cookers. This is not to say that one can't find good barbecue that isn't cooked over 100% wood, but the odds of it are certainly greatly diminished. Plus, experience has shown that many (not all, mind you, but many) of the restaurateurs who take the more expedient route with their fuel source are also prone to cut a few corners in other aspects of their barbecue and side dishes as well.

Here's a very important piece of advice when it comes to Carolina barbecue restaurants: *Call ahead*. In the Midlands and Lowcountry of South Carolina, many joints operate only a handful of days each week. Some, like Jackie Hite's in Leesville, South Carolina, serve only lunch and close down by midafternoon, while others are just dinner spots. These limited hours date back to the early days of commercial barbecue businesses, which tended to be run as casual operations that were a sideline to someone's regular mode of employment. A barbecue man might cook a hog or two on a Thursday and stay open until the meat was gone, which might be as late as Saturday night but could occur well before noon. In the Piedmont of North Carolina, restaurants tend to have more regular hours, though some close their doors on Sunday and others on Monday. If you drive 100 miles to try one of the highly recommended joints in this book without double-checking their hours of operation in advance, you may pull into an empty parking lot in front of a darkened building with a locked door. That's the kind of heartbreak from which it's really hard to recover.

Also, be sure you're prepared to pay for your meal. These days, more and more barbecue restaurants will take credit and debit cards, but some of the more old-school places are still cash only, and you'll need to have some greenbacks in your wallet when you arrive. In the heading for each restaurant, this guide specifies the days of the week and the times of day the establishment is open and whether it accepts those trendy new plastic charge cards. But hours and policies are prone to change, so, again, *call ahead*!

I wouldn't go so far as to say with certainty that the restaurants in this guide are the very *best* in the Carolinas. What I will say is that they represent the full sweep of the Carolina barbecue tradition and that they are *among* the very best that the two states have to offer. Daring to rank restaurants or declare one better than another is a dangerous endeavor, one that's likely to earn you nothing more than a sock in the nose. Here in the Carolinas, hometown barbecue restaurants are near and dear to our hearts. For many of us—especially those who were raised in small towns or out in the more rural parts—it's the food that we grew up eating. The style of barbecue served at whatever restaurant was our family's favorite becomes, to our minds, what defines "real barbecue." That definition involves far more than just the method of cooking, the type of sauce, or the dishes that come on the side. It's about the entire experience: the decor of the restaurant, the layout of the tables, whether it's all-you-can-eat or pay-at-the-counter. Perhaps most important, it is deeply associated with our interactions with the people with whom we share our table as well as with the others from the community who dine around us.

When Carolinians leave home and move somewhere far away, their childhood barbecue joints can become powerful distillations of home, symbolic evocations of what home is and what home means. When Carolinians are away and can't get their hands on it, they dream about coarse-chopped pork and red slaw or pulled pork with a side of hash and rice. Just check the comments on the Facebook pages of any long-lived joint that has acclimated itself enough to 21st-century technology to actually have a Facebook page: They'll be filled with the lamentations of former regulars now exiled far away and pining for a taste of that particular place's barbecue. When such exiles return home to visit, having lunch or dinner at their family's favorite restaurant is a perfect way to reconnect and feel like they're truly home.

I am leery of slighting any sort of institution with which people form such strong emotional connections. But, in the end, there's only so much space in a single book, and only so much give in the waistline of my pants, and I had to draw the line somewhere. I polled every barbecue connoisseur I knew, and I made the not-so-onerous effort of trying to eat at as many of their recommended joints as I could. There are bound to be a few sins of omission, and for those I apologize in advance.

As for those restaurants that did make the cut, when you visit any one of them, you can be assured that you're getting a taste of a tradition that dates back hundreds of years—a tradition, in fact, that antedates even the arrival of European colonists on Carolina's shores. If we can't confidently say that barbecue was invented in the Carolinas, we can at least maintain that it has one of the country's oldest and most vibrant barbecue traditions. In fact, there's a good case to be made that barbecue as it is still practiced in Eastern North Carolina and the Pee Dee region of South Carolina is the closest approximation to the way barbecue was cooked in the 18th and 19th centuries, when entire communities gathered together to share a feast based upon meat from animals cooked whole over wood coals in pits dug in the ground.

The details and trappings may have changed over the decades, but the fundamental essence of Carolina barbecue—meat cooked low and slow over hardwood coals—remains the same. And that is something that each and every one of us can savor.

A BRIEF HISTORY OF BARBECUE IN THE CAROLINAS

Quite a few South Carolina barbecue partisans have declared that barbecue was invented on the coast of the Palmetto State, and they've dubbed their home state the birthplace of barbecue. Their logic is this: Native Americans had a method of cooking meat on a raised frame of green sticks over a bed of coals—neither roasting nor smoking but something in between. The Spanish colonists, who introduced pigs to the New World, established a short-lived settlement they called Santa Elena on what is now Parris Island, South Carolina. Therefore, these commentators conclude, barbecue must have been invented at Santa Elena when the meat and the cooking technique came together.

Being a native South Carolinian, I would very much love for this to be the case. Unfortunately, there's not a scrap of evidence showing that pigs were ever cooked in this fashion at Santa Elena, much less that it was the very first place where the culinary marriage occurred. You could use the same argument to claim that any number of spots in the Caribbean or Florida were the birthplace of barbecue, for the Spanish took pigs with them wherever they went, and the method of cooking that gave its name to barbecue was practiced up and down the Atlantic Seaboard and throughout the Caribbean islands.

Philologists point to the Caribbean, and they generally agree that the word itself originated among the Taino Indians, whose term for that frame of green sticks was *baribicu*, which became *barbacoa* in Spanish and *barbecue*

What Is Virginia-Style Barbecue?

Of the original colonies, Virginia was where barbecue took the most firm root as a social institution, and barbecues remained an important part of community life in the Old Dominion until well into the 20th century. But, today, unlike the Carolinas, which have several flourishing barbecue traditions, no one really talks about "Virginia-style" barbecue.

There are a fair number of barbecue restaurants in Virginia these days, though none are recognized as American classics. The advertising for a lot of Virginia joints, in fact, confirms that this once-proud barbecue state now has an inferiority complex. Buz & Ned's claims to be "Richmond's only real barbecue," but the history on its website has its founders exploring and sampling great barbecue joints across America (including those in Lexington, North Carolina) and bringing 150-year-old recipes to Richmond. The Silver Pig Barbecue Restaurant near Lynchburg claims to have "the best Carolina-style chopped barbecue, Brunswick stew and sides known to man, woman, or child!" Three L'il Pigs in Daleville (just north of Roanoke) boasts "the tastiest, slow-cooked, hickory-smoked North Carolina-style barbeque anywhere in the valley."

So what happened to make barbecue die out in the state where it once held such culinary sway? That's a difficult question to answer. Across the United States in the early to mid-20th century, barbecue was making a transition from being served large scale at free public gatherings to being a commercial product sold in individual portions at restaurants. In the 1920s and 1930s, Virginia had as many good old-fashioned election and church-picnic barbecues as anywhere else. Somehow, though, no legendary barbecue restaurants developed in Virginia that could rival the likes of Stamey's in Greensboro, the Skylight Inn in Ayden, or any of the two dozen joints in Lexington, North Carolina. People in Virginia still love to eat barbecue; they just don't seem to have much of a distinct local feeling for the dish.

in English. European colonists took readily to the technique, and by the early 18th century the English were cooking barbecue from the Carolinas all the way up to New England. Believe it or not, during the 18th century there were plenty of barbecues held in Massachusetts: Benjamin Lynde Jr. of Salem recorded in his diary for August 31, 1733, "Fair and hot; Browne, Barbacue; hack overset." This made him the first person known to have used the term *barbecue* in writing to refer to an event instead of just a method of cooking. There are many other references to barbecues being held in New England during the colonial days, though by 1800 the practice seems to have faded out in the region.

Barbecue took root more strongly in Virginia, where it became firmly entrenched as a social institution. Virginians brought with them from their homes in southern and western England a culture of roasting and a love of feasting. They also brought pigs, which flourished on the acorns and chestnuts of Virginia's forests and became the colony's primary source of meat. By the 1750s, having a barbecue was one of the most popular forms of entertainment in Virginia, and it was far more than just a meal. A "barbecue day" started early in the morning and ran well into the night, with residents of all ranks joining together for feasting, drinking, and dancing.

There's not as much documentation about barbecue in the early days of the Carolina colonies, but it was certainly present by the early 18th century. In 1709, John Lawson, the surveyor general of North Carolina, recorded in *New Voyage to Carolina* that the natives would catch "bright, scaly Fish . . . and barbakue them, till they are crisp, then transport them, in wooden Hurdles, to their Towns and Quarters." In his *Natural History of North-Carolina* (1737), John Brickell recorded that the Native Americans used barbecue racks to dry salted venison over hickory coals and also to cook wild turkeys. The latter, he noted, "they Barbecue and eat with *Bears-grease*, this is accounted amongst them a good Dish."

The earliest written reference to the colonists themselves having barbecues in the Carolinas appears in an imitation of Horace that was published in London's *Gentleman Magazine* in 1753. It was written by one "C.W." residing in Charles Town, South Carolina. The writer is reveling in the spring, which by the Charleston calendar was the end of "the season," and the planters who had come to town with their families to sell their rice were wrapping up their business and preparing to head back to their plantations to begin a new growing year. But first, the poet implored, they should enjoy themselves a little: "Let's each hold a gen'rous barbicu feast / And with toddy and punch drink rich wine of the best." Apart from this lone passing reference, I have been unable to uncover any other mention of barbecues being held in Charleston before the Revolutionary War. Charleston society in the 18th century preferred more formal entertainments such as balls and banquets, and its culinary tastes ran more toward wild game, rice dishes, and shrimp instead of roasted pork.

Down the coast in Beaufort, though, barbecues seem to have been more popular. William J. Grayson, a prominent South Carolina man of letters, recalled that during his childhood in Beaufort the older men of his community, who had fought in the Revolution, constituted "a jovial and somewhat rough race, liberal, social, warm-hearted, hospitable, addicted to deep drinking, hard-swearing, and practical-joking . . . fond of dinner, barbacues, and hunting clubs." For that generation, barbecues were rambunctious, all-male parties, and each guest was expected to match his fellows drink for drink. Anyone who refused, Grayson wrote, was considered to have violated "barbecue-law" and was subjected to some form of punishment. One guest who so transgressed, a young man newly arrived from Scotland who refused to drink to intoxication, was sentenced to a 1-mile footrace. He was given a 5-yard head start and had to outrun the entire "barbecue posse," as Grayson put it, or submit to drinking as much as the rest. Aided, no doubt, by his relative sobriety, he "outran his pursuers without trouble."

The Beaufort Hunting Club maintained a "barbecue house" about a mile outside of town, and it was destroyed by a hurricane in 1804. A poet named Findlay commemorated the event in a mock-heroic verse entitled "On the Fall of the Barbacue-House," which was published in the *Charleston Courier*. In his poem, Findlay recalls the "sacred temple—where, in mirthful glee, the jovial sons of Pleasure oft convene" and where "Grog's mellow radiance set their souls on fire." Interestingly, the poet does not mention pork at all but instead the "famed SIRLOIN" and "Turkey-cock," and he makes clear that this early form of Carolina barbecue was quite spicy. The meats "feel the pangs / Of pungent Cayenne, Mustard's biting power / And many a stimulant to me unknown." The barbecue house was apparently never rebuilt.

In terms of the evolution of Carolina barbecue, the events held in Beaufort seem part of an isolated pocket. The main barbecue tradition in the Carolinas did not spread inland from the coast but instead was brought southward by settlers from Virginia as they made their way down the eastern edge of the Appalachians into the Piedmont of North and South Carolina. Charles Woodmason, an itinerant Anglican minister assigned to the western parishes of South Carolina in the 1760s, recorded in his journals that he had experienced "the velocity and force of the Air—By smelling a Barbicu dressing in the Woods upwards of six Miles." One of the leading occasions for a backwoods barbecue was a militia muster, which would bring men together from across the county for a day of drills and, afterward, a lot of socializing. Horse races and civic celebrations were prime times to barbecue a pig or cow, too.

In 1766, tensions were high over the recently enacted Stamp Act, which levied taxes on legal documents, newspapers, and magazines. North Carolinians weren't particularly pleased by the measure, and the militia companies from several counties expressed their feelings by marching to the town of Brunswick and refusing to let a cargo of stamped paper be landed. Alarmed by the unrest, North Carolina's governor, William Tryon, tried to placate the militia men. For the next muster in New Hanover, Tryon arranged a feast for the troops that included a whole barbecued ox and several barrels of beer. You can't fault him for trying, but the gesture did little to win over the bitter Carolinians. When called to the feast, the soldiers mocked Tryon's hospitality, poured the beer into the ground, and pitched the ox untasted into the Cape Fear River. This event

A Purely Democratic Barbecue

In June 1778, the citizens of New Bern, North Carolina, celebrated a victorious Revolutionary War campaign in what would soon become the most prominent form of patriotic celebration in the Carolinas: holding a barbecue. The local newspaper described it as follows:

> By way of celebration for this event, starting at one o'clock there was a barbecue (a roast pig) and a barrel of rum, from which the leading officials and citizens of the regions promiscuously ate and drank with the meanest and lowest kind of people, holding hands and drinking from the same cup. It is impossible to imagine, without seeing it, a more purely democratic gathering.... There were some drunks, some friendly fisticuffs, and one man was injured. With that and the burning of some empty barrels as a *feu de joie* at nightfall, the party ended and everyone retired to sleep. (*North-Carolina Gazette*, July 10, 1778)

took place a good seven years before a bunch of Yankees donned Mohawk garb and tossed three shiploads of tea in the Boston Harbor, but for some reason the Boston Tea Party is the protest that gets all the attention.

The accounts that survive of barbecues in the Carolina backcountry suggest that many were rather rough and unsophisticated. They were usually held in the woods or in dusty open fields, with improvised tables and whatever dishes and utensils the guests brought with them. In 1773, William Richardson, a Charleston merchant, attended a horse race in the Camden District of South Carolina and described the accompanying barbecue in a letter to his wife. He noted with derision the "clouds of dust arising everywhere" and "the Quarter of Beef Barbacuing in this dust and nicely browned indeed, but not with fire." The tables for the event consisted of three planks laid across some "cross-sticks," covered with rather dirty cloths, and set with a mishmash of knives, forks, and pewter plates. In addition to the quarter of beef, two whole hogs were cooked for the occasion, which Richardson described as "half roasted . . . with the blood running out at every cut of the knife." He advised his wife, "Don't tell this to any of your squeemish C Town ladies for they will not believe you."

Most guests must have enjoyed barbecues far more than Richardson did, for by the early 19th century they had become ingrained in the social and political institutions of the Carolinas. Barbecues became the customary way to celebrate the Fourth of July, and by the early 19th century a surprisingly formal and regimented set of rituals were followed in one community after another across the Carolinas. Residents would come from all over the county and gather at a common spot, where they would form a procession and be led by the local militia to the county courthouse or a church for the day's ceremonies. These almost always opened with a prayer, then the Declaration of Independence would be read aloud, followed by music played by whatever passed for the local band. The ceremonies invariably concluded with a prominent citizen delivering an oration on such patriotic themes as the importance of the Constitution or the principles of the Revolution.

Once the speechifying was finished, the citizens would reform their procession and march to a shady grove where a barbecue feast awaited. After they finished eating, it was time for the toasts. These kicked off with the "regular toasts," always 13 in number to represent the original colonies. Each was delivered by a prominent person chosen in advance for the honor. The 13th toast was almost always devoted to honoring American women—or, as it was frequently phrased, "the American Fair." These would be followed by as many "volunteer toasts" as members of the crowd were inclined to offer, and many times they numbered 30 or more. The themes of the toasts might range from

Fourth of July Barbecue Toasts

In Columbia, South Carolina, on the morning of July 4, 1827, a gathering of citizens, led by the Richland Volunteer Rifle Company, marched to the local Presbyterian church, where the pastor led them in prayer, Ensign Braithwaite read the Declaration of Independence, and Colonel E. H. Maxcy delivered an "eloquent and appropriate oration." The assembly then marched to Mrs. Sistrunk's Spring, where "a sumptuous barbecue was served up," followed by many rounds of toasting. The *South Carolina State Gazette* recorded the following 13 regular toasts:

1. *The 4th of July*—A day dear to freemen, hated by tyrants—May each return of it inspire every American with the spirit of '76.
2. *Washington*—"Fame spread her wings, and with her trumpet blew,
    Great Washington is come! What praised is due?
    What title shall he have? She paused and said,
    Not one! His name alone strikes every title dead."
3. *The Union*—In the emphatic language of the father of his country, may we "frown indignantly upon the first dawning of every attempt to alienate any portion of our country from the rest."
4. *South Carolina Legislature*—She cannot set a more noble, or less dangerous precedent, than the late gift to the "Sage of Monticello"—may such representatives always have the support of the people.
5. *Jefferson and Adams*—May the hand of heaven, which dissolved these deathless patriots on the Jubilee of this holiday of Freedom, protect their descended mantle from the sacrilegious hand of faction and disunion.
6. *The Army and the Navy of the United States*—Sentinels on the watch tower of freedom—at the signal of invasion they shall lead the van for millions of its defenders.
7. *The Heroes of the Revolution*—We will cherish the memory of the dead, and the glory of the living.
8. *The President of the United States.*
9. *The Governor of South Carolina.*

(continued)

10. *The Holy Alliance*—The otto of despotism, the profaners of the temple of liberty. *"Procu, O! Procul, este profani."*

11. *Riflemen*—The invincibles under Morgan, the keen shooters at the Cowpens, the "fighting quakers," under Coffee at New Orleans—May they ever preserve the character which they won in those times of peril.

12. *Charles Carrol of Carrolton*—The last on our roll of blood bought charter—his companions have left him to guard its purity and strength.—When the herald of freedom shall have passed the rich horizon of a protracted day, may he announce to his colleagues, the triumph of the cause, to which they devoted their lives, their fortunes, and their sacred honors.

13. *The Fair Sex*—The soldiers concern, his hope, his reward—They have no equal in his estimation but Honor, no superior by Fame.

These were followed by 15 volunteer toasts celebrating everything from the advocates of the Woolen Bill to General Lafayette.

celebrating democracy and American ideals to honoring war heroes and advancing political causes. The toasts themselves were of great interest to the community, and the local newspapers usually recorded them verbatim in their accounts of the celebrations.

The Fourth of July was by far the most popular occasion for a barbecue, but in the antebellum Carolinas the events were also held in conjunction with militia musters and for all sorts of other civic celebrations. They were almost always held outdoors, usually beneath the trees of a shady grove and near a running spring, which provided much-needed water. This was long before the era of refrigeration, so the animals would typically be brought directly to the cooking site to be slaughtered and dressed. Pork is by far the dominant barbecue meat in the Carolinas today, but that wasn't necessarily the case in the early days. The livestock for a barbecue was usually donated by members of the community, and they gave whatever they had on hand and could spare. In addition to pigs and chickens, it was common to see beef cattle, oxen, sheep, lambs, and goats served at Carolina barbecues.

For the pit, workers dug a long shallow trench in the earth, about 4 feet wide and anywhere from 6 to several hundred feet long depending upon the size of the gathering. Oak and hickory logs were piled into the pit, set ablaze, and allowed to burn until reduced to coals, which were spread out evenly through the pits. As was the case throughout the South, the laborious work at community barbecues tended to be performed by African-American slaves, and there was far more to it than just digging the pit and chopping the wood. The animals being cooked were usually split lengthwise and run through with long green sticks or iron bars before being laid across. Alongside the pit were pots of basting liquid, and the men tending the pit would move up and down either side, basting the meat with long-handled brushes or mops. Periodically, they would lift the carcasses and turn them over, and there was always a small pit of hardwood off to the side to ensure a steady supply of coals, which they shoveled into the pit to keep the heat constant.

Barbecue fans today make a lot of fuss about the many varieties of sauce that are found in different parts of the Carolinas. Back in the 19th century, none of those variations existed. Cooks tended to baste the meat on the pit with a mixture of either melted butter or lard mixed with water or vinegar and then salt and red and black pepper. That sauce was used just for basting, for the meat would be served dry. The squeeze bottles of sweet and spicy sauces didn't arrive on the scene until the 20th century.

It didn't take very long for politicians to figure out that, in an era before television and mass communications, barbecues were a great way for them to get their messages heard by a large number of voters. At first, they crashed the local Fourth of July celebrations, and while the attendees were enjoying their barbecue, the office seekers would jump up on stumps and address the crowd, which is the origin of the expression "stump speech." Before long, supporters of candidates started pooling their resources to host barbecues for the sole purpose of campaigning, and these efforts were some of the earliest examples of political-party organization in the Carolinas.

As one might guess from the sheer number of toasts drunk at Fourth of July celebrations, in the early decades of the 19th century, barbecues were notoriously drunken and rough-and-tumble affairs. In an interview with the Works Progress Administration, Samuel D. Latham described the barbecues at the militia musters he attended as a boy at Caldwell Cross Roads in Fairfield County, South Carolina. After the drilling was over and the barbecue eaten, he recalled, "Hard liquor would flow; and each section would present its 'bully of the woods' in a contest for champion in a fist and skill fight.... It was primitive prize fighting."

That started to change in the 1830s, as what used to be considered the backcountry of the Carolinas ceased to be a frontier society and became more secure and sedate. A backlash arose against all the drinking and carousing that went on at barbecues, especially during election time and on the Fourth of July. "A people whose patriotism needs to be forced into activity and life," the editor of the *Cheraw Gazette* harrumphed in 1837, "by the stimulants of alcoholic liquors and rich dinners may make good *subjects*, but not good *citizens*." The temperance movement in the South was just getting underway, and reformers trained much of their attention on barbecues. They began holding

"Nat Joined the Temperance Society"

Julian A. Selby, who grew up in antebellum Columbia, South Carolina, captured this anecdote in his book *Memorabilia and Anecdotal Reminiscences of Columbia, S.C.* (1905):

> Nat Monteith was a good-natured free and easy individual from boyhood up. He was a great lover of "pot-liquor," and whenever cabbage would be prepared for dinner, the cook would inevitably call to him ... to come and get some of the homely beverage. There had been quite a revival among the advocates of temperance, and a "Cold Water Army," for the benefit of the boys, had been organized—backed by a barbecue in the Court House grounds, northeast corner of Main and Washington streets. Next day the cook called to him that she had his "pot-liquor" ready. "No, Aunt Jane, can't take it: joined the temperance society."

their own "cold water" barbecues on the Fourth of July, trying to draw citizens away from the competing whiskey-soaked affairs. Allen Fuller, the secretary of the Salubrity Temperance Society in Liberty, South Carolina, noted that at the local wet Fourth of July barbecue, "The candidates for office were there, and dealt out the liquor in profusion, and profanity, drunkenness, and quarrelling were the order of the day." The temperance society's event, by contrast, was not only more peaceful and respectable but also offered "the means of advance the temperance cause in this vicinity." There were still plenty of toasts drunk at these events, but they were, as one attendee put it, "cold water toasts . . . which nearly froze on the lips."

Before the Civil War and emancipation, African-American slaves may have had to do the hard work preparing community barbecues for white Carolinians, but they also cooked barbecue for themselves and their families and friends. Up until the early part of the 19th century, slaves in the Carolinas tended to have a relative amount of leeway to travel between plantations and cities and to attend church meetings, funerals, and even barbecues. Barbecues, in fact, were a favorite form of recreation on Sunday, when most slaves were not required to work and were allowed to gather with family and friends.

Such events allowed African Americans to socialize and interact with each other, and over time these gatherings began to be seen as threats by slaveholders in the Carolinas, especially after slaves in other states started using them as cover to plan revolts. In 1800, an enslaved blacksmith named Gabriel conceived a plan for a massive revolt in the area around Richmond, Virginia, and he staged several barbecues to attract followers to join him in his plans. When informants leaked word of the plot to the authorities in Richmond, Gabriel and 20 other conspirators were arrested and executed. In 1831, a party of slaves that included Nat Turner took a pig and some brandy and gathered for a barbecue in Southampton County, Virginia. From there, they launched a revolt they had been planning for months, initiating a two-day assault that ended up in the deaths of 55 white Virginians and, in the violent suppression that followed, the killing of more than 100 African Americans.

It was the bloodiest slave revolt in American history, and it struck fear in the hearts of slaveholding Southern societies. In the Carolinas and elsewhere, governments passed one measure after another to clamp down on the few remaining liberties that both enslaved and free blacks once enjoyed, including the ability to gather for barbecues and other feasts. During the rest of the antebellum era, slaves got to eat barbecue on just a few occasions per year, typically on Christmas Day and either the Fourth of July or a late-summer harvest celebration. The plantation owner would often provide a pig or a sheep for the barbecue, and the slaves would augment that with produce from their own garden patches. On occasion, slaves did take it upon themselves to hold their own barbecues despite the risks, stealing a hog and cooking it off in the woods for an illicit event. In the last few decades of the antebellum era, however, the ability of African Americans in the Carolinas to enjoy barbecue was sharply curtailed.

In the white communities, as barbecues became less drunken brawls and more sedate social occasions, they began to be enlisted for all sorts of other purposes. In the 1840s and 1850s, as the first railroad companies were being established in the Carolinas, the "railroad barbecue" became an early form of venture capital. In 1847, for instance, the citizens of Chester, South Carolina, staged a barbecue to solicit funds to complete the railroad from Columbia to Charlotte, a route that would pass directly through their town. After the guests "partook of an Excellent barbecue," the subscription books were opened and the townspeople pledged $150,000 toward the effort, securing a matching pledge from the state legislature that eventually resulted in the completion of the line.

Barbecues not only funded the railroads but also celebrated the happy day when the new line arrived in a town, an event that promised decades of future economic success for a community. In June 1842, thousands of citizens turned out to welcome the arrival of the first passenger train to reach Columbia, which had left the Line Street depot in Charleston at 6 a.m. that morning and arrived in Columbia around 4 p.m. It was greeted by the Washington Light Infantry and some 5,000 Columbia residents who, after a round of welcome speeches by local dignitaries, adjourned to a nearby grove to feast on barbecued sheep, pigs, and calves.

After the Civil War, barbecue remained the premier form of civic gathering and celebration in the Carolinas, and it took on a particular importance in the lives of African Americans even before the war ended. On January 1, 1863, several thousand black residents from the Sea Islands near Beaufort, South Carolina, made their way by boat and wagon to Camp Saxton, which by then was in Federal-controlled territory. Ten oxen had been procured for the gathering, and they were roasted over coals in pits dug in the ground. The Eighth Maine band played music for the ceremony, and, following a short prayer, President Lincoln's Emancipation Proclamation was read aloud to the assembled crowds. The moment the speaker read the last word, the assembled people—now officially free—spontaneously burst into singing "My Country 'Tis of Thee." Orations and more patriotic songs followed before the crowd finally sat down to a modest wartime feast of barbecue beef, hard bread, and water flavored with molasses and ginger. Susie King Taylor, a former slave who had become a schoolteacher on St. Simons Island, remembered the meal as "a fitting close and the crowning event of this occasion." It wasn't served "as tastily or correctly as it would have been at home," she noted, "yet it was enjoyed with keen appetites and relish."

The celebration held at Camp Saxton was repeated in communities throughout the Carolinas once they came under Federal control and the Emancipation Proclamation could be enforced. During the Reconstruction years, January 1 was celebrated as Emancipation Day, an important holiday for black Carolinians, commemorated each year with a big barbecue and a reading of the Emancipation Proclamation. As the shadows of the Jim Crow era descended, white and black Carolinians became increasingly divided by legalized segregation, and the two communities maintained their barbecue traditions in separate but parallel paths that on occasion intersected. Barbecues remained a popular way to celebrate the end of the harvest, and farmers would slaughter a hog and cook it to share with all the workers who just finished bringing the crop in. Barbecue also was used to draw people to school fund-raisers and to feed attendees at gatherings of social and civic clubs.

This period saw the rise of "barbecue men," noted cooks who earned a reputation for their skills and were enlisted to provide smoked meats for all sorts of public and private events. In the Midlands of South Carolina, Hezekiah "Kiah" Dent emerged as the region's most respected barbecue man. A farmer and Confederate veteran, he provided the barbecue for everything from gatherings of the Knights of Pythias (a fraternal organization) to massive Labor Day picnics in Columbia. Dent regularly cooked the pigs for the reunions of the Richland County Confederate veterans, too. When Kiah Dent died in 1908, the Columbia *State* noted that "no one ever partook of a feast prepared by him who went away other than thoroughly satisfied."

Cooking barbecue in Southern Pines, North Carolina. From *Frank Leslie's Illustrated Weekly*, December 19, 1891

The phenomenon of the barbecue man preceded the rise of barbecue restaurants, and it continued well into the 20th century. Frank T. Meacham, the superintendent of the Piedmont Experimental Station in Statesville, was one of the most noted of the Tar Heel State's barbecue men. He started cooking for events connected to the Experimental Station, such as the annual Iredell County farmers' picnic. As his reputation grew, he traveled across the state to preside over the pits at barbecues staged by chambers of commerce, the Kiwanis Club, the Boy Scouts, and countless churches. By the 1920s, he had become so well known that newspapers would refer to public barbecues as being "prepared a la Meacham style."

Starting around the turn of the 20th century, barbecue in the Carolinas began evolving from something served for free at large-scale public functions to something to be sold as an article of commerce. Some barbecue men realized they could charge for their services to cook at school fund-raisers and gatherings of social organizations. This eased barbecue into the commercial world, and that transition was accelerated by the urbanization of the Carolinas. Railroads, textile mills, and cotton and tobacco markets created hundreds of new towns throughout the region. By the early 1900s, about one out of every six Carolinians lived in a town or city.

In a rural environment, it took a big occasion, like a candidates' debate or a Fourth of July celebration, to draw enough people together to justify barbecuing a whole hog. As towns and cities grew, they provided enough of a market to create a reliable clientele for regular businesses. Around 1900, barbecue stands started popping up on downtown street corners in towns across the Carolinas. These often were created by entrepreneurs who saw a chance to earn a little money selling food to the farmers who had come in from the countryside to conduct business when the court was in session or the tobacco markets were open. Many of these entrepreneurs were themselves farmers who looked at barbecue as a way to bring in a little cash income on the side. These early businesses weren't terribly sophisticated. In some cases, cooks just sold barbecue from the back of a wagon, while others might set up a tent or a rudimentary stand on a street corner to provide a little shelter.

Many of the legendary barbecue restaurants in the Carolinas trace their origins to precisely this sort of casual business. In the late 1800s, Skilton Dennis started loading up a wagon on Saturday afternoons and taking home-cooked barbecue into Otter Town, North Carolina, to sell to the farmers who had come into town for the weekend. In 1890, Otter Town changed its name to the more respectable sounding Ayden, and Dennis's son, Skilton M., and his grandson Bill continued the informal business in the early 20th century.

Nunn's Barbecue Stand: North Carolina's First Barbecue Restaurant?

In February 2011, when Charlotte was selected to host the 2012 Democratic National Convention, First Lady Michelle Obama found herself on the hot seat for praising the city's charm, hospitality, and "of course, great barbecue." Carolina barbecue fans howled in derision, insisting that while there are any number of places in the Carolinas where you can find great barbecue, the Queen City has never been accused of being one of them. John Shelton Reed, a retired University of North Carolina sociologist and coauthor of *Holy Smoke: The Big Book of North Carolina Barbecue*, had perhaps the best rejoinder of all. "Complete the sentence," he instructed the Associated Press. "As a barbecue town, Charlotte is one, not what it used to be; two, like Minneapolis for gumbo; three, good enough for Yankees; four, not far from Shelby." Not even the editorial board of the *Charlotte Observer* would come to the defense of the city's barbecue, commenting, "Everybody knows to get the best stuff, you gotta drive north to Lexington." And that makes it all the more ironic that the home of the very first barbecue restaurant in North Carolina may have been Charlotte.

In April 1899, Mrs. Katie Nunn took out a classified ad in the *Observer* announcing that she was opening a grocery store and barbecue stand on 13 South Church Street. Her husband, Levi, would do the cooking in a large pit he had built out behind the store. This was a good two decades before Sid Weaver and Jess Swicegood started selling barbecue from tents across from the courthouse in Lexington. These days, pork is synonymous with North Carolina barbecue, but Mr. Nunn's menu also featured beef and mutton, the former a rarity and the latter an impossibility in a Tar Heel barbecue joint today.

Very little is known about the Nunns, and their forays into the world of barbecue selling were short lived. In 2012 Kathleen Purvis of the *Charlotte Observer* set out to track down whatever information she could about the Nunns. She discovered that, by the end of 1899, the Nunns' grocery store had been replaced by a candy manufacturer, and the Nunns left Charlotte not long after, moving to Norfolk, Virginia, where Levi Nunn found work as a housing contractor. But, for a brief spell in 1899, they may well have been running the first commercial barbecue operation in the Carolinas.

Eventually, Bill Dennis rented a booth on a street corner where he sold his barbecue along with corn bread made by his wife, Susan, and in the 1920s he moved into a building on 2nd Street. Bill Dennis's descendants went on to open several more restaurants, including two—Bum's and the Skylight Inn—that are still in operation today.

Farther west in Lexington, North Carolina, Sid Weaver and George Ridenhour put up a tent on the corner across from the county courthouse and started selling barbecue in 1919. Not too long after, Jess Swicegood set up a competing tent nearby and started selling barbecue, too. At first they cooked only during court weeks, but by the end of the 1920s there was enough business from farmers coming into town on Saturday to justify operating every weekend. Weaver and Ridenour added a tin roof and siding and converted their tent into a semipermanent stand, and Jess Swicegood followed suit. In the 1920s, Sid Weaver was still cooking the meat in the backyard yard of his house and bringing it down to the stand on the courthouse square to sell. That changed by the 1930s, when he upgraded to a permanent restaurant made of cinder blocks, complete with a cash register, tables, and a counter with stools. This pattern was repeated in town after town as barbecue vendors enclosed their stands, added seating, and created more formal restaurants.

Adam Scott, a janitor and elevator operator from Goldsboro, started cooking barbecue on the side for local parties and receptions. Before long he was selling barbecue from his backyard every weekend, and in 1933 he enclosed the back porch of his house and transformed it into a dining room. He continued to enlarge the restaurant over the succeeding years. Fifty miles north in Rocky Mount, a merchant and horse trader named Bob Melton followed a similar course. He would cook a whole hog on occasion in a pit dug in the ground and serve it to friends on some bottomland he owned along the Tar River. As more and more people took a liking to his barbecue, Melton started selling meat by the pound and attracted a regular stream of townspeople down to the river for lunch every Saturday. So he built a shed with rough tables inside, and later he screened that in to keep out the flies. A small permanent dining room followed, which Melton expanded several times over the years. In 1929, he was selling a plate of barbecue and boiled potatoes for 45 cents and barbecue sandwiches for 15 cents. Soon, Melton's reputation was attracting travelers heading up and down US 301, the main thoroughfare from up north to Florida in the days before I-95. Bob Melton's Barbecue remained a classic North Carolina barbecue restaurant long after its founder's death in 1958. In 1999, the flooding following Hurricane Floyd forced the family to move the restaurant to a strip mall, where it lasted just a few more years before closing its doors in 2005.

Adam Scott's Divinely Inspired Sauce

These days, it's not easy to sample the whole hog barbecue from Scott's in Goldsboro, one of the oldest barbecue restaurants in operation anywhere in the country. Its founder, Adam Scott, got started in the business way back in 1917, and it's now run by a third generation of Scotts, though with very limited hours: open for lunch only on Thursday and Friday. Getting your hands on Adam Scott's famous sauce is a far easier proposition. Each year, the Scott family sells upward of a million bottles of the spicy Eastern North Carolina–style sauce in yellow labeled bottles in grocery stores across the state.

In addition to cooking barbecue, Adam Scott was a preacher in the United Holy Church of America. He claimed that, after experimenting futilely for 20 years trying to come up with the perfect sauce for his pork, the ingredients suddenly came to him one night in a dream. It's a basic vinegar sauce loaded up with plenty of salt and black and red pepper, but there are several other herbs and spices of some sort in the mix, too, and they settle out and form a thick layer at the bottom of the bottle. When you shake it up to distribute the ingredients, it makes for one supremely spicy sauce. (Adam's Scott's son, A. Martel Scott, is said to have spiced up the recipe a good bit from his father's version when he started bottling it for sale.)

In *North Carolina Barbecue: Flavored by Time*, Bob Garner tells the story of one man who learned a hard lesson about the heat of the Scotts' sauce. One night in 1957, the Goldsboro police received a call reporting that a man was breaking into Scott's Barbecue. When the officers arrived, they found a broken window but no sign of the perpetrator. Just as they were about to leave, they heard noises coming from the storeroom in the back, and there they found the would-be burglar hiding inside a 55-gallon drum half filled with the Scotts' sauce. The longer he had steeped, it seems, the more uncomfortable he had become, until the heat had finally made him shift in the barrel, giving his location away. The cops hauled the miscreant off to jail, where he spent the rest of the night in a cell in his sauce-soaked clothes. The next morning, Martel Scott was called down to the station, but he refused to press charges. He figured the poor man had already suffered enough for his crimes.

Gable's Motel in Florence, South Carolina, circa 1950s

As automobiles became more affordable, more and more Carolinians took to the road, and an array of new businesses popped up along the roadside to cater to them. The owners of country stores, gas stations, and motels found that they could earn a little extra money by cooking a whole hog on Friday and selling the meat to hungry motorists over the weekend. Cooper's Country Store in Salters, South Carolina, and Scott's Variety Store in Hemingway are two surviving examples of this phenomenon. In many cases, barbecue sales eventually eclipsed the owner's original enterprise and turned into their main line of business.

After World War II, drive-in restaurants became the rage in towns and cities across the Carolinas. Hungry families could now order dinner without leaving their cars and have it delivered by carhops wearing white aprons and paper hats and maybe even roller skates. The typical drive-in menu included hamburgers, hot dogs, and french fries, but wood-cooked barbecue was usually the featured item. The restaurants of the Bessinger family in Charleston and Columbia (see Bessinger's Barbeque and Maurice's), Fuzzy's in Madison, North Carolina, and the Skylight Inn in Ayden are just a few of the legendary

Carolina barbecue restaurants that got their start as drive-ins in the 1950s and 1960s.

Before barbecue restaurants, there were few regional variations in barbecue styles in the Carolinas, or in the United States as whole, for that matter. In the old days of free outdoor barbecues, farmers donated whatever livestock they could spare for the event, which usually included at least one whole hog but might also be sheep, goats, or even a cow. The side dishes were contributed by the community, too, and they tended toward things that could hold up all day outdoors without any refrigeration, like sliced tomatoes and cucumbers, watermelon, and loaves of white bread.

All that changed with the rise of restaurants. Most started off as small operations, and the cooks by necessity settled on a streamlined set of things to serve. They tinkered with their sauce recipes, adjusting the amount of black and red pepper and adding newly available commercial condiments like ketchup and prepared mustard. An informal barbecue apprenticeship system helped codify the style in a particular region, as restaurateurs like the legendary Warner Stamey (see sidebar, Shoulders & Light Red Sauce chapter) hired young men to work in their pits, and those cooks later went on to open their own places, taking with them the techniques and recipes they learned from their mentor. By the 1950s, most of the distinctive elements of the different styles of barbecue in the Carolinas—yellow mustard-based sauce in the South Carolina Midlands, chopped pork shoulder and red slaw in the North Carolina Piedmont—had been codified in each region's restaurants and on the palates of their customers.

Barbecue as a restaurant food reached its peak around 1960. It was being sold from quick-serve stands on street corners, drive-in restaurants along the highway, and in more formal sit-down restaurants alongside steaks and chops. Countless farmers and butchers and mill workers had discovered that they could cook a whole hog or a couple of shoulders on a wood-fired pit and make a modest living while getting to be their own bosses. But the business got tougher as the restaurant industry evolved. Calculating entrepreneurs started squeezing costs out of their operations by streamlining their menus, focusing on food that took less skill and labor to prepare and, therefore, could be sold more cheaply to undercut the competition. Drive-in operators ditched their flatware and china in favor of plastic utensils and paper trays, and simple items like burgers and hot dogs began to eclipse barbecue as the preferred quick-serve item. Many of the sons and daughters of barbecue-restaurant owners, having grown up knowing the hard labor required for an increasingly diminishing return, decided they had no desire to continue on in the family business and looked for careers elsewhere.

By the 1970s, even those who wanted to keep cooking barbecue felt tremendous pressure to give up their wood-burning pits and convert to gas or electric cookers. Hardwood was becoming scarce and more expensive, adding even more cost pressures. Why pay a premium to haul and split logs and preside over a smoky, grease-laden pit for 12 hours a day when you could install a fancy new stainless steel oven with a handy thermostat that let you set a desired cooking temperature and head home for a good night sleep? In 1979, when Allie Patricia Wall and Ron L. Layne wrote *Hog Heaven*, their pioneering guidebook to South Carolina barbecue joints (see "*Hog Heaven*" sidebar in Yellow Mustard & Hash chapter), they found that more than half had already made the switch to electric or gas.

But Carolinians loved their barbecue too much to let it fade away forever into a fast-food world of quick-serve burgers and cut-rate fried chicken. Newspaper columnists like Dennis Rogers of the *Raleigh News & Observer* and Jerry Bledsoe of the *Greensboro News and Record* started championing the cause of traditional Eastern- and Piedmont-style North Carolina barbecue, defending it from the assaults of modernity and the ignorance of Texans and others who persistently confused beef with barbecue. Television reporters like Bob Garner of WUNC-TV in Chapel Hill began taking cameras into the classic barbecue restaurants of the Carolinas, interviewing the pitmasters and celebrating their unique culinary legacy on air. These days, a new generation of restaurateurs is embracing the old style of cooking on real wood, opening new restaurants that look to the past but keep the art of barbecue moving ahead into the future. Today, the barbecue tradition is very much alive and thriving in the Carolinas, and it shows no sign of losing its renewed energy any time soon.

BARBECUE CALENDAR

Although most Carolinians these days get their barbecue from restaurants, they are by no means the only source. In fact, some of the best barbecue in the two states can be found only on special occasions. Since the 18th century, Carolinians have staged barbecues for civic celebrations and to raise money for charitable causes, and they're still doing so today. The rising popularity of barbecue competitions over the past few decades has added an entirely new type of event to the barbecue landscape, too. Here's a rundown of some of the most popular and representative special barbecue events that are held regularly in the Carolinas.

South Carolina BBQ Shag Festival

When: April
Where: Hemingway Recreational Complex, Hemingway, SC
Started: 1988
scbbqshagfestival.org
This community festival in Hemingway blends South Carolina's official state "picnic cuisine" with its official dance: the shag. There's a barbecue cook-off each year along with crafts, carnival rides, music, dancing, and games.

Newport Pig Cooking Contest

When: April
Where: Town Park, Newport, NC
Started: 1978
newportpigcooking.com
This annual event in Newport, North Carolina, bills itself as America's largest whole-hog pig-cooking contest. More than 80 teams show up to cook an entire pig each, and after the judging is over the meat is taken to a chopping tent where volunteers convert it into chopped-pork plates, which are sold to the public. There are rides, crafts, and music to entertain the crowds, too. Admission is free, and proceeds from the barbecue sales go to selected local non-profit organizations.

A Note on Barbecue Competitions

Dozens of barbecue competitions, large and small, take place in the Carolinas each year, but not all of them are prime occasions for eating barbecue. Some are adjuncts to larger festivals and not designed for the general public to feast on barbecue. Of those that do promise pulled pork to the public, oftentimes the barbecue prepared by the competition teams is enjoyed only by the judges and the teams themselves, and a commercial vendor provides barbecue for the general attendees (though if you're gregarious enough, you can usually talk your way into a few tasty samples from the teams). Such competitions are frequently coupled with another type of entertainment, like a music festival or antique auto show, since the barbecue alone isn't sufficient to draw a large crowd. Many are short lived, too, being staged for a year or two before fading from the scene. This chapter includes some of the more popular and long-lasting barbecue competitions in the Carolinas. For full lists of barbecue competitions—and there are lots of them—consult the websites of the South Carolina Barbeque Association (scbarbeque.com), the North Carolina Barbecue Society (ncbbqsociety.com), and the Kansas City Barbeque Society (kcbs.us), all of which sanction barbecue contests in the Carolinas.

ROBERT DONOVAN

BBQ Festival on the Neuse

When: May
Where: Pearson Park, Kinston, NC
Started: 1981

bbqfestivalontheneuse.com

This annual event is held on the banks of the Neuse River in downtown Kinston, and it claims to be the largest barbecue cook-off in North Carolina. Like most barbecue festivals, it has plenty of live music, amusement rides, arts and crafts, a car and truck show, and there's also a corn-hole tournament, a farmers' market, and a wine garden featuring North Carolina wines.

The Blue Ridge BBQ & Music Festival

When: June
Where: Harmon Field in Tryon, NC
Started: 1994

blueridgebbqfestival.com

The Blue Ridge BBQ & Music Festival is one of the most successful barbecue competitions not just in the Carolinas but in the entire country. It's a Kansas City Barbeque Society event, so it draws cooks from all over the country and has become more a showcase for Tennessee, Alabama, Texas, and Kansas City 'cue than North Carolina varieties (in 2014, the highest-ranked North Carolina team finished seventh overall). The event features live music on two stages, a craft fair, rides, kids' games, a classic car show, and, of course, plenty of barbecue. Proceeds benefit the Carolina Foothills Chamber of Commerce and its Chamber Foundation.

Annual Roasting of the Pig

When: July
Where: Beech Mountain Resort, Beech Mountain, NC
Started: 1977

beechmountainchamber.com

In Beech Mountain, North Carolina, they gather each year to celebrate Independence Day with a big barbecue on the weekend just before or after July Fourth. Lots of pork butts and turkey, too, are slow cooked and served to the crowd, who enjoy it along with music, dancing, and children's games. Though the first snow won't fall for several months, guests can still ride the ski lifts at the slopes, and the festivities close with a grand fireworks display at dark.

South Carolina Festival of Discovery

When: July
Where: Greenwood, SC
Started: 2000

festivalofdiscovery.com

Crowds pack Main Street in uptown Greenwood to listen to blues and eat barbecue. In addition to a Kansas City Barbeque Society–sanctioned barbecue competition, some of the best blues artists from around the state perform on the big stage.

Poplar Tent Presbyterian Annual Barbecue

When: First Thursday in October
Where: Poplar Tent Presbyterian Church, Concord, NC
Started: 1945

poplartentchurch.org

In 1945, members of the Poplar Tent Presbyterian Church dug a pit in the ground and cooked five hogs, which they sold to the public, raising $80 for the church. They've been doing it ever since. Volunteers begin making slaw on Monday morning, mix the sauce on Tuesday, and light the fire in the barbecue pits at 3 a.m. on Wednesday morning; at 10 a.m. on Thursday morning, 12,000 pounds of barbecue and over 500 gallons of Brunswick stew are ready to serve the crowds. The proceeds are used to maintain the church building and programs, continuing a long North Carolina tradition of church fund-raising barbecues that dates back to the 19th century.

Lexington Barbecue Festival

When: One of the last two Saturdays in October
Where: Uptown Lexington, NC
Started: 1983

barbecuefestival.com

Lexington is the capital of Piedmont North Carolina barbecue, so it's only fitting there's been a festival to celebrate it every year since 1983. And barbecue fans turn out in droves—over 200,000 of them in 2013. It's a street festival that takes place on a 9-block stretch of Main Street right in the heart of downtown, and admission is free. Hundreds of craft and gift exhibitors are on hand to sell their wares, and there are arts and crafts competitions, performances by local and national musical acts, rides and games for children, and an antique-car show for good measure. Barbecue, of course, is the highlight of the day.

Crowd at the 2013 Lexington Barbecue Festival. THE BARBECUE FESTIVAL/*THE DISPATCH*

Served from three main tents, it's the genuine Lexington style: sandwiches and trays of chopped pork and red slaw made by seven local pitmasters. No barbecue festival would be complete without racing pigs on the Hogway Speedway or an elaborate pig sand sculpture, and the Lexington Barbecue Festival has both.

Squealin' on the Square

When: October
Where: Laurens, SC
Started: 2000
mainstreetlaurens.org
Every October, the historic public square in downtown Laurens is roped off for the weekend-long Squealin' on the Square festival. There are kids' games, arts and crafts, and music, but the main focus is on the Kansas City Barbeque Society–sanctioned barbecue competition and, of course, eating lots of barbecue from local vendors.

Mallard Creek Barbecue

When: Fourth Thursday in October
Where: Mallard Creek Presbyterian Church, Charlotte, NC
Started: 1929
mallardcreekbbq.com

The largest and most famous church barbecue in the Carolinas is the one hosted annually by the Mallard Creek Presbyterian Church, which has been doing it for more than 80 years. It all got started in 1929. The congregation had borrowed some money to build classrooms for their Sunday school, but in the wake of the stock market collapse, they were in danger of defaulting on their loan. Will Oehler, a longtime member, offered to barbecue a couple of pigs and a goat for the congregation to sell to the public. The event raised $89.50, enough of a success that the church decided to repeat the event the following year. They've been doing it ever since, and always on the fourth Thursday in October.

Early on, the pigs for the pits were donated by farmers who were members of the church, and H. Y. Galloway slaughtered and dressed them at his house. They were cooked over hickory coals in a pit dug in the ground and served along with Brunswick stew, coleslaw, rice, and pie. In the 1940s, the church members started taking the pigs to an abattoir for slaughter, and they built a screened-in cookhouse with cement block pits. As the crowds grew, potato salad replaced the rice, and applesauce took the place of the pies.

These days, the Mallard Creek Barbecue draws more than 20,000 attendees. Volunteers cook more than 8 tons of pork shoulders and hams several days before the event, and they've had to add metal cookers to supplement the open pits. Once ready, the meat is spread out on long wooden tables, hand chopped, and seasoned with a vinegar sauce, then it's stored in two large refrigerator trucks and reheated on the morning of the event. Brunswick stew—some 2,500 gallons of it—is cooked in a row of iron pots in specially made brick cookers and stirred with long wooden paddles. The Saturday before the event, members gather at the Community House to prepare 2 tons of coleslaw.

When Thursday arrives, the crowds descend midmorning and stay until the food runs out in the early evening. For $9, you can get a pork plate with slaw, applesauce, and Brunswick stew, or, for the same money, three sandwiches with coleslaw on a hamburger bun. Guests eat and socialize at long rows of wooden tables with folding chairs, decorated with bright flowers, bottles of barbecue sauce, and loaves of white bread in the bag. Though diners can buy sodas, the coffee is free, as has always been the tradition, and they'll

How to Tank an Election in North Carolina

Anyone aspiring to hold public office in the state of North Carolina needs to be ready to eat a lot of barbecue. From the obligatory meet and greet at the Mallard Creek Presbyterian Church to the endless rounds of smaller fundraising barbecues, pit-cooked pork has been connecting candidates with voters for more than two centuries. Those who lack the stomach for it may well find their entire campaign hamstrung. Just ask Rufus Edmisten, the former North Carolina attorney general who made a gubernatorial run in 1984. Early in the campaign, after a long summer making the obligatory rounds to dine on whole hog in the east and chopped pork shoulder in the west, Edmisten finally snapped.

"There is one thing that is blessed about tonight," Edmisten said while speaking at a forum for gubernatorial candidates in Raleigh. "We haven't had any of the damnable barbecue. I know it's heresy. But I have got some principles. I've eaten enough barbecue. I am not going to eat any more. I'm taking my stand and that's it."

The comments were published in newspapers across the state, and the Edmisten campaign immediate went into damage control. "I must have been possessed by demons the night I said that ridiculous thing about barbecue," he told the *Raleigh News & Observer*. "I remember saying it, but I wasn't in control of my faculties." Edmisten made a point of dining at several barbecues a week as the campaign continued, and he declared to voters, "I do feel cleansed now. I will never say anything bad about North Carolina's standard-bearer again."

Whether North Carolina voters forgave him for his heresy is unclear. He won the Democratic primary but he lost the general election to Republican Jim Martin by 10 points. Analysts blamed a long-standing political grudge that caused several key Democratic leaders to cross party lines and endorse Martin, but it's reasonable to suspect Edmisten had simply been unable to recover from that early barbecue gaffe.

drink more than 400 gallons of it. For those who want to get their barbecue to go, four drive-thru lines run under a covered shed, where volunteers hand out sacks of sandwiches and plastic tubs of Brunswick stew.

It didn't take North Carolina politicians very long to figure out that the Mallard Creek Barbecue was a great way to get in front of thousands of potential voters just before election day, and the event became an obligatory campaign stop for any local or statewide office seeker. As the number of campaigners increased, the church cordoned them off in a separate area roped off by colored flags. Walking the line and shaking the politicians hand is now an essential part of the annual Mallard Creek experience.

Whole Hogs & Vinegar Sauce: Eastern North Carolina & the Pee Dee

Eastern North Carolina and the Pee Dee region of South Carolina maintain the closest approximation of the original style of American barbecue—a set of recipes and techniques dating back to the colonial era. And that means cooking whole animals (that is, hogs) over hardwood coals and basting them with a fiery pepper-laced vinegar sauce. In this part of the Carolinas (or, at least, at the restaurants that still cook with real wood), they tend to cook on open pits: waist-high structures made of either cinder block or brick with an opening at the bottom into which glowing hardwood coals are shoveled. Whole hogs are splayed out on an iron rack or grate inside the pits, with just temporary coverings like sheet metal or flat pieces of cardboard. It's not far removed from the way whole pigs were cooked over open trenches dug in the ground 200 years ago, only the pits raise the meat up to waist level so the cooks don't have to stoop over to tend the coals.

With whole hog barbecue, the leaner hams and tenderloin meat gets mixed in with the fattier shoulder, so the final product can have a drier texture than the shoulder-only variety found farther west. But when properly basted and finished, Eastern-style barbecue can be exceptionally tender and flavorful—long strands of delicate pork steeped with tangy heat. The region's sauce is as basic as it comes: a simple blend of vinegar, salt, black pepper, and red pepper, the latter of which may be finely ground cayenne, dried red pepper flakes, or both. A few restaurants sneak in a little sugar to sweeten the version used at the table, but most don't. They are, however, likely to take a liberal hand with the red pepper, resulting in a sauce that can raise a sweat on your brow and leave your lips tingling.

It's a sad state of affairs that so many barbecue restaurants in Eastern North Carolina today cook their pigs with gas and mince it with mechanical choppers, resulting in gray bits of pork devoid of smoke flavor and unable to

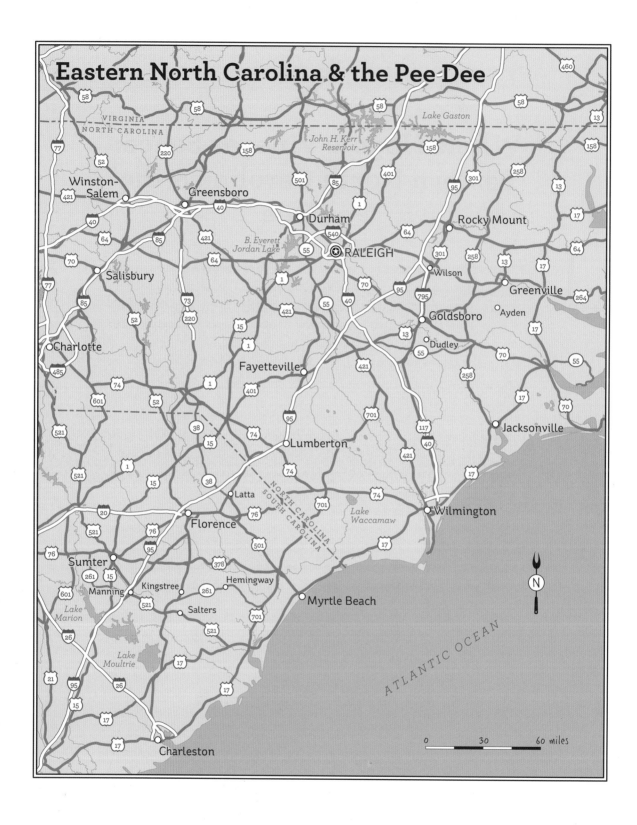

Eastern North Carolina & the Pee Dee

be revived by any amount of hot pepper–vinegar sauce. But, a few holdouts still do things the old-fashioned way with real wood, and it's very much worth the effort to seek these traditionalists out.

When touring the barbecue joints of the Pee Dee and Eastern North Carolina, you are in many ways experiencing an older way of life that is slowly but steadily fading away. This is farm country, and the towns where most of the classic barbecue joints are to be found today came into being in the 19th and 20th centuries for the sole purpose of supporting the farming community. They were home to the tobacco and cotton markets where farmers sold their crops, and to the dealerships where they bought tractors and parts, the feed stores where they purchased supplies, and the banks where they secured loans to see them through to the next harvest.

The barbecue style of the region has a direct link to this agricultural past, when in the late autumn families would slaughter hogs they had raised themselves and cook them on a pit to share with friends and neighbors. Many of the restaurants in Eastern North Carolina and the Pee Dee were established by farmers as a sideline business. They might slaughter a hog (often one of their own or one bought from a nearby farm) and cook it to sell on Friday and Saturday. Starting with a simple take-out stand, over time they added enclosed

What and Where Is the Pee Dee?

The "Pee Dee" is used as shorthand for the northeastern corner of South Carolina. It's named after a river, the Great Pee Dee, which in turn was named after the Native American Pee Dee tribe. The lower watershed of the Pee Dee River largely defines the region, and some people include the coastal counties of Horry and Georgetown in their definition, while others don't. The Pee Dee is predominantly rural, with Florence (population 37,056) its largest city.

Pork sandwich with white slaw and corn sticks from Grady's. ROBERT DONOVAN

dining rooms and expanded the side items served with the barbecue until, eventually, they had a full-service restaurant and a big parking lot to accommodate hundreds of hungry diners at a time. Later, as paved automobile highways began to be constructed, the owners of gas stations and country stores would do the same thing, cooking a whole hog to sell to their customers on weekends and, eventually, evolving into something approaching a restaurant, with side dishes and utensils and everything.

Even today, the side dishes in Eastern North Carolina tend to be rather simple, straightforward preparations. You'll often find "barbecued" potatoes that, despite the name, are just plain white potatoes boiled and cut in chunks. In the Pee Dee, a slice or two of white bread is common, but north of the border the accompanying bread is more likely to be made from a cornmeal batter in one of several forms: corn bread, hush puppies, or corn sticks (see recipe, In the Kitchen chapter). The latter are made from batter that's baked in a mold and then deep-fried to give them a crunchy, hush-puppy-like texture. The coleslaw in these parts tends to be made from cabbage that is shredded, not

BARBECUE LOVER'S THE CAROLINAS

chopped, with a mayonnaise-based dressing and often a little pickle or celery seed. In Eastern North Carolina, Brunswick stew is a popular accompaniment to a plate for pulled pork. Some Pee Dee restaurants have adopted the hash and rice that's served in the Midlands and Lowcountry of South Carolina, while others offer perloo or chicken bog, rice dishes unique to the region.

Perloo & Chicken Bog

It's spelled a lot of ways: *pilau, perloo, purlo*. And it's pronounced in just as many ways, too. But, no matter how you spell it or say it, the word refers to an old Lowcountry delicacy, a savory dish or rice cooked with chicken and spices. Karen Hess, the author of the *Carolina Rice Kitchen* (1992), dug deeper into the history of the dish than anyone else, and her description is perhaps the best: "Long-grain rice that has been washed and presoaked is added to simmering aromatic broth ... then covered and cooked until nearly dry." In the 18th and 19th centuries, perloo was the signature dish of the Carolina rice plantations the surrounded Charleston. Somewhere along the line, traditional Lowcountry perloo migrated up to the Pee Dee, and in the process diverged into a variant called "chicken bog."

Perloo and chicken bog can be found on the buffets at many of the barbecue restaurants in the Pee Dee, and the difference between the two is simple: Chicken bog is wet (hence the "bog" part of the name), while the grains of rice in perloo are dry and stand loose and distinct from each other. But, this doesn't mean perloo is a boring dish. Far from it. Done properly it's a tasty treat, the rice grains infused with the savory spices and broth, the whole assemblage steamed to just the right firm but toothsome texture. It's a combination that goes just swimmingly with a plate of slow-cooked barbecue.

So, if you see that funny P word on the next Pee Dee buffet you visit, take a few spoonfuls of chicken and rice and put them on your plate. You won't be disappointed.

In recent decades, many restaurants have expanded their offerings, instituting all-you-can-eat buffets with dishes ranging from baked beans and collards to fried catfish and chicken. But barbecue is still the main draw, and these restaurants have become not just places to get something good to eat but also important institutions in the social life of their communities. It's where locals gather to eat, socialize, and enjoy one another's company. It's where civic clubs hold their meetings and where people go as much for the conversations to be had as for the food they can eat.

There are still a lot of active farms throughout the region, but they're growing fewer by the year as younger generations seek out different lines of work or move away altogether. The increasing automation and commoditization of agriculture means that farmers don't need as big a crew of workers as they once did, and in Eastern North Carolina in particular the rise of factory hog farming has meant a relentless march toward fewer farms producing on an ever-increasing scale. Fallow fields are giving over to weeds and scrub brush, and cotton, tobacco, and soybean lands have been steadily converted to timber. You'll see an awful lot of pine trees driving through Eastern North Carolina and the Pee Dee.

If you want to strike out and explore the region, you'll need a full tank of gas, for the barbecue joints are relatively few and far between. In North Carolina, you'll need to hit a couple of key towns, including Greenville, Ayden, and Goldsboro, where some of the best barbecue joints are concentrated. In the Pee Dee, you'll be heading down a lot of two-lane country highways with nothing but pine trees on either side, but it's well worth the time spent. While there may not be a whole lot of them, the good barbecue joints in the eastern part of the two Carolinas tend to be really, really good, and there are a few that rank right up among the best in the Carolinas—which, by extension, make them among the best in the world. It's there that you have the best odds of getting a sense of how barbecue probably tasted back in the era before automobiles, electricity, and even restaurants themselves.

Brown's Bar-B-Que

809 N. Williamsburg County Hwy., Kingstree, SC 29556; (843) 382-2753 **Founded:** 1981 **Cooking Method:** Gas on closed metal pits **Serves:** Lunch daily; dinner Wed–Sat **Cards Accepted:** Yes

Brown's Bar-B-Que got it start back in the 1980s when Thomas Brown started cooking barbecue under a shed outside of Kingstree. That led to a small takeout restaurant with picnic tables, which was replaced around 1990 by the current long, pale-yellow building. It's operated today by Thomas Brown Jr. and his wife, Angela, who carry on the tradition of whole hog barbecue.

The Browns go through seven pigs a day, and almost every scrap winds up on the buffet in one form or another. The pork is pulled into long strands with generous white chunks and bits of the crisp brown outer meat left in, and it's pre-sauced with a salty blend of vinegar and red pepper flakes. The ribs are pulled out separately on the buffet, and they, too, are soaked through with the same pepper-laced sauce, which is among the fieriest in the Pee Dee and will leave your lips tingling.

The lesser parts of the pig are put to good use, too. The cracklings are fried into salty chunks that are crisp but still chewy inside. The Browns make their hash with the heads and the livers, which they grind together with onions and seasonings. The end product is a thick, sort of gray, lumpy sauce that's rich with liver, and—surprisingly, considering the heat of the barbecue sauce—it's actually rather mild. They also make a unique concoction they call "BBQ gravy," essentially the spicy pepper vinegar that was poured onto the hogs while they cooked, which is later put on the buffet for folks to season their greens and string beans. There are even pigs' feet on the buffet, their gelatinous meat tinged pink by a tangy sauce.

In addition to all the permutations of pork, there's plenty more to choose from on the big L-shaped buffet and the separate salad bar that flanks it. The vegetables rotate, but they are often picked fresh from the Browns' own garden, like collards and cabbage in the winter or okra, squash, and corn during summer. The potato salad is tinged with sweet pickle and slightly yellow from mustard. Be sure to try the chicken bog, for Brown's version is an especially good example of this Pee Dee specialty—a fragrant blend of tender chicken, rice, sausage, and seasonings. To wrap things up, there's a full dessert station offering a range of sweets that might include, on any given day, banana pudding, German chocolate cake, white cake topped with sweet coconut frosting, and homemade pecan pie.

For Kingstree, Brown's is not just a barbecue joint but a beloved family restaurant and a popular gathering places. The big dining room can accommodate hundreds of diners, and a gap in the sliding-curtained wall offers a peek into the private dining area in the back, where the local Rotary Club meets. A rarity in the Pee Dee, Brown's is actually open for lunch all seven days of the week and for dinner Wed through Sat giving the folks of Kingstree plenty of opportunities to gather together over a big barbecue meal.

B's Barbecue

751 B's Barbecue Rd., Greenville, NC 27858 **Founded:** 1978 **Cooking Method:** Whole hog over charcoal on open metal pits **Serves:** Lunch Tue–Sat **Cards Accepted:** No

It's easy to remember the address for B's Barbecue, for it's located on B's Barbecue Road (actually, at the intersection of B's Barbecue Road and NC 43). The restaurant occupies a tiny building that was once a country store, and it closes whenever the food runs out, which can happen even before the lunch rush is over. They don't have a telephone, much less a website. Heck, they don't even really have a parking lot, just an expanse of gravel where cars wedge in at haphazard angles under the big oak trees and overflow out onto the side of the highway. B's recently made one concession to modernity, however, replacing the old rusty sign that once topped the small white building with a brand new bright blue version that announces "B's Barbecue: Born in Eastern NC." Everything else is pretty much as it has been since the 1970s.

The menu is simple: just whole hog barbecue and barbecued chicken, which are available on a plate, a dinner, or in a sandwich. They're cooked in a screened-in pit building out behind the restaurant that holds what are effectively gigantic metal grills with big lids, for B's is one of the few restaurants around that fires their pits with charcoal. The whole hogs—anywhere from 8 to 14 a day—are cooked overnight, then chopped by hand, the cook taking care to remove all the gristle and inferior bits. B's barbecued chicken is just as good as the pork, with smoky, juicy meat and crisp skin. The only side dishes are white slaw, potatoes, green beans, and long, skinny corn sticks. The potatoes are boiled with ketchup, which give them a pale red cast, and the corn sticks

are nice and crunchy with a sort of grits-like texture inside. B's sauce has a touch of white sugar with the vinegar, salt, and black and red pepper, and it's served in old Royal Crown Cola bottles.

B's was started by William and Peggy Lawhorn in the late 1970s (the "B" comes from William's nickname, Bill), and it's now run by their three daughters. They have no plans to make any changes to this Eastern North Carolina classic, and that's just the way their customers want it.

Bum's Restaurant

566 3rd St., Ayden, NC 28513; (252) 746-6880; bumsrestaurant.com
Founded: 1966 **Cooking Method:** Whole hog on open brick pits over hardwood coals **Serves:** Breakfast and lunch Mon–Sat, dinner Mon and Wed–Fri **Cards Accepted:** No

Lathan "Bum" Dennis retired from the Navy in 1966 and purchased the City Cafe from John Bill Dennis, his father's first cousin. He renamed the establishment Bum's Restaurant, and it's been a fixture in downtown Ayden ever since. It's not so much a barbecue joint as a meat 'n' two diner that includes pit-cooked barbecue alongside fried chicken, Black Angus steaks, beef stew, and chicken and pastry. The barbecue gets top billing, though, and for good reason. Cooked the old-fashioned way—whole hogs cooked over real wood on open pits—the chopped pork is juicy and smoky with bits of crisp skin chopped into it.

The Legacy of Skilton Dennis

Starting in the late 1800s, Skilton Dennis regularly loaded up a wagon on Saturday afternoons and took home-cooked barbecue into Otter Town to sell to the farmers who had come in for the weekend. In 1890, Otter Town changed its name to the more respectable-sounding Ayden, but Dennis kept bringing his barbecue in to sell, and he eventually sired an entire line of barbecue cooks. (Popular legend has it that Ayden is a shortened version of "a den of thieves," since Otter Town was a notoriously rough place. Historians throw a little cold water on that tale, maintaining that a man named Joab Harrington picked "Aden" from a map of the world and submitted it as a suggestion to the US Post Office. The post office agreed to the change, with the stipulation that the letter *y* be added. And thus Otter Town became Ayden.)

Skilton Dennis's son, John, and his grandson Bill followed in the patriarch's footsteps, taking the informal business into the 20th century. Eventually, Bill Dennis rented a booth on a street corner, where he sold his barbecue along with corn bread made by his wife, Susan, and in the 1920s he moved into a building on 2nd Street. One of Bill Dennis's sons, Emmett, continued operating the restaurant after Bill passed away, and a second, John Bill, set up shop in a 17-foot trailer with a barbecue pit from which he sold just pork, corn bread, and drinks. John Bill later built a dining room around the trailer and transformed it into a permanent restaurant, too.

Today, Ayden boasts two world-famous barbecue restaurants, and both trace their roots back to these early Dennis joints. Josie Dennis was Emmett and Bill John's sister, and her son Pete Jones started working at his Uncle Emmett's place as a boy. When he turned 18, he set out on his own and opened a curb-service drive-in on the edge of town, calling it the Skylight Inn. As was standard for drive-ins in that era, he sold hot dogs, hamburgers, and sandwiches alongside the barbecue his uncle had taught him to cook. Lathan "Bum" Dennis, Pete Jones's cousin, worked both for Pete and for their uncle John Bill. In 1966 Bum bought out John Bill's operations and renamed it Bum's

Restaurant. Today both Bum's and the Skylight Inn use the same corn bread recipe developed by Susan Dennis way back in the 1920s.

If you ask the Dennis and Jones families, they'll maintain that Skilton Dennis was the first person to sell barbecue commercially in North Carolina. From what I can tell, they might just be right. At a minimum, they are carrying on a proud family tradition that is now well into its second century.

DENNY CULBERT

Ayden calls itself the collard capital of the world, and the town holds an annual collard festival, so it's little wonder that the greens at Bum's are so good. Locally grown and light green in color, they're called "cabbage collards," and Bum's cooks them in a slow-simmered stock made from three kinds of ham. The corn bread is crisp, unsweetened, and about a half inch thick, and it's made following a century-old Dennis family recipe. Brunswick stew, red potatoes, potato salad, coleslaw, and sweet potato muffins are popular sides, too, and for dessert, the warm meringue-topped banana pudding is legendary.

The Dennis family has been cooking barbecue since the 19th century, when Skilton Dennis (see "The Legacy of Skilton Dennis" sidebar, this chapter) became known for cooking whole hogs for church gatherings. The

The Origin of Brunswick Stew

Brunswick stew is a classic North Carolina barbecue side dish, but it is commonly found down in Georgia and over in eastern Tennessee, too. (Curiously, it tends to leap right over the middle part of South Carolina, where the standard side dish is hash—see "Hash & Rice" sidebar, Yellow Mustard & Hash chapter.) Where Brunswick stew originated is one of those inflammatory questions that tends to gets barbecue fans all hot and bothered. Two different Brunswicks—one a city in Georgia, the other a county in Virginia—lay claim to having originated the dish. Curiously, North Carolina has both a Brunswick County and a town of Brunswick of its own, but few Tar Heels have claimed that their state invented the dish.

So, how did Brunswick stew get to North Carolina? Did it come up from Georgia or down from Virginia? Georgia partisans point to a tangible piece of physical evidence: a historical monument outside of the town of Brunswick consisting of a 25-gallon iron pot on a stone base bearing the inscription "In this pot the first Brunswick Stew was made on St. Simons Isle, July 2 1898." It might be true that the first Brunswick stew *on St. Simons* was cooked in that pot, but it was by no means the very first Brunswick stew. That famous concoction had been served in Virginia for over half a century before the St. Simons claim, appearing in newspaper accounts of Virginia barbecues as far back as the 1840s. In 1849, the *Alexandria Gazette* described it as "a genuine South-side dish, composed of squirrels, chicken, a little bacon, and corn and tomatoes, ad libitum."

As best as I can tell, Brunswick stew was first devised by a rolling stone named James Matthews, a veteran of the War of 1812 who bounced around Brunswick County, Virginia, in the 1820s, mooching off friends as a house guest and performing odd jobs in return. He was a great squirrel hunter, and, as one man writing in 1886 recalled, "it was his way of cooking the squirrels which gained him such popularity and eclat with the ladies."

Matthews had a simple recipe for stew. He cooked squirrels in water with bacon and onions until the flesh was falling from the bones, then skimmed out the inedible parts and finished the stew with butter and bread crumbs. After his death, Matthews was succeeded by a series of local stew masters, and over time they added tomato, onion, corn, and potatoes to the recipe. By the 1840s the stew had spread beyond Brunswick County and was being served at barbecues throughout Virginia. It soon snuck down into North Carolina and, eventually, to Georgia, too. Why it skipped over South Carolina remains a mystery. (See the Brunswick Stew recipe, In the Kitchen chapter.)

restaurant is run today by Larry Dennis, Bum's son, and his wife, Teresa. The slogan "Wood Cooked Barbecue" is proudly emblazoned in white letters on the front window, a declaration of pride for barbecue purists in Eastern North Carolina. While plenty of barbecue restaurants in the Piedmont of North Carolina serve breakfast, Bum's is one of the few in the eastern part of the state that opens at the crack of dawn, serving a full slate of eggs, pancakes, and french toast six days a week.

Cooper's Country Store

6945 US 521, Salters, SC 29590 **Founded:** 1937 **Cooking Method:** Whole hog on closed metal pits **Serves:** Barbecue available all day, Mon–Sat **Cards Accepted:** Yes

If you're heading eastward on US 521 from Manning toward Georgetown, keep your eye peeled for the Exxon sign on the right side of the road about 2 miles past the town of Salters. When you see it, pull into the parking lot of the old white grocery store, head inside, and make your way to the little counter in the back. That's where you'll find the barbecue.

In 1937, the year US 521 was completed, Theron Burrows built a combination Esso gas station and grocery store in a prime spot at the intersection of the new highway and SC 377. Originally known as Burrows's Service Station, the white wooden building is a rare surviving example of the architecture of country stores in the early automobile era, particularly the big second-story porch that extends out over the lone gas pump. After Burrows passed away in 1974, the business was taken over by his daughter, Adalyn Cooper, and her husband, George. They started cooking pork and chicken on a portable barbecue pit, then in the 1980s they built permanent pits under a big wooden shed, where the barbecue for Cooper's Country Store is still cooked today.

Russell Cooper started working for his Uncle George back in the 1980s, and he runs the business today. The lone Exxon pump out front is a modern, up-to-date version that takes credit cards, but just about everything else about the store is a throwback to an older time—well-worn wooden floors, shelves crowded with groceries and tools and all sorts of useful items, deer heads mounted on the wall. Country hams from Virginia hang from white wooden racks, and locally made sausage is displayed in the glass cases where you order the barbecue. You can buy buckets of lard and hog heads, too, in case you're in the market for such things.

The barbecue is cooked by Levern Darby using the techniques he learned from his mother, who used to barbecue whole hogs on a pit just around the corner from Cooper's. On weekends, she took the meat to the store parking lot

and sold it out of the trunk of her car. Later, when the Coopers decided to sell barbecue from the store, they hired Levern Darby to make it for them.

The pork is pulled into long, tender strands, and it's soaked through with a generous dose of pepper-laced vinegar sauce. If you've tried and failed to re-create Pee Dee–style barbecue with a bottle of vinegar-based barbecue sauce bought from a store, there may be a reason: It's not as simple as just adding sauce to roasted pork. Darby and the Cooper's crew cook their pigs for 12 to 14 hours, skin up at first, then flipped over on their back for the rest of the time. To finish it, they fill the cavity with vinegar and pepper and crank up the pits, bringing the sauce to a simmer inside the hog and effectively braising the meat. "We don't . . . take it off the pit and throw it in a pan and just dump raw vinegar," Russell Cooper explained to oral historian Rien Fertel in 2012. "It's boiled in the cavity. That's the way the old-time people did it, and that's the way we do it."

The result is some tender, fiery barbecue. You can buy pulled pork by the pound in plastic containers or on a simple barbecue sandwich—just the meat inside a plain hamburger bun. You can also buy a whole or a half of a bar-becued chicken and what's billed as "cooked red hash," though there doesn't seem to be a scrap of tomato or anything red in it except for ample flecks of red pepper. It's more a creamy spread with long, tender shreds that, apart from the red pepper and a few chunks of white onions, is quite akin to the pork *rillettes* you might find on the charcuterie plates at the high-end restaurants down in Charleston. When you spoon some hash over a pile of white rice, it makes for a splendidly rich side dish that's filling enough to stand as a meal on its own. Little wonder that generations of beach travelers have made it a tradition to stop off at Cooper's to stock up on barbecue and hash on their way to the coast.

The Opening of Rocky Mount's Barbecue Park

In May 2014, the city of Rocky Mount, North Carolina, held a celebration for the grand opening of Barbecue Park, perhaps the only city park in the country commemorating slow-smoked meat. "This park allows citizens to reflect on Rocky Mount's rich barbecue history," explained Parks and Recreation director Kelvin Yarrell at the opening, "and to understand why barbecue is such a huge part of Rocky Mount's heritage." The park is dotted with signs memorializing the Eastern North Carolina barbecue tradition, including now-departed local restaurants like Buck Overton's Barbecue, Brown's Chicken and Barbecue House, Josh Bullock's Barbecue, and the granddaddy of them all, Bob Melton's Barbecue, one of the state's first sit-down barbecue restaurants.

The park is located on the banks of the Tar River at the site of Melton's former barbecue house, which opened in 1933 and was destroyed in 1999 by the flood caused by Hurricane Floyd. It's equipped with soccer fields, a fishing pier, walking trails, and a playground. Local Eagle Scouts raised $7,500 to pay for the barbecue history signs. And, yes, at the opening ceremony, they served free barbecue to all comers.

ROBERT DONOVAN

Grady's Barbecue

3096 Arrington Bridge Rd., Dudley, NC 28333; (919) 735-7243

Founded: 1986 **Cooking Method:** Whole hog over oak and hickory on an open brick pit **Serves:** Lunch Wed–Sun **Cards Accepted:** No

In 1986, Gerri Grady's brother-in-law decided to open a barbecue restaurant in Dudley, North Carolina. Gerri offered to help him out with the cooking, and on opening day the brother-in-law discovered that he didn't much enjoy running a barbecue restaurant. But, Gerri Grady liked it just fine, so she and her husband, Stephen, stepped in and bought it. They've been running Grady's Barbecue ever since.

It's one of the smallest restaurants in the state, just a small white-painted cinder-block building and a few booths with red wooden seats inside. A sign on the wall promises "Highly Seasoned Foods," and the offering lives up to the commitment. The Gradys serve chopped pork along with potatoes, coleslaw, and hush puppies enclosed in little white paper envelopes. All their veggies— collards, cabbage, black-eyed peas—are hand cut and cooked fresh each day. Gerri Grady still brews the ice tea in a pot on the stove, and her homemade sweet potato pie is a favorite of regulars.

As for the barbecue, it starts with whole hogs split into sides, along with racks of chicken quarters, which Stephen Grady cooks over oak and hickory coals in brick pits following the style he learned from his grandfather, a noted barbecue cook in the neighborhood. He cooks the meat fresh four nights a week, starting it off at 11 p.m. and finishing it up around 8 a.m. the next morning. And that helps explain why Grady's keeps rather unusual hours, opening its doors at 10 a.m. from Wed through Sun and closing down at 3 p.m. on weekdays and 4 p.m. on Sat and Sun.

McCabe's Bar-B-Que

480 N. Brooks St., Manning, SC 29102; (803) 435-2833 **Founded:** 1990
Cooking Method: Whole hogs on a closed pit over oak and hickory
Serves: Lunch Thurs–Sat **Cards Accepted:** No

Here's a tip for navigating the room the first time you visit McCabe's. Make your way to the right side of the buffet and pick up a Styrofoam plate. The woman behind the counter will ask what your party would like to drink (which, by all rights, should be sweet tea), and someone will fill the cups for you while you load your plate from the steam table. There's no need to pay right away—that comes after the meal. Just look around the room and find the table that's been selected for you: It's the empty one with the cups of tea awaiting and a full pitcher for refills.

Even as barbecue joints go, McCabe's is a modest place. It occupies a pale-green building set back from the street on the north side of Manning proper. Inside there's just a single small room with white-painted wood walls and about a dozen booth-style tables, a short buffet counter and cash register positioned along the far wall. It also has some of the most limited hours of any South Carolina barbecue joint, being open just three days and only through the midafternoon, but the locals know that during those brief hours they can find some of the best barbecue in the Pee Dee.

McCabe's cooks whole hogs in enclosed metal pits in the screened-in room that extends off to the right behind the restaurant proper. The meat is hand pulled and pre-sauced, resulting in long, thin strands that are slightly spicy and subtly smoky with little hits of crunch from outside brown. McCabe's buffet has a smaller selection than many, but every item on it is top notch. That includes green beans, stewed tomatoes, cabbage, sweet potatoes, hush puppies, and coleslaw. Of particular note is the perloo, a savory rice dish that's not often found in barbecue restaurants outside the Pee Dee region. The turnip greens may well be the best greens in the state: finely chopped and slow cooked with little bits of pork that give it a sweet, smooth richness. The superb fried chicken has a crisp, light batter, and McCabe's hash and rice—a thick, reddish concoction that's richly gooey and not too spicy—is as a good as anyone's.

Although the pulled pork is pre-sauced on the buffet, I recommended adding a couple of extra squirts from the squeeze bottle of thin reddish sauce that

awaits at your table. The pork steeps in that peppery, slightly sweet vinegar as you work your way through the contents of your plate. At the end, you're left with a delicious pool of tangy, spicy broth at the bottom of the Styrofoam plate and it's absolutely heavenly when you mop it up with the last remaining strands of pulled pork.

McCabe's remains a low-key place, and it has not gotten nearly as much media attention as some of the better-known barbecue joints in the Carolinas have, though it has appeared twice in *Southern Living*, and in 2010 *Garden & Gun* included it in its roundup of the best-kept secret barbecue pits in the South. (The framed articles hang on the wall in the small dining room.) But, thanks to word of mouth and its location close by I-95 in Manning, McCabe's has long been a favorite detour for South Carolinians heading to the Grand Strand beaches, and it's more than worth your while to stop by, too.

Parker's Barbecue

2514 US 301, Wilson, NC 27893; (252) 237-0972 **Founded:** 1946
Cooking Method: Whole hog on gas-fired pits **Serves:** Lunch and dinner daily **Cards Accepted:** No

Like a lot of Eastern North Carolina barbecue joints these days, Parker's cooks with gas, but it's still worth a visit because it is a genuine civic institution in the town of Wilson. On weekends, diners queue up in a long line that snakes

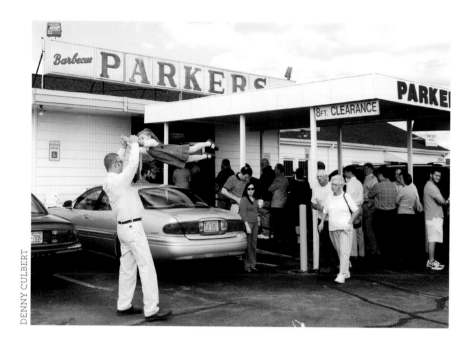

DENNY CULBERT

its way clear out into the parking lot. As they finally reach the front door, each group is greeted by the owners before being ushered to their tables by young waiters in white aprons and old-style paper hats.

Ralph Parker, the last of the three original partners, passed away in July 2013 at age 89. The business is carried on today by Eric Lippard, Donald Williams, and Kevin Lamm. Their whole hog barbecue is finely chopped and seasoned with a spicy vinegar sauce. The full menu includes fried chicken, grilled chicken, and fried shrimp and flounder, plus oysters when they're in season. Parker's can really turn it out, too, cooking 150 pigs and 8,000 fried chickens a week to feed over 20,000 customers.

The barbecue is served on buns as sandwiches, on barbecue plates accompanied by slaw and corn bread, or as dinners with a choice of Brunswick stew, boiled potatoes, french fries, or string beans. Parker's slightly sweet coleslaw is finely chopped and tinged yellow with mustard, and their sides include boiled potatoes, something you see in Eastern North Carolina but not very often anywhere else. In a sort of sectional compromise, they serve both long, tubular hush puppies and skinny corn sticks. For sauces, there are two options: a vinegar sauce laced with crushed red pepper and Texas Pete (see "Texas Pete" sidebar, Shoulders & Light Red Sauce chapter) or, in an unusual twist, just a bottle of straight cider vinegar.

Barbecue Presbyterian Church

It seems only fitting, considering its residents' love for wood-roasted pork, that North Carolina is home to the Barbecue Presbyterian Church. It's located about 15 miles outside the town of Sanford, North Carolina, which is itself about 40 miles southeast of Raleigh. The church dates all the way back to 1758, and the congregation built their first building—a one-room structure made from logs—in 1765.

As for the unique name, it actually comes not from the food that North Carolinians loved to eat even back in the 18th century but, rather, from the method of cooking itself. According to the church's official history, Red McNeill, a new settler in the area, saw steam rising from a nearby creek, and it reminded him of the pits he had seen down in the Caribbean. He named the rivulet "Barbecue Creek," and the church took its name from it.

NICHOLAS MCWHIRTER

Parker's has been serving the same food now for almost 70 years and in the process has earned an army of loyal fans. "People come in, and they're family also," co-owner Kevin Lamm told interviewer Rien Fertel in 2011, "and they feel a part of this place, and they have a connection." That connection is what keeps the institution of Parker's Barbecue going strong well into the 21st century.

The Pit

328 W. Davie St., Raleigh, NC 27601; (919) 890-4500; thepit-raleigh .com **Founded:** 2007 **Cooking Method:** Whole hog over charcoal on closed metal pits **Serves:** Lunch and dinner daily **Cards Accepted:** Yes

Occupying a restored 1930s meatpacking building in Raleigh's downtown warehouse district, The Pit blends the old and the new in the world of barbecue. On the one hand, they serve real pit-cooked whole hog barbecue dressed in a classic Eastern North Carolina sauce. Alongside, they offer traditional fare like coleslaw, black-eyed peas, and heirloom cabbage collards, which are light green in color, sweeter in flavor, and founded almost exclusively in Eastern North Carolina. At the same time, there are exposed brick walls, tealights on the tables, and a full bar. They take reservations (which you can even make online) and have valet parking, too. It's even run by a restaurant group, Empire Eats, which operates five restaurants in downtown Raleigh.

Inside the restaurant, the barbecue is cooked in custom-designed metal pits that have big industrial ventilation systems to whisk the smoke out of the building. The whole hogs are cooked over Kingsford charcoal and seasoned with hickory chips soaked in vinegar and pepper. With its other meats, The Pit breaks outside other Eastern North Carolina conventions, serving Texas-style brisket, chopped turkey, and baby back ribs. Perhaps most iconoclastic of all, though, is the barbecued tofu: slices of soy protein shaped like chicken nuggets, which are grilled and tossed with slices of squash, zucchini, and cherry tomatoes and can be dressed by diners with barbecue sauce. A full slate of appetizers includes deviled eggs, fried pimento cheese, and bacon bruschetta, and for sides there are sweet potato fries and red beans and rice. The Pit's house-made banana pudding is particularly tempting: vanilla pudding, vanilla wafers, sliced bananas, and marshmallow creme layered in white ceramic bowls, topped with meringue, then baked in the oven until the meringues peaks are toasted golden brown.

It's definitely an unusual hybrid of the traditional and the trendy, but The Pit has managed to win over a lot of diners in the Research Triangle. It went over so well that Empire Eats opened a second Pit location, lovingly nicknamed "D-Pit," in nearby Durham in 2011.

Scott's Bar-B-Que

2734 Hemingway Hwy. (SC 261 at Cow Head Road), Hemingway, SC 29554; (843) 558-0134; thescottsbbq.com **Founded:** 1972 **Cooking Method:** Whole hog on open cinder-block pits using oak, pecan, and hickory **Serves:** Lunch Wed–Sat; dinner Thurs–Sat **Cards Accepted:** No

Folks in the Hemingway area know that if they have an oak or pecan tree down in their yard, they can call Rodney Scott, and he and his crew will come out with chain saws to cut it up and cart it away. That wood is destined for Scott's burn barrel, which is fashioned from old industrial piping, now warped and wrinkled from years of heat, with truck axles inserted near the bottom to hold the burning logs. New logs are periodically tossed in the top, and as they burn, coals fall through the axles to the bottom, where they're scooped out by the shovelful, carried into the cookhouse, and layered into the openings in the bottom of the cinder-block pits. "We use mostly oak," Rodney Scott says. "And we use more pecan than we do hickory. We don't find a ton of hickory growing in this area." It's a unique and impressive operation, and it involves plenty of

DENNY CULBERT

manual labor. Scott keeps his pigs on the pits skin-side up for 12 hours, then flips them over and finishes them with a thorough mopping of fiery vinegar-and-pepper sauce. The resulting pulled pork is intensely smoky and tongue-tinglingly spicy and as good an example of the craft of barbecue as you'll find anywhere.

It all got started back in 1972 when Roosevelt and Ella Scott, who had been living in Philadelphia, moved back home to South Carolina and opened Scott's Variety Store at Brunson Crossroads, just west of Hemingway. The Scotts learned to cook barbecue from Roosevelt's Uncle Thomas and began selling it alongside the dry goods and sodas at the store. Before long, barbecue moved into the forefront. Rodney Scott, Roosevelt's son, has now taken over the primary cooking duties, and he says they go through an average of 15 hogs per week.

The menu at Scott's is pretty basic. Most customers buy pulled pork by the pound, though you can get a pork plate with coleslaw and baked beans plus two slices of white bread for either making a sandwich or just eating alongside as you see fit. The sauce is among the spiciest in the Carolinas, and while the pulled pork is already pretty fiery just from the mopping it gets on the pit, you can heat it up even more with a good dose from one of the squeeze bottles on the table. Scott's serves barbecued chicken, too, and they recently added a new item to the menu: a smoked rib eye steak, which they sell only on Saturday. "I had a bunch of steaks in my freezer," Rodney Scott explains, "and I could not figure out what I was going to do with them. So I kept trying to figure out how to make a really great steak." He ended up marinating the rib eyes in the family's barbecue sauce for about 24 hours, then smoking them on the barbecue pit.

But Scott's whole hog barbecue is still the center of attention. You can eat some at a couple of tables in the corner of the store, but the bulk of Scott's sales are takeout. They also do a brisk business selling whole hogs for weddings, family reunions, and other gatherings, too. (A large cooked whole hog runs around $400, or you can bring your own pig and they'll cook it for you for $100.) Be sure to grab one of the plastic ziplock bags of fried pork skins. They are crisp and airy and, odds are, won't make it all the way to wherever you're heading.

Write-ups in the *New York Times* and appearances on TV shows like *CBS Sunday Morning* have helped make Rodney Scott a star of South Carolina barbecue, and he's frequently invited to cook at events like New York's Big Apple Block Party. Hemingway may be, as Scott puts it, "an hour and a half from anywhere," but barbecue fans from all over now make pilgrimages to Scott's to see what the fuss is all about "*Lots* of out-of-towners show up here now," Scott says. "From Myrtle Beach, from Charleston. We've had people in from Connecticut, Florida, Chicago, and I'm just talking about this week."

A Devastating Fire Sends a
Cook into Exile

On the day before Thanksgiving in 2013, one of the pigs cooking on the pits at Scott's Bar-B-Que caught fire, and the flames reached the wooden wall of the cookhouse, shot upward, and set the entire roof ablaze. The building was a total loss, but the family was determined to rebuild. Rodney Scott kept the business going by cooking on four spare pits he had out behind the store, plus a couple of portable pits he dragged in temporarily.

To rebuild, he was able to tap into the network of friends he had built cooking barbecue at events across the country. The Fatback Collective, a group of 20 or so cooks, restaurateurs, and writers, helped him stage the "Rodney in Exile" tour, wherein Scott traveled around the South cooking barbecue alongside other famous pitmasters and fine-dining chefs, too. The proceeds from these events raised three-quarters of what Scott needed to rebuild the cookhouse (the rest he secured from bank loans). "We came to the conclusion that we should do this right," Scott says. "We decided to upgrade to all codes and all regulations, so this thing would be [around] more than a few more years." And that means a new pithouse made from noncombustible metal, plus better exhaust systems and a new prep area for pulling pork.

But don't expect any changes to the main building of Scott's Variety Store, which was untouched by the fire. It will remain as much a throwback as ever, with its battered metal roof and white-painted cinder-block sides with bright cyan trim—an iconic representation of the old style of country stores. "The store we don't plan to do a whole lot with," Scott says. "We plan to leave some original history alone."

Don't expect any differences in the barbecue either. "The only change I plan to make is to pump out as much more pork as possible," Scott says. "As far as the style and procedure, I plan to keep that all the same, the same way I do it now."

Shuler's Bar-B-Que

419 SC 38 West, Latta, SC 29592; (843) 752-4700; shulersbbq.com
Founded: 1996 **Cooking Method:** Pork shoulders over oak coals on
a metal rotisserie pit **Serves:** Lunch and dinner Thurs–Sat **Cards
Accepted:** No

Shuler's occupies a big log-cabin-style building off the side of SC 38 a couple
of miles outside of Latta, South Carolina. Like most barbecue joints in this part
of the state, it's an all-you-can-eat buffet and is open just Thurs through Sat.
Owner Norton Hughes cooks pork shoulders, chicken, and dry-rubbed ribs on
a giant rotisserie pit fired by shovelfuls of wood coals. The pulled pork is quite
good, but for me the real stars are the dry-rubbed ribs, which are thick, meaty,
and very smoky—a rarity in this part of the Carolinas. The side dishes on the
buffet are well above average, too, and they include fried chicken, fried corn,
marinated slaw, collards, and mac 'n' cheese. Lynn Hughes's sweet potato soufflé and homemade "little biscuits" are crowd favorites, as are her from-scratch
desserts like peach cobbler and red velvet cake.

Shuler's started out with just a single high-roofed dining room in 1996,
but they won over so many fans that they had to add on what they call "the
back porch," a second large dining area enclosed by broad glass windows. If
you snag a table on that porch, you can eat your barbecue overlooking a large,
peaceful pond, which is a very fine way to spend an evening.

Skylight Inn

4618 S. Lee St., Ayden, NC 28513; (252) 746-4113; skylightinnbbq.com
Founded: 1947 **Cooking Method:** Whole hog on open brick pits over
oak **Serves:** Lunch and dinner Mon–Sat **Cards Accepted:** No

You won't mistake the Skylight Inn for any other barbecue joint in America, for
it's the only one whose roof is topped by big white dome with a giant American
flag flying above it. Back in 1980, National Geographic published a book called
Back Roads America that declared the Skylight Inn made the best barbecue in
the country, and feature stories in *Southern Living* and other magazines soon
followed. The Skylight Inn was still a pretty tiny restaurant at the time, but by
1984, as the publicity began drawing bigger and bigger crowds, Pete Jones
and his sons, Bruce and Jeff, decided it was time to expand. "If we're going to
be the barbecue capital," Bruce Jones told his father, "let's put a dome on the
top." And that's exactly what they did.

"We've been cooking the same way since we opened," says Samuel Jones,
Bruce Jones's son and now the third generation of pitmasters to cook at the

Where's the Beer?

Folks visiting the Carolinas from, say, Memphis or Kansas City may be surprised when they stop off at the local barbecue joint and discover they can't order a beer. Carolina barbecue restaurants are almost universally dry with a few notable exceptions, like Po Pigs Bo-B-Q near Edisto Beach, which has a glass-doored reach-in cooler with a few bottles of beer. Beer's relative absence from Carolina barbecue joints might be attributable to the fact that so many of the two states' classic restaurants originated as casual street-corner stands or drive-ins. It's common in the Carolinas for barbecue restaurants to close their doors by 8 p.m. or even earlier. In places like Memphis and Texas, where beer is routinely sold alongside barbecue, a lot of the restaurants got started as nightclubs, and their proprietors began cooking a little barbecue to sell to patrons who got hungry while drinking and dancing out late.

John Shelton Reed and Dale Volberg Reed advance an alternate theory in *Holy Smoke: The Big Book of North Carolina Barbecue* (2008). "Beer goes best with a sweet sauce," they write, "like what they use in Memphis or Kansas City." On the converse side, they maintain, "the vinegar base of most North Carolina sauces cries out for something sweet to complement it." Perhaps, but a lot of the restaurateurs opening new barbecue joints these days don't seem to have the same aversion to alcohol as their predecessors. At 12 Bones Smokehouse in Asheville, you can order a draft beer from one of several local breweries. Southern Belly BBQ, a nouveau 'cue joint in Columbia has plenty of domestic and imported bottled beers. A few of the newer establishments not only sell beer and wine but even have a full bar, too. Fiery Ron's Home Team BBQ in Charleston, for instance, sells its own signature frozen drink called the Gamechanger, a potent variant of the rum-and-pineapple-based Painkiller, and features live music that plays until well after midnight. The Pit, a slick city joint in downtown Raleigh, is doing what it can to put the "bar" in barbecue, too, offering what they claim to be "the best pound for pound beer list in North Carolina," plus specialty cocktails like Sweet Propane, which blends house-infused vanilla moonshine with orange soda.

While it does look like things are starting to change, for now at least, most Carolinians still take a sober view of barbecue, at least when they're dining out. The majority consensus remains that beer may be something you can drink in ample quantities while staying up all night cooking a whole hog, but when you sit down to eat it at a restaurant, it's best washed down with a cup of sweet tea or perhaps a little Cheerwine (see "Cheerwine" sidebar, Shoulders & Light Red Sauce chapter).

Skylight Inn. They use simple open brick pits with iron rods to hold the split whole hogs, and lightweight metal lids cover them while they cook. There's not even an opening at the bottom for adding coals: They're simply scattered by the shovelful around the pigs so they fall to the floor of the pit.

"We use primarily oak," Jones explains, "and a little hickory if we can get it. We burn [the wood] down in chimneys, then as it produces the coals, they are fired into the pit." After about 16 hours of cooking, the finished pig is quartered and then deboned and hand chopped with cleavers on big butcher blocks, the whack of metal on wood echoing out into the dining room. "The main thing that sets ours apart from everyone else's is the fact that we chop the skin into the pork," Samuel Jones says. They season the meat as they chop it, sprinkling on handfuls of salt and pouring on cider vinegar and Texas Pete (see "Texas Pete" sidebar, Shoulders & Light Red Sauce chapter) from big plastic bottles. The bits of skin incorporated into the mix add a pleasing crunch to each bite

The Joneses are barbecue minimalists, serving only corn bread and coleslaw alongside the chopped pork. The famous corn bread, cut into flat squares that are just an inch thick, is made from a simple batter of cornmeal, water, and salt that's poured into pans lined with the smoky drippings from the pit-cooked pigs. To wash it down, there's just sweet tea and soft drinks in old-school glass bottles.

Pete Jones launched the Skylight Inn in 1947 when he was only 17 years old. Originally it was a full-menu drive-in complete with burgers and hot dogs,

NICHOLAS MCWHIRTER

but in the mid-1960s he scaled back and started serving barbecue only, selling it on a tray, on a sandwich, or by the pound to go. Samuel Jones, Pete Jones's grandson, runs the operation today, though at first, he wasn't sure he wanted to go into the family business. "As a child," he says, "I looked at it as a prison. But, when I was in college I started looking at it through a different set of spectacles. It's been a way of life for our family for all these years."

These days, Samuel Jones is committed to preserving the same slow, labor-intensive whole hog tradition that his family has practiced since the 19th century. And he's quickly racking up as many accolades as his grandfather. A few years ago, the Southern Foodways Alliance crowned him one of the "kings of Southern barbecue," and he's cooked at special events in places like New York City and Napa Valley, sharing the distinctive Eastern North Carolina style with barbecue lovers across the country. But, to get the full effect of the whole hog barbecue at its minimalist best, you have to make a visit to the barbecue capital of the world.

Wilber's Barbecue

4172 US 70 East, Goldsboro, NC 27534; (919) 778-5218; wilbers
barbecue.com **Founded:** 1962 **Cooking Method:** Whole hogs on open
pits over hickory and oak **Serves:** Breakfast, lunch, and dinner daily
Cards Accepted: Yes

Like Bum's in Ayden, Wilber's is not just a barbecue joint but a full-menu restaurant, serving fried fish, liver, and pork chops at lunch and dinner as well as
breakfast in the mornings. The interior looks the way most small-town restaurants did 40 years ago: brown paneled walls and red-checkered cloths on the
table. The place is big, too, with two dining rooms that can seat 300 people.

The star of the show, though, is the chopped pork barbecue, and Wilber
Shirley and his staff still make it the same way as when he opened the restaurant in 1962. They cook whole hogs and a few pork shoulders for 8 to 12 hours
on two rows of open pits in a brick building behind the main restaurant. To fire
the pits, they burn oak logs down to embers in the dirt next to the cookhouse
and carry the glowing red coals by the shovelful to spread under the cooking
pigs. When they're done, the meat is removed from the bones and chopped on
a broad cutting board by a man wielding a cleaver in each hand. Finally, the
barbecue gets a good dosing with a spicy blend of vinegar, black pepper, and
red pepper.

You can sample that meat on a pork tray, which comes with coleslaw and
hush puppies, or the larger pork plate, which adds potato salad, too. They're
served on round plastic plates with little compartments molded into them,
a spherical scoop of potato salad in one of the quarter-moon slots, a scoop
of green-flecked coleslaw in the other, the main compartment holding a big
mound of finely chopped pork. The potato salad is sweet and tinged a pale
yellow from mustard, while the hush puppies
are crisp and golden brown. A plastic pitcher
of tea (sweet, of course) awaits on your table so
you can help yourself to refills. Wilber's Brunswick stew is worth sampling, too, a rich reddish
blend with corn and limas. Roll it all together,
and you have a classic Eastern North Carolina
barbecue experience.

Shoulders & Light Red Sauce: The Piedmont

Trying to identify all the good barbecue joints in the Piedmont of North Carolina is sort of like trying to count the fish in the ocean. The region teems with hickory-smoked pork, and what passes for second-tier barbecue in towns like Lexington and Salisbury might well be considered the best 'cue in a three-county radius if it were found somewhere else. The folks in the Piedmont have clung tightly to their barbecue traditions, and a large proportion of their restaurants today date back to the 1950s and 1960s, having managed to keep their businesses thriving through the bleak years of the 1970s and 1980s. Their current operations are not all that much different than they were a half century ago.

The term *Piedmont* is taken from the French, and it literally means "foot of the mountains." In the Carolinas, it's the region that runs roughly from the fall line westward to the edge of the Blue Ridge mountains. As you head west into the Piedmont, the terrain becomes rolling and hilly, the soil transitioning from sandy dirt to the region's distinctive red clay. From a barbecue perspective, the Piedmont begins somewhere just west of the state capital of Raleigh and continues westward until traditional barbecue fades out around the edge of the Appalachians.

As siblings are wont to do, North Carolinians on either side of the divide between the East and the Piedmont argue bitterly over whose style of barbecue is superior. Quite a few conciliatory commentators have tried to talk reason, pointing out that the divide amounts to little more than fine points of doctrine. In the Piedmont they tend to cook just the shoulders instead of whole hogs. And their sauce starts off pretty much like the Easterners', only in the Piedmont they add in a little ketchup or tomato to give it a slightly red tinge and a bit of sweetness. Someone who grew up eating, say, the sauceless smoked brisket of Texas or the barbecued mutton of Kentucky might not even notice much difference at all between the two North Carolina styles.

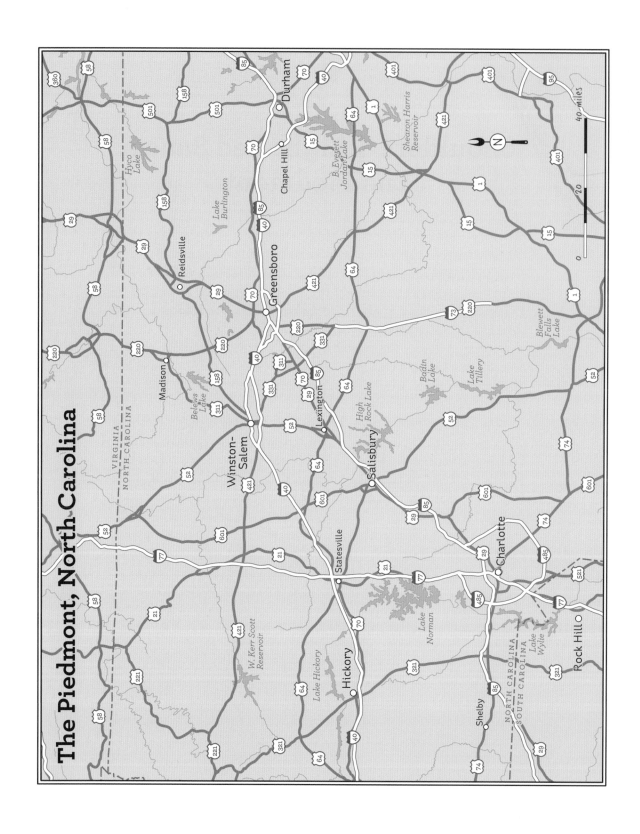

The Piedmont, North Carolina

But, if you spend enough time traveling through the Tar Heel State and sampling the barbecue you find along the way, the differences between the Piedmont and Eastern styles become glaringly apparent. Chip Stamey of Stamey's in Lexington explains the difference between the regions' styles in terms of the how the traditions developed. "We weren't as much based in the farm as they were down East," he told one interviewer. The whole hog tradition in the East, he explained, originated from slaughtering a hog to share with neighbors and to thank everyone who'd been in the fields when a crop was brought in. In Lexington, which came along a little later, it was less a farm-based way of cooking and more a commercially oriented one. "We're not going to waste the bacon and the ham. That has a use other than cooking barbecue. . . . The least expensive part of the hog was the pork shoulder."

That explanation not only accounts for the difference in meats but in the patterns found in Piedmont restaurants, too. Unlike the traditional open pits you find in the East, at one Piedmont restaurant after another, you'll see a very similar style of redbrick cookhouse adjoining the main building. Rising above it will be anywhere from one to six tall brick chimneys with pyramidal tops. After a few trips through the region sampling the barbecue, those chimneys become a comforting sight: the harbinger of a good meal to come. These closed brick pits are constructed sort of like giant fireplaces. Hardwood coals (usually oak, hickory, or both) are spread by the shovelful in the firebox underneath the cooking chamber, and their heat and smoke are held in by vertical metal doors that are kept closed while the meat cooks. This is a direct-heat method, not a form of smoking. The pork shoulders rest on racks about 2 feet above the coals, the heat and smoke rising up and over them and finally out of the chimney high above.

The menus at Piedmont joints are as standardized as the pits, and the region has its distinctive set of terms to use when ordering a meal. You can ask for a plate, a tray, or a sandwich, and you can request your pork chopped, coarse chopped, or sliced (chopped seems to have the edge in terms of popularity). At most restaurants, though it's never explained on the menu, patrons can request different categories of pork: white or brown, inside or outside, fat or lean. (We'll get to what all those terms mean in due time.) Tomato-laced "barbecue slaw," deep-fried hush puppies, and french fries are the omnipresent side dishes.

Many of the barbecue restaurants in this part of the state got their start back in the 1950s and '60s as drive-ins or fast-food restaurants, and they retain many of the characteristics of that format today. In and around Lexington, North Carolina, you'll consistently find signs saying "Sound horn for service," and upon your honk a carhop will come out with a pad and pen and take your order in the car. Old drive-in favorites like hamburgers and hot dogs are typically served alongside the barbecue.

Piedmont restaurants have the broadest hours of operations of any region in the Carolinas, tending to be open six days a week for both lunch and dinner. A few are even open on Sunday, too. Over the years, a lot of joints

Eastern versus Piedmont Barbecue: The Curious North Carolina Divide

Somewhere around the capital city of Raleigh, an invisible but not at all imaginary line bisects the state of North Carolina, dividing it into two semihostile camps. Folks to the east of that line are dead set in their barbecue ways and believe to their souls that those to the west are scandalously mistaken. Those on the western side of the divide have about the same thing to say about the easterners.

To outsiders, the difference between the barbecue in these two regions might seem subtle at most. In the east, they cook their pigs whole. In the Piedmont, the use just certain parts of the pig—the shoulder parts, to be precise. Easterners employ a spicy sauce made from vinegar, salt, and black and red peppers, while Piedmonters have a spicy sauce made from vinegar, salt, and black and red peppers plus a touch of tomato or ketchup. For natives, though, these amount to doctrinal difference, and they inspire a sort of intolerant fervor that divides North Carolinians even more sharply than Democratic and Republican politics or Duke and UNC basketball.

have expanded their offering to a full restaurant menu, and many even serve breakfast, something you never see down in the Midlands of South Carolina. Being full-service restaurants, most have accommodated modernity enough to accept credit cards, but do be sure to check ahead: A few holdouts, like Little Richard's in Winston-Salem, are cash only.

If you're hungry for classic wood-cooked barbecue, take a ride down the I-85 corridor from Greensboro to Salisbury, or west on I-40 from Chapel Hill to Statesville. You'll pass through the densest concentration of good barbecue restaurants to be found anywhere in the Carolinas, and perhaps anywhere in the country. And that means you'll be in for plenty of good eating.

Allen & Son Barbeque

6203 Millhouse Rd., Chapel Hill, NC 27516; (919) 942-7576 **Founded:** 1970 **Cooking Method:** Shoulders on closed brick pits over hickory **Serves:** Lunch Tues–Sat; dinner Thurs–Sat **Cards Accepted:** Yes

Keith Allen of Allen & Son Barbeque is a do-it-yourself kind of guy, and he's not prone to taking the easy path. He cooks all the barbecue served at his restaurant himself, and it's open from Tues through Sat. That means Allen wakes up at 2 a.m. each morning and has the fires going by 3. "On Monday when I'm off," he says, "I go haul wood. All hickory when I can." He splits that wood himself using a maul and a steel wedge.

Keith Allen is the son in Allen & Son, and his father, James, was the one who first got the family into the restaurant business. James Allen was a car salesman who, in the 1950s, suddenly decided to open a gas station with a small grill on the side selling hot dogs and hamburgers in Bynum, North Carolina. When his lease was up, he couldn't renew it, so he bought a drive-in barbecue restaurant from a man named Henry Hearn and renamed it Allen & Son. Young Keith Allen learned the barbecue trade there, helping fire the pits, chop the pork, and make the sauce.

While he was in college, Keith Allen paid the bills doing landscaping, catering, and working as a butcher at an A&P grocery store. One day in 1970, he was eating lunch with a friend at a barbecue restaurant north of Chapel Hill, and he commented that he thought the owner could do a better job running the operation. Allen's friend told him, if you can do better, why don't you buy it? So, Allen did, borrowing $3,000 and buying the restaurant with a certified check during his lunch hour the following Saturday. He went to work at his new business on Monday and has been there ever since.

James Allen passed away in the early 1970s, and Keith Allen found himself with two barbecue restaurants on his hands. He ended up selling the original

Allen & Son operation in Pittsboro to another family, who kept the name but long ago switched over to cooking with gas. Allen focused his attention on the restaurant he had founded. Over time, he eliminated all the frozen and prepared food and replaced it with family recipes made from scratch.

The main site of Keith Allen's labors is the cinder-block cookhouse behind the restaurant. In the front are the deep fryers that cook the hush puppies, plus a stove where Brunswick stew and barbecue sauce simmer in gigantic steel pots. In the back is the pit room itself, one entire wall a massive expanse of brick enclosing two pits with vertically mounted metal doors and, in the middle, a fireplace and chimney. Inside the doors of each pit is a wide compartment in which the pork shoulders, ribs, and chicken cook on big metal racks that, in a unique system, can be rolled out into the room for loading and unloading. Allen burns hickory logs in the fireplace, which has a set of andirons fashioned from short pieces of railroad track that are now blackened from years of smoke and ash. He uses a long-handled shovel to scoop glowing red embers from the chimney and spread them under the racks in each pit. "I do it every 30 minutes," Allen says. "For 10 to 12 hours." He stacks his ribs on top of the pork shoulders to insulate the ribs from the direct heat of the coals and keep them tender.

The result of all this labor is some of the best pork barbecue to be found in the Carolinas. Stylistically it straddles Eastern North Carolina and the Piedmont. Allen chops the shoulders on a broad cutting board using two long, machete-like cleavers he calls "lamb breakers," then seasons them with a thick red vinegar sauce. Despite its vivid red color, there's not a touch of tomato or ketchup to it. It's his father's recipe, unchanged since the 1950s, and red pepper gives it both its color and its fiery bite. The meat has great smoked flavor, especially the outside brown, and the tangy, spicy barbecue is a perfect complement. In a nice touch, a bottle of extra sauce is brought to your table warm.

For a long time, Allen served his barbecue only on a sandwich or on a plate, though a few years ago, in deference to Piedmont sensibility, he added a tray with just barbecue, slaw, and hush puppies. That slaw is the white variety found more commonly to the east, while in Piedmont fashion each order comes with a wicker basket of round, crisp hush puppies. Perhaps the best bet on the menu is the "stew & BBQ" combination, which pairs that delightful chopped pork with slaw and a bowl of orangish-red Brunswick stew that's a lot thicker and smoother in consistency than many Carolina varieties but still studded with the requisite corn, limas, and potatoes. Be sure to save room for dessert, since the pies, cakes, and cobblers are all made from scratch and rotate each day. On my last visit, I lucked into a delicious blackberry cobbler

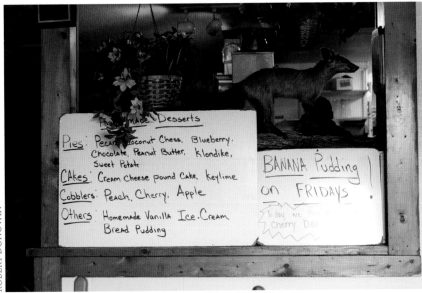

ROBERT DONOVAN

with a dark molasses sweetness and perfectly flaky pastry topped with a scoop of Allen & Son's homemade vanilla ice cream, which has the nice icy texture of old-fashioned hand-churned ice cream.

This splendid food is served in a modest atmosphere that is exactly what one wants in a classic barbecue joint: a mix of brown wood paneling and cinder-block walls painted pale green, simple tables topped with green-and-white checkered tablecloths. Keith Allen somehow manages to squeeze in a few hours for hunting on the side, and a mounted deer head adorns one wall while a stuffed fox perches atop the board where they post the daily dessert options. Allen & Son closes early on Tues and Wed, serving only through the late afternoon, though they serve dinner until 8 p.m. Thurs through Sat. Someone else has to close the place up, though, since Keith Allen is usually in bed by 8. At 2 a.m., after all, he has to get up and do it all over again.

A Note on the Term Piedmont

Though the barbecue made west of Raleigh is often called "western North Carolina style," that's not geographically accurate. The style is spread through a long swath of the central part of the state, ranging from Shelby up through Lexington and encompassing Greensboro, Winston-Salem, and parts of Raleigh. The mountainous western part of North Carolina doesn't have much of a distinctive barbecue style at all, and what is to be found in those parts tends to be a fusion of styles from all over, including from far outside the bounds of the Carolinas. That's why the purists, in the interest of accuracy, call what's served in Lexington and Salisbury and Greensboro "Piedmont-style barbecue." But, if you say "western North Carolina style," that's OK. Everyone will still know what you mean.

Barbecue Center

900 N. Main St., Lexington, NC 27292; (336) 248-4633; barbecue
center.com **Founded:** 1955 **Cooking Method:** Shoulders over hickory
and oak on closed brick pits **Serves:** Breakfast, lunch, and dinner
Mon–Sat **Cards Accepted:** Yes

Half a mile north from downtown Lexington proper, the Barbecue Center maintains an old drive-in feel, including a covered awning extending off the back
of the low brick restaurant where you can still get car service. The restaurant
got its start as the Dairy Center, an ice-cream shop, and the owners ended up
adding a small barbecue pit so they would have something to sell in the winter.
The restaurant still serves a lot of ice cream, including towering 5-pound, three-
scoop banana splits topped with chocolate syrup, whipped cream, and cherries.
But somewhere along the line the name was changed from the Dairy Center to
the Barbecue Center to better reflect what had grown to be the main draw.

A team of waitresses rove the brown-paneled dining room, and none
seems assigned to a particular table. One might take your drink order, and
another passing by will take your food order, and yet another might swing past
a few minutes later and ask if you're doing OK. If you've ordered a pork tray
or a pork plate, you're probably doing OK, for it's really great barbecue. Moist
and slightly smoky, it's pretty finely chopped and has a generous dose of dip
already mixed in. When you hit a chunk of outside brown, there's a heavenly
burst of smoky flavor.

The Barbecue Center's red slaw has a cool, tangy flavor, and the hush puppies are quite good, too. Each is hand cut with a spatula and dropped into
the fryer, resulting in thin, irregular fingers that are crispy almost all the way
through. The restaurant doesn't sell traditional Brunswick stew but a unique
variant upon it: Q Soup, a sort of vegetable soup with pork barbecue in it.
There's also a barbecue salad that loads 4 or 5 ounces of chopped pork atop a
bed of lettuce and tomato.

That pork starts off as 16-pound shoulders, seasoned only with salt, which
are cooked for 8 hours over hickory and oak. Some of the dark and light meat is
separated for slicing, and the rest is chopped with cleavers on a huge butcher
block and dressed with the restaurant's signature dip. They've been making the dip the same way for over 40 years, a simple blend of water, vinegar,
ketchup, sugar, salt, and pepper brought to a boil.

Sonny Conrad started working as a carhop for his brother-in-law Doug
Gosnell in 1955, when the restaurant was still named the Dairy Center. Gosnell had learned to cook barbecue from Warner Stamey (see "Warner Stamey"
sidebar, Shoulders & Light Red Sauce chapter), and after Conrad bought the
restaurant in 1968 he kept on cooking it the same way. Sonny Conrad also
helped plan and launch the Lexington Barbecue Festival (see Barbecue Calendar chapter), and it became a tradition for him to present the first barbecue
sandwich each year to the mayor of Lexington. Mr. Conrad passed away in
2013, but the business is carried on today by his wife and sons, keeping one of
the stars of the Lexington barbecue constellation shining bright.

Barbecue Salad

Piedmont barbecue restaurants tend to have pretty broad offerings, which invariably include a selection of salads. When it comes to the greenery, you'll often find listed among the chef salads and Caesars an odd duck known as a "barbecue salad." The exact contents vary from spot to spot, but generally it's a very basic green salad—iceberg lettuce, tomato, cucumbers, and the like—topped with 4 to 6 ounces of chopped pork barbecue. It seems like a reasonable compromise, for even those who are watching their waistlines may need a barbecue fix.

Carolina Bar-B-Q of Statesville

213 Salisbury Rd., Statesville, NC 28677; (704) 873-5585; carolina bar-b-q.com **Founded:** 1985 **Cooking Method:** Pork shoulder on brick pits **Serves:** Lunch and dinner Mon–Sat **Cards Accepted:** Yes

Not far off of I-77 in downtown Statesville, there's a pale yellow building with a steep-slanted green-shingled roof. On that roof, the words *Carolina Bar-B-Q* are displayed in big white letters that wrap around the silhouette of a pig. Inside, a green model train circles the dining room on a suspended track near the top of the blond-paneled wall. There are wooden booths with orange backs plus six-top tables with fruit-decorated tablecloths. The extra-friendly waitresses will call you "sweetie" when you arrive and send you away with a cheery "Have a blessed day." And, they'll serve you Statesville's version of Piedmont North Carolina barbecue.

Carolina-Bar-B-Q has a very broad menu that includes fried chicken, buffalo wings, country ham, and fried shrimp and flounder dinners. Sides run the gamut from barbecue staples like french fries and slaw all the way to meat 'n' three

standbys like corn on the cob and fried squash. But, the slow-cooked pork is the real center of attention. They cook shoulders for 10 to 12 hours, then strip away the fat and gristle by hand and pull the meat off the bone. It's lightly seasoned with dip in the kitchen, but so subtly you might not even realized it's been sauced.

A lot of restaurants in this area will steam the buns for their chopped pork sandwich, but at Carolina Bar-B-Q they toast theirs. You can choose red or white slaw (choose red), and the resulting sandwich—with a warm bun, crisp slaw, and tender, smoky meat—is excellently balanced and delicious. Two bottles of sauce—one mild, the other spicy—await at your table, along with the requisite bottle of Texas Pete (see "Texas Pete" sidebar, Shoulders & Light Red Sauce chapter) The mild sauce is a thick, sweet tomato-based sauce that's almost brown in color and quite uncharacteristic of the Tar Heel State. The hot sauce is much more in line with the region's traditional version—thin, slightly red—and it really isn't all that hot.

The barbecue-oriented side dishes are quite respectable, too. Beneath their crunchy brown crust, the big spherical hush puppies are fluffy and a little sweet. The Brunswick stew is slightly sweet, too, and it gets a dose of smoky flavor from the big shreds of barbecue amid a generous portion of potatoes, carrots, corn, green beans, peas, and limas, making it a worthy representative of this Piedmont classic.

Cheerwine: The House Wine of Barbecue

People who grew up in the Carolinas might tend to forget that visitors to the region may not be familiar with Cheerwine. For locals, it's no more exotic than a can of Pepsi Cola or a cup of ice tea. Since 1917, the cherry-flavored soft drink has been produced by the Carolina Beverage Company of Salisbury, North Carolina. Far fizzier than your ordinary soft drink, it has a deep red color similar to that of wine, but that's about the only similarity between the two beverages. (And, no, there is no alcohol in Cheerwine.)

NICHOLAS MCWHIRTER

Cheerwine is omnipresent in barbecue joints in the Piedmont region, and the Carolina Beverage Company recently took to advertising it as "BBQ's best friend." These days, the beverage is sold from West Virginia all the way down to Florida, but the Carolinas are still where it is most known and loved. If you're stopping into a Piedmont barbecue joint for the first time, you owe it to yourself to at least give it a sip alongside a plate of chopped pork. Sweet, fruity, and quite bubbly, it marries just right with smoky pork and a tangy vinegar sauce.

Cook's Barbecue

366 Valiant Dr., Lexington, NC 27292; (336) 798-1928; cooksbbq.com
Founded: 1969 **Cooking Method:** Pork shoulders on closed brick pits over hickory wood **Serves:** Lunch and dinner Wed–Sun **Cards Accepted:** Yes

Cook's Barbecue is technically a Lexington joint, but to find it you have to drive a good 15 minutes south of town to the end of a country road called Valiant Drive. Set back from a large parking lot is a big building made of dark rough-hewn planks. It's a sprawling place with a concrete floor, an angling roof with exposed rafters, brown wood walls, and a working fireplace. At the height of noon, it's cool and quite dark inside. Every time I've eaten there, several police cars were parked in the lot and uniformed officers were eating inside, and that's always a promising sign.

You owe it to yourself to order the compactly named Combo with Beef. Pork isn't mentioned explicitly, but why would it be? This being North Carolina, it sort of goes without saying that you'll get chopped pork on the plate (or sliced or coarse chopped for a 50-cent surcharge). That pork is paired with what may well be the best beef brisket in the state of North Carolina. Sliced fairly thick, it has a tender but still chewy texture and a good dose of smoke. In a move that would make a Texan shudder, it comes dressed with a tangy sweet sauce, but to this Carolinian's taste buds it complements the beef quite nicely. Still, this is the Tar Heel State, and the big scoop of smoky chopped pork outshines the beef—a little salty, a little spicy, and all around delicious. Two squeeze bottles of sauce are brought to the table with the combo, one the thick, sweet, tangy brown sauce for brisket, the other a traditional Lexington-style dip made from ketchup, vinegar, and crushed red pepper that's a bit spicier than average. In a nice touch, both bottles come to the table warm so they don't cool the meat when you apply them.

Cook's hush puppies are tiny golden-brown orbs—the smallest and some of the best I've found in the Carolinas—and they're quite sweet beneath their crunchy exterior. The cool red slaw has a touch of onion to it. In addition to the barbecue plates, trays, and sandwiches, the menu offers burgers, hot dogs, and fried fish and chicken sandwiches. They even have a salad bar.

Outside Brown

A lot of barbecue lovers in the Piedmont are particularly attached to what is known in the region as "outside brown." It simply means the meat from the outer parts of the shoulder that has been transformed into brown, crisp bits by its proximity to the heat. Many diners ask to have a little outside brown mixed into their barbecue because it adds a pleasantly chewy texture and extra smoky flavor to the meat. Some will even ask for an entire tray of outside brown. That option is never called out explicitly on the menu, but the next time you order a chopped pork plate, tray, or sandwich in a Piedmont joint, just ask, "Can I get some outside brown?" You'll taste why Piedmonters make such a fuss about it.

Cook's Barbecue dates back to 1969, when Doug Cook built a pit and kitchen on the lot next to his house and started selling barbecue from a take-out window. It was a bare bones operation at first, offering just chopped pork plates and sandwiches along with hush puppies, french fries, and slaw. As business picked up, Cook built a small dining room with planks he milled himself, and around 1980 he added on a bigger dining room in the back. In 1984, he sold the business to Don Payne, a childhood friend, who kept the restaurant's name. In 2001, Brandon Cook, Doug Cook's son, took over pitmaster duties, and a Cook was cooking at Cook's again. These days, Brandon Cook uses all hickory wood, slow roasting his shoulders for about 5 hours, then flipping them over to the skin side for another 5 hours or more. All in all, it's a very impressive operation, and an encouraging sign of a new generation of barbecue pitmasters choosing to carry on the old, slow traditions that make Piedmont barbecue such a delight.

Fuzzy's Bar-B-Q

407 N. Highway St., Madison, NC 27025; (336) 427-4130; fuzzysbbq .com **Founded:** 1954 **Cooking Method:** Shoulders over hickory coals on closed brick pits **Serves:** Breakfast, lunch, and dinner daily **Cards Accepted:** Yes

This Madison, North Carolina, landmark was founded in 1954 by T. H. "Fuzzy" Nelson, who got his nickname because as a child he was attached to an old hat that he wore down to nothing but fuzz. On one wall of the restaurant hangs blown-up black-and-white photographs of the original building, a small drive-in with tall glass windows and a neon sign out front offering "Curb Service." That original 18-stool grill was replaced by the current building in 1974. It's a big fast-food-style place, all plate-glass windows on the front and sides, a counter, and windows into the kitchen along the white-tiled back wall. Its dozens of wooden booths can seat 150 patrons, and the barbecue is still cooked fresh each day in the brick pits in the back. Apart from Easter, Thanksgiving, and Christmas, they're open every day for breakfast, lunch, and dinner.

Fuzzy's pork is chopped fine, and it has a nice, smooth texture and a good dose of smoke to it. The thin red sauce with which it's dressed has a touch of sweetness and a sharp pepper bite, and an extra cup of it is served alongside the plates and trays. Most unique are the long, skinny hush puppies that are cooked funnel-cake style, with the cornmeal batter squeezed into the hot oil and allowed to twist and fold into long fried squiggles that are nicely crisp on the outside and chewy in the middle.

Fuzzy's Quest to Bring North Carolina Barbecue to New York City

In 1978, T. H. "Fuzzy" Nelson headed to New York City, with visions of following in the footsteps of Ray Kroc and Colonel Sanders and making barbecue the next quick-service food to take America by storm. He was lured there by Barry Farber, a New York radio talk show host and Greensboro native, who had started importing Nelson's barbecue and was selling 100 pounds a week at Alex Parker's Cafe de la Bagel in Times Square. With Nelson as their barbecue consultant, Farber and Parker planned to build pits in the South Bronx and open their first restaurant in Harlem. Fuzzy's brief stint in the Big Apple earned him a mention in the *New Yorker*'s Talk of the Town, but the restaurant chain never panned out, and he returned home to Madison to resume his flourishing wholesale barbecue business.

For another decade, Barry Farber persisted in his quest to bring Fuzzy's North Carolina–style barbecue to hungry New Yorkers. He convinced a restaurant named Ellen's, which was located on lower Broadway across from city hall, to serve chopped pork that was shipped in frozen from Fuzzy's wholesale operation, and he even taught them the proper way to serve it: on a steamed (not toasted) bun with red barbecue slaw and vinegar-and-tomato sauce. A few weeks in, Farber dropped by for lunch and found, to his dismay, that Ellen's had switched to serving the barbecue open faced on a seeded hard roll with a white, mayo-based coleslaw on top. But, the sandwiches were selling well, so Farber let it go, frustrated once again in his long-running quest to transplant Piedmont North Carolina barbecue to the Big Apple.

Fuzzy's daughter and two sons carry on the operation today, and they still offer curb service: Just park in the spaces along the right side of the building. In addition to the barbecue, the colorful trifold menu offers an array of salads, seafood and grilled chicken plates, burgers, and sandwiches. At breakfast, there are pancakes, biscuits, breakfast sandwiches, and three-egg omelets, too.

Hill's Lexington Barbecue

4005 N. Patterson Ave., Winston-Salem, NC 27105; (336) 767-2184
Founded: 1951 **Cooking Method:** Shoulders over hickory coals
Serves: Breakfast, lunch, and dinner Tues–Sun **Cards Accepted:** Yes

A lot of barbecue restaurants in the Piedmont are open for breakfast, but Hill's is one of the rare few that actually serves barbecue as a breakfast item. It's one of the meat options (along with bacon, sausage, ham, and—yes—brains) on their breakfast plates, which also include eggs, your choice of grits, gravy, or hash browns and either toast or biscuits. Put smoky chopped pork alongside a bed of crisp shredded hash browns and scrambled eggs and you've got a breakfast to remember. (Be sure to opt for the biscuits: They come two to a plate, and they're wonderfully fluffy and buttery.)

Once lunchtime rolls around, the menu expands to offer the standard assortment of Piedmont barbecue staples along with a broad slate of steaks, burgers, fried chicken, and ham. The big white sign out by the road features a strutting pig decked out in a top hat and tails. In keeping with that

ROBERT DONOVAN

Lexington: The World Capital of Barbecue?

Lexington, North Carolina, has a population of just under 20,000 (18,936 per the 2010 census, if you want to be exact,). It also has at least 18 barbecue restaurants in operation today, giving it about one restaurant for every 1,000 people. The Campaign for Real Barbecue (see "Taking the True 'Cue Pledge" sidebar, Shoulders & Light Red Sauce chapter) confirmed that 10 of those restaurants are still cooking the "proper" way over real hardwood coals. Memphis and Kansas City are municipalities that have their own recognizable barbecue style, but they're both big cities. How many towns of under 20,000 people can claim a barbecue style of their own? The term *Lexington style* is often applied to the barbecue in the Piedmont in general, for, indeed, the town's legendary pitmasters helped create and spread the mode of cooking that the entire region is now known for.

For the sheer density of barbecue per capita, as well as the enduring devotion of local residents to the style of barbecue that their local pitmasters helped create almost a century ago, it seems only logical to declare that Lexington, North Carolina, is, indeed, the world capital of barbecue.

sophisticated mode, Hill's serves its barbecue on real plates, and its pork tray comes not in a flat cardboard container but rather on a stainless steel metal tray. That pork is chopped into short shreds, and it's notably tender and juicy, with a generous proportion of outside brown adding nice smoky bursts. By itself, Hill's thin red dip is dominated by the flavor of ketchup, but when you pour it over the pork, the tomato moves to the background and the barbecue really comes alive with tangy vinegar and a fair amount of spice. The red slaw is finely minced and quite peppery, too. You can also get the pork sliced or, in Hill's parlance, "blocked," which to me is more of an accurate description of what is usually termed "coarse chopped."

Joe and Edna Hill opened the restaurant in 1951, bringing to Winston-Salem the Lexington-style of cooking barbecue that Joe learned from Warner Stamey (see "Warner Stamey" sidebar, Shoulders & Light Red Sauce chapter). It originally operated in a small building with room for just 35 customers not far from its current location. Today it fills a long brick building with two large dining rooms flanking a central area with a counter and stools. Their banana pudding recipe dates back 50 years to a cook named Joe Johnson, and many declare it to be North Carolina's best. Unlike most, it's served warm, piled high in a small ceramic bowl with real meringue that's toasted a golden brown on the exterior. No wonder that well-attired pig out front is strutting so proudly.

Lexington Barbecue

100 Smokehouse Ln., Lexington, NC 27295; (336) 249-9814; lexbbq .com **Founded:** 1962 **Cooking Method:** Pork shoulders over oak and hickory coals in closed brick pits **Serves:** Lunch and dinner Mon–Sat **Cards Accepted:** Yes

Locals tend to refer to Lexington Barbecue as "Honey Monk" or just "The Monk," while others refer to it as "Lexington Barbecue #1," though that numeral appears nowhere on the building or the menus and there's no "Lexington Barbecue #2" to be found. As it turns out, owner Wayne Monk's brother ran a stand called "Lexington Barbecue #2" for a while, but after it closed Monk dropped the "#1" from his original restaurant. The name has stuck around anyway, perhaps in recognition that, in a town crowded with great barbecue restaurants, Lexington Barbecue consistently gets the nod as many residents' favorite. And they show up in droves for it: At 2 p.m. on a weekday, the large parking lot is still packed, and diners stream in and out throughout the afternoon.

Wayne Monk was just 26 years old when, after working with Lexington barbecue legend Warner Stamey (see "Warner Stamey" sidebar, Shoulders & Light Red Sauce chapter), he decided he wanted to open a restaurant of his

own. More than 50 years later, he's still serving classic Lexington-style pork from the same white barn-like building beside US 29/70. You don't have to come inside to get good barbecue: Just park on the side by the pit, toot your horn, and someone will come take your order from your car. But, it's quite worth heading in. You can grab one of the green-capped stools in the front room and eat at the counter, watching the half dozen or more folks behind it chatting up the regulars and packing up boxes of take-out food.

The barbecue is cooked behind the restaurant in a brick pit building with a half-dozen chimneys rising above it, putting out wafts of tempting hardwood smoke. They generally cook over locally sourced oak, though they will use hickory when they can get it. The pork shoulders are salted and then cooked for 10 to 11 hours, covered with sheets of cardboard to keep ashes from falling back down on the barbecue and to hold the heat in, too. They don't baste, and they don't put any sauce on the meat until it's on the plate or bun and about to be served.

The pork comes sliced, chopped, or coarse chopped, and you can get it on a tray with slaw and your choice of a rolls or hush puppies, or on a plate, which adds french fries. And that barbecue comes out fast, too, seeming to hit your table before your order even has time to get back to the kitchen. My favorite is the chopped pork sandwich, which has a generous portion of barbecue topped with red slaw on a steamed bun.

The hush puppies are thin and crisp and not at all sweet, but both the sauce and the red slaw get a good dose of sweetness from tomato ketchup

("We put ketchup in about everything except the ice tea," Monk told interviewer Jed Portman of *Garden & Gun* magazine in 2012). On each table is a bottle of the restaurant's Smokehouse Hot & Tangy Barbeque Sauce. It's ruddy brown with spices and heavily laced with chili powder, and the label declares that it's for "barbeque chicken, chops, beans, etc." You can try it on pork barbecue, too, if you want to be a little heretical, but if you do, use a moderate dose: The sauce is quite tasty but will leave your tongue tingling. After a sandwich or a big plate, the homemade cobblers, particularly the peach, are the perfect way to round out the meal.

It's hard to put a finger on just what makes the barbecue at Lexington Barbecue so good, but Wayne Monk and his team definitely have it down to a science. They keep it simple and stick with what's worked over the decades,

The Origins of Honey Monk

Wayne Monk opened his barbecue restaurant in 1962 when he and a partner, a man named Honeycutt, purchased a restaurant called the Knob Hill Drive-Inn. They hated the name, so they decided to come up with a new one. One night the two partners were horsing around, put their two names together, and came up with "Honey Monk." Monk didn't realize Honeycutt was serious until he came to the restaurant one day and saw workmen outside changing the sign. Monk stuck with that name until around 1980, when he owned the restaurant outright, and finally started calling it Lexington Barbecue, which sounded much more respectable to his ear. To this day, though regular customers still make out checks to "Honey Monk," and Wayne Monk still cashes them.

and the results have been accolades from barbecue lovers across the country. In 2003, the prestigious James Beard Foundation awarded Monk an American Classic Award for his decades of devotion to the art of barbecue, confirming what the locals have known all along: Lexington Barbecue is among the very best barbecue restaurants anywhere.

Little Richard's

4885 Country Club Rd., Winston-Salem, NC 27104; (336) 760-3457; eatmopig.com **Founded:** 1991 **Cooking Method:** Open pit, shoulders over hickory wood **Serves:** Lunch and dinner Mon–Sat **Cards Accepted:** No

Approaching Little Richard's from the west on Country Club Road, the first thing you see as you crest the hill is a big brick chimney with clouds of smoke rolling out of it, its top almost level with the road itself. It's as good advertising as a barbecue joint could ever need, especially if you are driving with your windows down and can smell the hickory.

ROBERT DONOVAN

Little Richard's is rather unusual among Piedmont restaurants in that it has a defined theme to its decor: the 1950s drive-in era. A big neon sign graces the front of the building, with "Little Richard's Lexington BBQ" in red and blue script and an animated pink pig galloping across the bottom. A retro-style jukebox with a rainbow of lights sits to the left of the front counter, and doo-wop and shag tunes swing out from the speakers in the dining room. A lot of legendary barbecue joints in the region actually got their starts as drive-ins in the 1950s, but Little Richard's only dates back to 1991. They do offer curb service, though, and the retro style seems a perfect fit for their traditional Piedmont barbecue

You pick your seat and order from a waitress, and she'll leave a handwritten green ticket on your table, which you take to the register up front to pay on your way out. The chopped pork tray arrives as a little gray cardboard boat piled high with meat and red slaw, a stainless steel fork in a paper envelope and a dozen spherical hush puppies in a paper-lined plastic basket. The pork is quite finely chopped and well soaked with dip, while the minced slaw is cool and tangy with generous flecks of black pepper. At first the barbecue seems to have a sharp vinegar bite, but after a couple of forkfuls your tongue adjusts and you may find yourself squirting on a second round of thin orange-red dip from the big bottle waiting by your table's napkin dispenser.

Barbecue sandwiches, trays, and plates are the primary offering at Little Richard's, though they do offer ribs on Wednesday and barbecue chicken on Friday and Saturday. There's a slate of burgers, hot dogs, sandwiches, and salads, too. For dessert, grab one of the premade plastic containers of homemade banana pudding. Beneath the clear plastic lid is a heavenly swirl of bright yellow pudding studded with crumbly vanilla wafers, slices of banana, and fluffy white whipped cream.

"Eat Mo' Pig" is Little Richard's slogan, and the residents of Winston-Salem have taken it to heart. The reception has been so great that owner Richard Berrier has opened a second location in the nearby town of Wallburg, where the gleaming new brick building with its green metal roof may lack the throwback charm of the original, but the barbecue is just as tasty.

Red Bridges Barbecue Lodge

200 E. Dixon Blvd., Shelby, NC 28152; (704) 482-8567; bridgesbbq
.com **Founded:** 1946 **Cooking Method:** Pork shoulders on closed
brick pits over hickory **Serves:** Lunch and dinner Wed–Sun **Cards
Accepted:** Yes

Red and Lyttle Bridges opened their first barbecue joint in 1946, and they
moved into the current building on US 74 in 1953. Red learned to cook from
Warner Stamey (see "Warner Stamey" sidebar, Shoulders & Light Red Sauce
chapter), the roving Piedmont North Carolina barbecue mentor who operated
a restaurant in Shelby for a few years in the 1930s. Red passed away in 1966,
but Lyttle carried on running the show for another three decades, working 12
hours a day until well into her 80s. With fiery red hair and a temper to match,
"Mama B" ran a tight ship, and those who worked for her recall her as a tough
boss but one who treated all her employees like family. Debbie Bridges Webb,
Red and Lyttle's daughter, and her children, Natalie Ramsey and Chase Webb,
carry on the business today, running everything the exact same way Mama B
would have wanted it.

You'll notice Bridges's throwback style even before you pull into the parking lot, starting with the big looping letters that announce "Bridges Barbecue" on the front of the building. That style continues inside, where there are

wood-paneled walls, booths and chairs with bright turquoise backs, and stylized light fixtures that look straight out of the Rat Pack era of the 1960s. Your waitress writes your order on a long strip of colored paper, and you'll take that to the register to pay after you eat.

Out back behind a white fence, a neatly stacked pile of wood stretches for dozens of yards. It's used to cook the barbecue fresh each day, and on occasion they do run out and have to close their doors early. Pork is the start of the show, of course, though Bridges serves chicken and turkey, too. There's a barbecue tray with a side of slaw, and the barbecue plate comes with two additional sides. You can ask for the meat to be minced, chopped, or sliced (chopped seems to be most patrons' default). Aficionados are passionate about the outside brown at Bridges, and for good reason—it adds crisp bites of smoky, almost nutty flavor to the chopped pork. The barbecue slaw, finely chopped in a reddish dressing, is worth attention, too.

For my money, though, the best way to bring the whole offering together is with a chopped pork sandwich. Bridges does it brilliantly: The meat is topped with barbecue slaw and layered between two halves of a soft hamburger bun. The whole thing is given a squeeze in a hot sandwich press before serving. The resulting assemblage—warm, crisp toasted bun giving way to a soft interior, the smoky pork merging with the tangy bits of crunch from the slaw—is a triumph of complementary textures and flavors. Combine it up with a few long, crisp hush puppies and some crinkle-cut french fries and you've got one of the best barbecue meals anywhere.

If you still have room, you should sample Bridges' pimento cheese sandwich, too. A rather uncommon article for Carolina barbecue joints, it's toasted in the sandwich press until the creamy, ruby-studded cheese is melted into a gooey, delicious treat.

Richard's Bar-B-Que

522 N. Main St., Salisbury, NC 28144; (704) 636-9561 **Founded:** 1935 **Cooking Method:** Shoulders on an open brick pit over hickory and oak **Serves:** Breakfast, lunch, and dinner Mon–Sat **Cards Accepted:** No

Richard's Bar-B-Que started out as T&F Barbecue, a seven-stool barbecue stand that opened in 1935 just around the corner from the Rowan County courthouse in Salisbury. The business changed hands several times over the years and eventually moved to its current location on Main Street. Richard Monroe, who started working there as a manager in 1974, eventually bought the restaurant and put his own name on it.

Hogwash: North Carolina's Barbecue Beer

Fullsteam Brewery in Durham has a unique mission: to perfect the art of Southern beer. For them that means looking not just to traditional brewing methods but also to the food and farm traditions of the Carolinas, incorporating heirloom grains and the produce of local farms into their brews. That philosophy has led to such creative flavors as a savory sweet-potato lager, a fragrant summer basil ale, and the malty, chocolatey Working Man's Lunch inspired by the traditional North Carolina pairing of an RC Cola and a Moon Pie.

With their Hogwash Hickory-Smoked Brown Porter, Fullsteam took their inspiration from another classic North Carolina food tradition. "We designed this specifically to go with North Carolina barbecue," says Sean Lilly Wilson, the brewery's founder and CEO (that's Chief Executive Optimist, according to his business card). "We take North Carolina six-row barley from Riverbend Malt House in Asheville and smoke it over hickory wood on a double barrel smoker."

The smoked barley gets blended in with nonsmoked grains, making up around 10 percent of the total volume. That's more than enough to imbue the finished beer with the rich, distinctive flavor of hickory smoke but not so much that it overwhelms the barbecue it is meant to accompany. "The beer tastes smoky until you have a bite of the meat," Wilson says. As for the infamous regional divides in North Carolina, he isn't playing favorites. "It works equally well with eastern- and western-style barbecue," he says.

So far, Fullsteam has released Hogwash in kegs only, so it's available solely in select bars and restaurants in North Carolina as well as at Fullsteam's own on-site tavern in Durham, where you can buy it in 64-ounce growlers to take home. A handful of barbecue joints, including the Pig in Chapel Hill and Mac's Speed Shop in Charlotte, have started selling Hogwash alongside their hickory-smoked pork. But Wilson doesn't expect it to rival Cheerwine (see "Cheerwine" sidebar, this chapter) as a classic Carolina barbecue drink any time soon. "The most potential," he says, "is for home enthusiasts to have along with meat." In part, he explains, that's because restaurateurs don't want the smoke of the beer to compete with the smoke of their meat. But there's a more practical limitation at work, too: The great majority of barbecue restaurants in North Carolina don't serve beer (see "Where's the Beer?" sidebar, Whole Hogs & Vinegar Sauce chapter).

The North Carolina Barbecue Society

Calling itself "The Fun Tribe," the North Carolina Barbecue Society (NCBS) has a two-fold mission: to preserve North Carolina's barbecue heritage and to promote the state as the barbecue capital of the world. The organization was founded by Jim Early in 2006. Four years prior to that, Early had published *The Best Tar Heel Barbecue: Manteo to Murphy*, a guidebook to the state's great barbecue restaurants. To compile his guide, he visited all of North Carolina's 100 counties and ate at over 200 barbecue restaurants. Early was a trial lawyer by trade, but he closed his Winston-Salem practice in 2007 to dedicate himself full time to the society.

These days, the society champions North Carolina barbecue in a range of ways. It publishes a monthly newsletter called *NCBS Pig Tales* to inform members of goings-on in the society and the world of barbecue at large. It stages barbecue "boot camps," where respected pitmasters teach attendees the basics of cooking whole hogs, pork shoulders, and the state's classic side dishes, and it trains them to become NCBS-certified barbecue judges, too. And, it created the North Carolina Barbecue Society Historic Barbecue Trail, an interactive online map that defines a meandering trail across the state, complete with driving directions. The trail takes aficionados from Murphy in the far western part of the state all the way to Ayden in eastern North Carolina, guiding them to 24 historic barbecue restaurants selected by the NCBS board as being representative of the state's genuine wood-cooked barbecue tradition. You can find the Trail and many more barbecue resources online at ncbbqsociety.com.

The brick building has a bright-red metal roof and a cheery red-and-white awning over the front windows. Inside, you can eat at a long counter with high wood-backed stools or at one of the many booths and tables in the dining room. Richard's shoulders are cooked on an open pit over hickory and oak embers, and they're chopped by hand into coarse shreds with a smoky blend of white meat and outside brown. You can also order the pork sliced, and it comes on a sandwich, plate, or tray, all of which have a generous amount of meat piled on. The spherical hush puppies are big and flecked with onion, and instead of ketchup the coleslaw has bits of chopped tomato in it. Though the restaurant is located squarely in the center of the Piedmont, Richard's spicy vinegar-and-pepper sauce is more akin to the stuff you'll find east of Raleigh, but it goes just fine with the smoky chopped pork. The rest of the menu includes a full line of burgers, dogs, and sandwiches along with a selection of meat-and-two plates. In the morning, they serve omelets, pancakes, and biscuits, and gravy breakfasts, too.

Short Sugar's Pit Bar-B-Q

1328 South Scales St., Reidsville, NC 27320; (336) 342-7487; short sugarsbar-b-q.com **Founded:** 1949 **Cooking Method:** Shoulders on an electric cooker, finished over hickory coals in a brick pit **Serves:** Breakfast Mon–Thurs; lunch and dinner Mon–Sat **Cards Accepted:** Yes

It's worth visiting Short Sugar's in Reidsville just to experience the throwback 1950s atmosphere. It's a low white building with lots of plate-glass windows and a tall white-painted brick column rising above it, the words "Short Sugar's" in capital letters on the side. Inside, you can sit at the lunch counter's leather-capped stools and watch as the waitresses bustle behind the counter, accompanied by the rhythmic whacking sound of a cleaver chopping pork on a cutting board. Outside, you can still get curb service and eat your sandwich or hot dog in your car under the big red awnings, as many of Short Sugar's customers do.

The restaurant's name has nothing to do with food. The story is that as a young man, Eldridge Overby, who was slight in stature, was out with his girlfriend, and her favorite song came on the jukebox. "I want to dance with my short sugar," she shouted, and "Short Sugar" he was ever after. Sadly, Overby was killed in a car wreck a few years later, and when his two brothers, Johnny and Clyde, opened a drive-in restaurant together, they decided to name it after their late brother.

North Carolina barbecue purists bemoan the fact that Short Sugar's shoulders get most of their cooking in electric smokers these days, but they are still finished over hickory coals in a brick pit in the back corner of the restaurant, and the pork is hand cut to order—sliced, chopped, or minced as the customer prefers. In a region where barbecue joints tend to be rigidly standardized in their offering, Short Sugar's food is as idiosyncratic as its name. The slaw, for instance, is white, not red. Their sauce (and they call it "sauce," not "dip") is vinegar based, but it's dark brown and sweet without a hint of tomato. It was created by Johnny Overby back in the opening days of the restaurant and hasn't changed a bit since.

The pork plates come with crinkle-cut fries, oblong hush puppies, and a couple of dill pickle slices. True to its drive-in past, Short Sugar's serves plenty of hamburgers and hot dogs, too, wrapped to go in white waxed paper. Pork ribs are available on Tuesday and Saturday nights. More than 60 years in, Short Sugar's is still family run, with David Wilson, Johnny Overby's son-in-law, and Wilson's son, John David, operating what is now a cherished Reidsville institution.

Texas Pete

In the Piedmont of North Carolina, there's one condiment that is found on the table of barbecue joints almost as frequently as ketchup: Texas Pete. Despite the name, this hot sauce has no relationship to the Lone Star State. For over 60 years, it has been made by the T. W. Garner Food Company of Winston-Salem and has been used to spice up countless plates of North Carolina barbecue.

According to the Garner company history, in the 1920s Thad Garner decided to take the money he had saved for college and buy a barbecue restaurant instead. Along with the building and equipment, he acquired the previous owners' barbecue sauce recipe, a crowd favorite. The restaurant folded quickly enough, but Thad and his father, Sam, started making batches of Garner's Barbecue Sauce and selling it throughout the state for 19 cents a bottle. They incorporated the T. W. Garner Food Company in 1946, and when they added a hot-pepper sauce to their line, they needed to come up with a brand name for the new product. Their marketing guy suggested "Mexican Joe" to invoke the fiery flavors found south of the border, but Sam Gardner insisted on an American name and suggested they use Texas instead. Harold Garner, Thad's brother and Sam's son, was nicknamed "Pete," and when they stuck the two names together, Texas Pete was born.

More than six decades later, the fiery, bright red sauce is almost ubiquitous on the tables of Piedmont barbecue joints. So if your chopped pork sandwich or sliced pork plate just isn't quite spicy enough for you, take a look around for a bottle of Texas Pete. You're pretty much guaranteed to find one.

Smiley's Lexington BBQ

917 Winston Rd., Lexington, NC 27295; (336) 248-4528 **Founded:** 2002 **Cooking Method:** Pork shoulders on brick pits **Serves:** Breakfast, lunch, and dinner Tues–Sun **Cards Accepted:** Yes

A 6-foot high statue of a pig stands just to the right of the front door at Smiley's, clad in a black apron and Carolina-blue ball cap, large cleavers in both of his hands—or front trotters or whatever one calls the things an anthropomorphic pig uses to hold cleavers. Smiley's has technically been around since just 2002, which would make it one of the newer players on the Lexington barbecue scene. But, you wouldn't know it from the classic feel of the restaurant itself nor from the excellent barbecue they serve, which can easily stand side by side with the old legends. The building Smiley's occupies has actually been a barbecue restaurant since the early 1950s, operating under the names "Dart's," "Jay's," and "Southern BBQ." Current owner Steve Yountz got his start in the business at the age of 13, working as a curb hop at the restaurant back when it was known as Southern BBQ. In 2002, he bought the business from then-owner David Guest and renamed it Smiley's.

ROBERT DONOVAN

The restaurant offers specials that vary by the day, and what's available is posted on a big wooden sign overlooking the parking lot. There might be a chop plate on Tuesday and rump roast on Thursday, while the crowd-pleasing barbecue chicken is served on Friday, Saturday, and Sunday. A cookhouse with closed brick pits extends off the back of the restaurant, and they're the same ones that have been used since the 1950s. The pork that emerges from those pits is cut by hand either into long shreds (the regular chopped) or into nice-size, stringy chunks (the coarse chopped). The sauce has a sweet tomato base, and it's thicker than most of what you'll find in and around Lexington. Dressed with that sauce, the barbecue is moist, tangy, and quite delicious.

Though most of the menu is straight-down-the-middle Piedmont North Carolina style, Smiley's serves sweet corn sticks, something more commonly found in the eastern part of the state. Smiley's slaw is a little coarser and crisper than other nearby joints, and slightly sweet hush puppies, crinkle-cut fries, and a creamy potato salad are among the highlights of the sides. Like many of the older joints around Lexington, they offer car service, but if you choose to dine inside, you'll do so in a modest dining room with pale-peach-colored walls and a brown tile floor—the perfect old school atmosphere for enjoying some excellent Lexington-style barbecue.

Stamey's

2206 High Point Rd., Greensboro, NC 27403; (336) 299-9888; stameys.com **Founded:** 1953 **Cooking Method:** Pork shoulders over hickory coals on closed brick pits **Serves:** Lunch and dinner Mon–Sat **Cards Accepted:** Yes

C. Warner Stamey, perhaps the greatest of all North Carolina barbecue mentors (see "Walter Stamey" sidebar, this chapter), capped off his notable career in Greensboro, where he opened Stamey's on High Point Road in 1953. After a few years, he handed the business off to his sons Charles and Keith, who added a second location on Battleground Road. The operation is continued today by Chip Stamey, Charles's son, and he sticks closely to the Lexington style of barbecue that his grandfather was so instrumental in defining.

"They flip a switch, we light a fire!" Stamey's website declares. That fire is made from 100 percent hickory wood, and they use it to cook pork shoulders for 10 full hours every day. The cooks burn logs in a furnace and shovel the coals under the meat on each pit, adding more every 15 or 20 minutes and turning the shoulders as they go. There are 10 of those pits, each of which can hold about 20 shoulders, and they are located in a separate building across the parking lot. There is also a single pit visible through glass windows when you

Taking the True 'Cue Pledge

John Shelton Reed and Dan Levine are barbecue purists. Reed, a retired University of North Carolina sociology professor, is the coauthor of *Holy Smoke: The Big Book of North Carolina BBQ* (2008) along with his wife, Dale Volberg Reed, and William McKinney. Levine, better known by his "nom de 'cue," Porky Le Swine, is one of the proprietors of the BBQ Jew website (bbqjew.com). For years each had bemoaned the ongoing plague of barbecue joints giving up the laborious but tasty practice of cooking over real wood fires in favor of the far more convenient gas and electric cookers. Finally, in 2013, they decided to do something about it, and the Campaign for Real Barbecue was born.

"Wood smoke defines Real Barbecue," the two declare on their website (truecue.org). "Without it, one has merely roasted meat—'faux 'cue.'" They enlisted 20 "patrons"—notable barbecue lovers, commentators, and eaters—as the champions in their cause (in the interest of full disclosure, I must declare that I am one of them). Then they undertook to track down every wood-burning barbecue restaurant they could find in the state of North Carolina and certify them as "True 'Cue" joints, and they plan to take the certifications nationwide. They also composed the True 'Cue pledge to allow the faithful to declare their allegiance to traditional barbecue, including promising to patronize wood-burning joints, celebrate those pitmasters who follow the old traditions, and call out those establishments who are taking the easy way out with electric or gas cookers.

ROBERT DONOVAN

So far, the Campaign for Real Barbecue has tracked down and certified close to 50 True 'Cue restaurants in the state of North Carolina, and they are in the process of verifying even more. It's all part of a focused effort to ensure that barbecue cooked over real wood remains a vibrant Carolina tradition for many years to come.

first enter the front door of the restaurant itself, but that's not used any more. "That was an innovation," Chip Stamey says. "It actually worked." The cooking surface opened out into a separate room so that the cooks could access the meat without being in the same room as the fire and smoke, and curious guests could watch the pit in operation through the plate-glass window. But, it couldn't cook nearly enough meat to support the restaurant's volume, and it didn't make sense to have people cooking in two different buildings. "It was a good idea," Stamey says, "but it didn't keep going."

Stamey's may be located in Greensboro, but it's a chapter-and-verse example of the Lexington style. "Even our wood is from Lexington," Chip Stamey says, for they get it by the dump-truck load from a supplier down in Davidson County. They serve their pork chopped or sliced, either on a plate or as a sandwich on a hamburger bun with slaw. The "dip," as barbecue sauce is inevitably called in this area, is thin and vinegary with a touch of ketchup. There's not a bit of mayonnaise in the homemade coleslaw, for it's a classic version of what's commonly called "red slaw" or "barbecue slaw": finely chopped cabbage dressed with ketchup, vinegar, red and black pepper, and sugar. The bright red Brunswick stew is thick and brimming with pork, chicken, corn, and limas, and the long, thin hush puppies are crisp on the outside and mildly sweet in the middle.

This is not to say that Stamey's doesn't have a few unique wrinkles. Their barbecue chicken, for instance, is not pit cooked but roasted in an oven, then

DENNY CULBERT

dipped in barbecue sauce before serving. What Stamey's calls a barbecue plate—pork with slaw and hush puppies on the side—would be called a "tray" a little farther to the south. (In and around Lexington, a "plate" has french fries in addition to the slaw and hush puppies.) The rest of the menu is pretty streamlined, too, especially for a Piedmont joint: hot dogs and chicken tenders for the non-barbecue fans, french fries and baked beans as side items. "That's my father's philosophy," Chip Stamey says. "Barbecue is sort of the ultimate fast food, though it's the slowest fast food to cook. But, once everything's ready you can really go fast with the barbecue. We like serving lots of people, and the less things that you do, the better that you can do those things."

For dessert, there's a selection of homemade cobblers, with peach as the house specialty. "My uncle [Keith] was a baker," Chip Stamey says. "He worked for Morrison's cafeteria before he went into the army. He learned to make really good dough and we decided to stop selling pies and sell peach cobblers. People ask why not banana pudding. Well, we make peach cobbler, and that's our big dessert."

Warner Stamey: Legendary Barbecue Mentor

Of all the cooks who helped define the unique regional styles of barbecue found in the Carolinas, perhaps the most influential was Warner Stamey. Stamey got started in the business in 1927 when, as a high school student, he began working part-time at Jess Swicegood's barbecue stand in Lexington, North Carolina. Three years later he moved to Shelby, where, using the techniques and recipes he learned at Swicegood's, he sold barbecue near the courthouse from a tent with a sawdust floor. Two Shelby residents, Alston Bridges (Stamey's brother-in-law) and Red Bridges (no relation), got their starts working in Stamey's restaurant, and they later branched out and opened their own places, Alston Bridges Barbecue and Red Bridges Barbecue Lodge, respectively.

In 1938, Stamey moved back to Lexington and bought out Swicegood's operations for $300; he later opened a second restaurant just south of town called Old Hickory Barbecue. Some of the many people who worked at Stamey's restaurants in Lexington include Doug Gosnell, who opened the Barbecue Center; Jimmy Harvey, who opened Jimmy's; Gene and Sylvia Whitley, who opened Whitley's; and Wayne Monk, who went on to open Lexington Barbecue—all in the town of Lexington. Wayne Monk taught Doug Cook, who opened Backcountry Barbecue and Cook's Barbecue, the latter of which is now run by Cook's son Brandon. Charlie McAdams also learned to cook at Warner Stamey's Lexington restaurant, and in 1947 he moved out to Mebane to open the A&M Grill. In 1951, Joe Hill headed to Winston-Salem and opened Hill's Lexington Barbecue. "Fuzzy" Nelson learned to cook barbecue at Hill's, and in 1954 he opened Fuzzy's in Madison. Leo Miller, another Stamey alum, opened Mr. Barbecue in Winston-Salem in the 1960s and later owned Three Little Pigs and Blackwelder's.

As for Warner Stamey himself, he ended his barbecue journey in Greensboro, where he opened Stamey's on High Point Road in 1953, which he eventually handed off to his sons Charles and Keith. It's still run today by his grandson Chip. Generations of barbecue men can trace their style back to Warner Stamey and, through him, to Jess Swicegood and his canvas tent across from the courthouse in Lexington. By learning the style of their mentors—how to cook and prepare the meat, the recipe for the sauce, the selection of side dishes to be served—the succeeding generations of barbecue restaurateurs helped codify and lock in the unique style of barbecue in the Piedmont region of North Carolina.

In a particularly unusual twist, the restaurant has its own coffee-roasting operation, which you can witness beside the retired pit through the glass windows up front. "That's just because I like coffee," Chip Stamey says. There was a small specialty grocery near the restaurant that roasted and sold coffee, and when they went out of business, Stamey decided to buy their roaster. "You roast pig, so why can't you roast coffee? And so we did. It's been a labor of love that just worked there because our chimney was there.

"Some people ask, 'Is that the barbecue chopper?'" Stamey says with a laugh. "No, it's not the barbecue chopper."

The spareness of the menu helps make Stamey's a well-oiled, high-volume operation. They may take their sweet time in cooking the barbecue, but they deliver it to customers at a rapid pace. The restaurant occupies a sprawling brick building with a big dining room with a high, open raftered roof. There's a drive-thru window, too, and about half their business is takeout. Located directly across the road from the Greensboro Coliseum, they do a land-office business when special events are being held, especially when the ACC basketball tournament is in town.

For my money, there's no better way to sample Stamey's barbecue than on a sandwich. Tender pork and crunchy coleslaw are piled on a warm steamed bun and wrapped in waxed paper. With each bit, the soft bun gives way to the chewy pork, which explodes with an intense smoky flavor that can come only from hours over hickory wood. Even if you order from the drive-thru and enjoy it as you speed down the highway in your car, you're still making a direct, tasty connection back to the early days of Piedmont North Carolina barbecue restaurants.

Tarheel Q

6835 W. US 64, Lexington, NC 27295; (336) 787-4550 **Founded:** 1984 **Cooking Method:** Shoulders on closed brick pits over hickory and oak **Serves:** Breakfast, lunch, and dinner Tues–Sat **Cards Accepted:** Yes

West of Lexington on US 64, almost to the county line, is a low cream-colored building with a gently sloping metal roof. Out front, a light-blue sign shaped like the state of North Carolina proclaims "Tarheel Q" with a bright red *Q*. It's one of the newer players on the Lexington scene (it's only been around since 1984), but it sticks firmly to the local traditions, which you can tell right away when you pull around the side of the building and see the brick pit room with four chimneys rising above it. Beside those chimneys is a covered chain-link pen holding tall stacks of split hickory and oak, and your nose can attest that

Keaton's: Not Exactly Barbecue, but Damned Good Chicken

The rusting sign over the restaurant says "Keaton's BBQ," but if you make the long journey to tiny Cleveland, North Carolina, to check it out, don't expect to find any chopped or sliced pork. Chicken is the name of the game at Keaton's, and it's fried, not cooked on a pit. B. W. Keaton opened the restaurant with his two brothers in 1953 and started cooking chicken in cast-iron skillets. As business increased, he installed custom-designed fryers that could hold two dozen pieces of chicken at a time. The barbecue part comes by way of the sauce, in which the chicken quarters are given a good dunking after they're fried. That famous sauce, which comes in both mild and hot varieties, is a dark-red vinegar-and-tomato based concoction that's very much a cousin of Lexington-style barbecue dip.

In the early days, Keaton's sold just fried chicken and beer and had only 10 booths and a bar, but over time both the restaurant and menu have grown in size. B. W. Keaton passed away in 1989, and his niece Kathleen Murray took over the operation. Fans still drive an hour or more to get their fix of the uniquely sauced fried chicken, and they happily take a number and wait in line for it to come out fresh from the fryer. No, it's not exactly what most Carolinians would call barbecue, but it sure is delicious.

Pit Cooking for the Masses: Brookwood Farms

Brookwood Farms (1015 Alston Bridge Rd., Siler City, NC 27344; 800-472-4787; brookwoodfarms.com) claims to be the only producer in America that's selling real pit-cooked barbecue to the food-service industry, and as far as I can tell they're right. At four o'clock in the afternoon each weekday, Brookwood's workers fire up more than a ton of hickory charcoal briquettes. They use them to fuel their brick-lined stainless steel pits, where they slow cook pork, beef, and chicken all night long. The next day, the meat is pulled or shredded, combined with one of four different sauces—mustard, vinegar, tomato, and a tangy western-style—then packed into plastic tubs.

Brookwood's cooking facility is located in Siler City, North Carolina, midway between Greensboro and Raleigh, and it produces more than 200,000 pounds of barbecue each week.

Much of that goes to Brookwood's high-volume restaurants in the Charlotte-Douglas International Airport and the Raleigh-Durham International Airport, feeding thousands of hungry travelers each week. They also sell their slow-cooked pork at the Charlotte Motor Speedway and in K–12 schools across the state, and consumers can pick up a 1-pound plastic tub of Brookwood barbecue in grocery stores throughout the Carolinas. It may be cooked in massive volumes and distributed far and wide, but it's still real pit-cooked barbecue. Would you expect anything less from a state as passionate about their barbecue as North Carolina?

they go through a lot of it, for as soon as you step from your car you'll bask in the aroma of real wood smoke.

The original Tarheel Q building suffered a fire in 2010 and was rebuilt, giving the interior a clean, new feel. It's obvious the minute you step through the door that the restaurant has a loyal following among the locals, for there's a continuous swirl of customers up front at the register waiting to pay. As is the rule in Lexington, Tarheel Q offers their pork chopped, coarse chopped, and sliced, and it comes on a sandwich, tray, or plate. The trays come with slaw, and they offer both a traditional Lexington red slaw and an Eastern-style white slaw, too. The plates add crinkle-cut fries. The pork is chopped by hand, and if you ask for it coarse, you'll end up with big cubes an inch or more on each side. The pork has a subtle but good smoky flavor, and the sauce is quite sweet and tangy. It's served warm, too—kept heated in a coffeepot. In addition to barbecue, the locals who crowd the dining room at lunchtime order steaks, fish, burgers, and sandwiches. You can even get a chili dog topped with the red barbecue slaw.

Wink's King of Barbecue

509 Faith Rd., Salisbury, NC 28146; (704) 637-2410 **Founded:** 1960s **Cooking Method:** Shoulders cooked over hickory wood on closed brick pits **Serves:** Breakfast, lunch, and dinner Mon–Sat **Cards Accepted:** Yes

The big yellow sign at Wink's in Salisbury is topped not by the traditional pig but rather by a lion, all the better to declare it the "King of Barbecue." The business was started by "Wink" Wansler back in the 1960s, and it was purchased by the Martin family in 1973. They've been running it for four decades now. Wink's moved to its present location in 2001, a large and rather nondescript brick building containing a big open dining room with a counter at one end. You can order breakfast all day long, including a sausage, egg, and cheese breakfast sandwich and big plates of flaky biscuits and thick, sausage-laced gravy.

Wink's still cooks pork shoulders over real hickory wood on the brick pit at the back of the restaurant. That pork can be ordered chopped or sliced, and it's accompanied by an orange tomato-and-vinegar sauce. On the barbecue tray, the pork is served beside a mound of Lexington-style red slaw, and, unlike most Piedmont joints, it comes not in a disposable cardboard tray but in a white ceramic au gratin dish. A basket of hush puppies comes alongside, and it includes a slice of "barbecue bread"—what others might call garlic bread or Texas toast. You can also order barbecue on a plate (and it's a real ceramic plate), which adds french fries and salad. For a sandwich, the chopped pork is piled on a warm bun, and it's topped not with red slaw but a tangy white version.

Barbecue gets the top billing, but Wink's is a seafood restaurant, too, offering an array of grilled and fried fish and shrimp, much of it caught right off the North Carolina coast, plus hearty dishes like meat loaf and foot-long hot dogs. Their grilled pimento-cheese sandwiches are legendary, too. One of the restaurant's specialties is a sort of sandwich made from two broad oatmeal cookies with cream cheese frosting layered inside; they're definitely worth saving a little room for.

A big sign hanging over the counter declares "We are Blessed." After polishing off a Wink's barbecue tray followed by an oatmeal-cookie sandwich, you'll probably be inclined to agree.

Yellow Mustard & Hash: The Midlands & Lowcountry of South Carolina

When people talk about South Carolina–style barbecue, they are usually referring to the Midlands style, a type of barbecue that originated in an eight-county region surrounding the capital city of Columbia, smack dab in the middle of the state. A few places in the Midlands, like Hite's in West Columbia, cook whole hogs, but shoulders and hams are by far the rule. Some spots, like Cannon's in Little Mountain, use both cuts; others, like Maurice's in Columbia, stick to hams alone. It results in a different type of barbecue than you'll find in the Pee Dee or Eastern North Carolina, where whole hog is supreme. The hams and shoulders are fattier, so the resulting barbecue is a little moister and more tender. In the Midlands it's as common to find that tender pork chopped into chunks as it is pulled into long shreds.

More than anything, though, the distinctive characteristic of the Midlands barbecue style is its eye-catching bright yellow sauce. Built on a base of yellow mustard, it is sometimes liberally sweetened and given a touch of tang from cider vinegar (as in the case of the Carolina Gold made famous by the Bessinger brothers). Other versions, like Wise's in Newberry and Jackie Hite's in Leesville, seem almost pure mustard. Most joints pre-sauce their meat generously, and there's even more available in squeeze bottles on the table. Admittedly, that dramatically colored sauce often gives pause to newcomers to Midlands barbecue. Indeed, when I moved from Greenville down to Columbia in 1992, my own palate, raised on a diet of Piedmont-style vinegar-and-tomato sauce, found the sweet, tangy mustard stuff to be quite a shock to the senses. But my advice to outsiders is to give it time. Mustard and pork, it turns out, are an excellent match, and the additional sweet, tangy notes are a fine accent to coarse-chopped or pulled ham and shoulder.

The Midlands is also hash and rice territory, and this classic barbecue-accompanying stew can put off newcomers, too, especially those with more

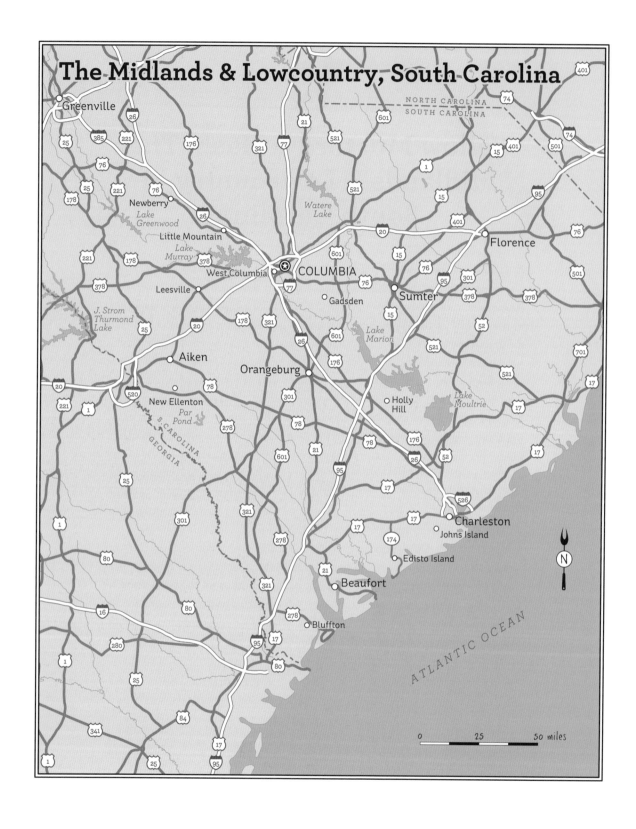

The Midlands & Lowcountry, South Carolina

Greenville

NORTH CAROLINA
SOUTH CAROLINA

Newberry

Lake Greenwood

Little Mountain

Lake Murray

West Columbia

Watere Lake

COLUMBIA

Florence

Leesville

J. Strom Thurmond Lake

Gadsden

Sumter

Aiken

New Ellenton

Par Pond

S. CAROLINA
GEORGIA

Orangeburg

Lake Marion

Holly Hill

Lake Moultrie

Charleston

Johns Island

Edisto Island

Beaufort

Bluffton

ATLANTIC OCEAN

N

0   25   50 miles

squeamish appetites. It's not exactly clear at first glance what might be in it, and it is true that hash originated as a way to use up the heads and the livers and all the rest of the pig you couldn't cook on a barbecue pit. But, most hash these days is made from inexpensive and inoffensive cuts like shoulder, and it's more a savory meat stew than anything else. If you look hard enough, though, you can find a few versions still made the old-fashioned way, and when you do, you'll know it, for the gray color and rich liver flavor give its ingredients away.

The Midlands are also the home of the barbecue buffet, a phenomenon not found in most regions of the country. It's the predominant form once you get down around Columbia, and it continues eastward all the way to the Low-country. Why the buffet took root so strongly in the region isn't exactly clear. It could be that these areas are more spaced out than, say, the joints in the Pied-mont portions of North Carolina, which tend to be found in the heart of towns and cities. To eat at classic Midlands restaurants, you're far more likely to have to get in your car and head to the outskirts of town or even many miles down a narrow country highway. They're the kind of eating places where people go on the weekend when they have ample time on their hands, not everyday places that people duck into for a quick bite.

If you talk to the owners of Midlands barbecue restaurants, you'll learn that most didn't start out offering a buffet but instead added them over time. Shealy's in Batesburg-Leesville claims to have been the first to introduce the buffet, which they initiated back in 1970. It's not something easily veri-fiable, but regardless of who introduced it, the barbecue buffet was greeted with open arms in the Midlands. By 1979, when Allie Patricia Wall and Ron L. Layne compiled their *Hog Heaven* guidebook (see "*Hog Heaven*" sidebar, Yellow Mustard & Hash chapter), more than a half of the barbecue restaurants they recorded in what they called the Central and Southeast districts were offering a buffet. These days, the all-you-can-eat steam table is more common than counter service at Midlands barbecue restaurants, though some places offer both forms. Bessinger's in Charleston is a double-sided restaurant with a "sandwich shop" on one side, where you order fast-food style at a counter, and a full country-cooking buffet on the other. At Wise's in Newberry and Jackie Hite's in Leesville, you enter the main dining room with the buffet via one door and a separate room for ordering takeout through another.

In terms of barbecue style, we can extend the Midlands region all the way down to the coastal areas around Charleston. The Lowcountry of South Carolina, historically speaking, does not have a strong barbecue tradition of its own. The historical record offers only a few passing mentions of barbecues being held in the region back in the 19th century, unlike the Midlands and

Upstate of South Carolina where every holiday, election, and civic celebration was an occasion to cook a whole hog or two. The Lowcountry has a rich culinary heritage based upon rice dishes like pilau and hoppin' John, fresh shrimp and fish from the Atlantic, and African imports like okra and benne (sesame) seeds. For some reason, though, it never developed its own barbecue

The German Connection: A Dubious Conjecture?

The presence of mustard in the barbecue sauce of the Midlands is often attributed to the German influence in what is known as the Dutch Fork, which takes its name from the spot where the Broad and Saluda Rivers meet to form the Congaree and from the number of Germans (or Deutsch) who settled in the area. Indeed, a suspiciously large number of the family names that adorn the signs of the region's barbecue restaurants are German in origin: Hite, Bessinger, Dukes, Shealy, Lever, Price. Germans, the explanation goes, have a fondness for mustard, and they ended up incorporating it into their barbecue sauce.

But German names dominate the barbecue in the Piedmont of North Carolina, too. The so-called German conjecture, first advanced by Gary Freeze, a professor of history at Catawba College in Salisbury, North Carolina, postulates that the barbecue families in that region—families with German names like Swicegood, Weaver, and Ridenhour—brought with them a fondness for vinegar-marinated smoked pork and, in particular, prized the shoulder of the hog. And, of course, the presence of immigrant German butchers in Texas and their fondness for smoked meats is often cited to explain the origin of Texas's famous sauceless brisket and beef ribs. Those Germans and their culinary preferences sure have gotten around.

style. Instead, barbecue styles were brought to it from somewhere else. The Midlands mustard-based style snuck down to the coast around World War II, when the expanding Navy Yard in North Charleston attracted thousands of new residents from the rural areas, including members of two influential Orangeburg Country barbecue families, the Dukes and the Bessingers. A little Pee Dee–style vinegar-and-pepper sauce has managed to infiltrate the greater Charleston area, too, and you'll usually find both mustard and vinegar sauces at restaurants in and around the city. (Lowcountry pilau, curiously, has managed to make its way in the reverse direction, sneaking up into the barbecue tradition of the Pee Dee in the form of chicken bog (see "Perloo & Chicken Bog" sidebar, Whole Hogs & Vinegar Sauce chapter).

Even if you weren't raised eating bright-yellow pulled pork with a side of hash and rice, it's well worth a visit to the Midlands to sample its distinctive barbecue culture. If you approach it with an open mind, you might come to believe that it's one of the most original and enjoyable of America's great regional barbecue styles.

Bessinger's Barbeque

602 Savannah Hwy., Charleston, SC 29407; (843) 556-1354; bessingers bbq.com **Founded:** 1960s **Cooking Method:** Pork shoulders over hickory and oak on closed brick pits **Serves:** Lunch and dinner daily, buffet Fri–Sun **Cards Accepted:** Yes

The Bessingers (see sidebar, this chapter) are one of the dominant barbecue families in the Midlands and Lowcountry regions of South Carolina, and the Bessinger's on Savannah Highway in Charleston is a prime embodiment of the family's signature style. It was founded by Thomas Bessinger and is now run by his sons Tommy and Michael, and it's located a few miles west of downtown on Savannah Highway (aka US 17). To my taste buds, the barbecue and the bright gold sauce at Bessinger's are virtually identical to the stuff served at Maurice's and Melvin's—separate operations that were founded by various other Bessinger brothers and have essentially the same menus.

Thomas Bessinger got his start working in his brothers' restaurants and, in the 1960s, decided he wanted his own place. So, he opened a new "Piggie Park" on US 17 on the west side of Charleston. Like many restaurants serving barbecue in that era, Bessinger's had a drive-in format with hamburgers and hot dogs sharing the menu with pit-cooked barbecue. Somewhere along the line the old drive-in building was replaced with a new long red wooden building, with a barnlike structure out front doing double duty as a sign for the restaurant and as a porch with swings for patrons to relax after polishing off a

The Bessinger Family

In the world of South Carolina barbecue, the story of the Bessinger family is the stuff of legend. And by legend, I mean a tale filled with myth and controversy and so many competing versions of events that it's hard to reconcile them into a single consistent narrative. But here's my best shot at it.

Joseph James "Big Joe" Bessinger was born in 1891 in Orangeburg County and was a farmer throughout his life. He cooked whole hogs in a dirt pit the old-fashioned country way, and in 1933, according to family lore, he came up with a secret recipe for a sweet golden barbecue sauce made with a base of yellow mustard. Was Joe Bessinger the very first person to create a barbecue sauce based on mustard? Perhaps; I've not found anyone else claiming to have done so earlier. But, there is one historical fact that isn't in dispute: In 1939, Joe Bessinger decided to try his hand at something other than farming, and he sold one of his cows and used the proceeds to open the Holly Hill Cafe in the town of Holly Hill, South Carolina. It was there that at least five of Joe Bessinger's sons—Joe David, Melvin, Robert, Thomas, and Maurice—learned to cook hogs over hickory woods and to make their father's signature sweet mustard-based sauce. But they were operating at the tail end of the Depression, and the cafe didn't last very long before Big Joe closed it down and went back to farming.

During World War II, several of Joe's sons, including Joe David and Melvin, served overseas. Melvin stormed Omaha Beach in 1944, and he was captured and imprisoned in a POW camp. After he returned home in 1946, he and his father opened Joe's Grill, also known as "Eat at Joe's." It was located in Holly Hill midway between Columbia and Charleston on US 176, which in that pre-interstate era was the main route between the two cities. Big Joe Bessinger died in 1949. Family legend tells of a lost will that was never found, and the ownership of the restaurant was apparently in dispute, but Melvin ended up taking over the operation. In a *New York Times* interview in 2001, Maurice Bessinger, one of Melvin's younger brothers, recalled that "Momma gave the restaurant to Melvin. . . . Melvin was always Momma's pet."

Melvin may have owned the Holly Hill restaurant, but his mother and brothers ran the business while he attended the Citadel in Charleston, from which he graduated in 1951. The rest of the Bessinger brothers felt the lure of the Holy City, too, and one by one they ended up moving down to Charleston and selling the same style of barbecue that they learned growing up in Orangeburg County. In the early 1950s, Joe Jr. opened the Piggie Park Drive-In on Rutledge Street, complete with intercoms for ordering and carhops to deliver the food to customers' automobiles. After returning from a tour of duty in Korea, Maurice Bessinger joined Joe Jr. and worked at the restaurant, too, but he ended up having a falling-out with at least one of his brothers and moved up to Columbia, where he opened his own Piggie Park Drive-In.

By 1958, Thomas Bessinger was managing the Piggie Park Drive-In on Rutledge Avenue in Charleston, and Joe Jr., was running Piggie Park Drive-In #2 on Dorchester Avenue. All this time, Melvin Bessinger was still running Joe's Grill up in Holly Hill. Then, in the early 1960s, I-26 from Columbia to Charleston was completed, and the traffic that once clogged US 176 dwindled to a trickle. Melvin decided to close the doors of Joe's Grill and join his brothers down in Charleston where there was more opportunity. By 1961, Burness Bessinger had come along, too, and he and his wife, Ida, were running the Piggie Park Snack Bar. Melvin was running Joe's Number 2 on Rivers Avenue in the expanding suburb of North Charleston. Thomas and Joe Jr. were still running the two original Piggie Park Drive-Ins on Rutledge and Dorchester Avenues.

Before long, the Bessinger brothers started spreading out all around the greater Charleston area. In 1961, Melvin opened his first Piggie Park Drive-In, and he quickly added two more locations, one in Beaufort and one in Orangeburg. Melvin's fledgling chain grew to eight locations by the 1980s, though he later pared them back to just two, both called Melvin's. His brother Thomas opened a Piggie Park west of the city of Savannah Highway, which he later renamed Bessinger's BBQ, and Robert Bessinger headed up to North Charleston to open two restaurants there, one of which has since closed. There's also a Joe Bessinger's barbecue in Summerville just outside of Charleston proper.

All of the Bessinger restaurants are similar in style and technique, and each traces that style back to patriarch Big Joe. They all serve a sweet yellow mustard sauce, though they vary slightly in flavor. Melvin's, Maurice's, and Bessinger's all feature "Big Joe" and "Little Joe" sandwiches on their menu. (Melvin claimed to have been the first to use the name, in honor of his dad; Maurice, of course, disputed that.) Hash and rice and big, puffy deep-fried onions rings round out the characteristics that make a Bessinger restaurant a Bessinger restaurant.

In September 2000, Maurice Bessinger hoisted the Confederate flag in front of all his restaurants in Columbia (see "Barbecue & Civil Rights" sidebar, this chapter), which prompted Wal-Mart, Sam's Club, and all the major grocery chains in South Carolina to yank his bottled barbecue sauce from their shelves. Maurice estimated that 98 percent of his sauce business evaporated and his multimillion-dollar bottle plant was standing mostly idle. His older brother Melvin spied an opportunity and started producing a barbecue sauce of his own, and he managed to take over the shelf space in the Bi-Lo grocery stores that used to be occupied by his brother's products. Maurice was enraged, and he spouted off to the press, "I taught Melvin everything he knows about barbecue sauce—but I didn't teach him everything I know." Melvin, of course, had a different take, saying that he was taught the recipe by his father and shared most it with his brothers as they came of age, but, per his parents' request, omitted two key ingredients.

Not surprisingly, a lot of consumers confused Melvin's sauce with Maurice's, and when civil rights groups started calling for a boycott of it, too, Melvin removed the name Bessinger from his label altogether. His attorney issued a press release declaring, "Melvin and his brother do not share political or social views. Despite their being brothers, they do not speak to each other." Robert Bessinger weighed in on his brothers' feud in 2001, saying, "They have an ego problem. Melvin wants to be the chief, and Maurice wants to be the major chief."

As Big Joe Bessinger's sons starting getting up in years, a third generation began taking the reins of their barbecue empires. Melvin retired in 2004 and passed away in 2012, and his wife, Betty, daughter Stephanie, and son David now operate the two remaining Melvin's locations. Two of Thomas's children, Tommy Jr. and Michael, have taken over the Bessinger's BBQ on Savannah Highway. Up in Columbia, Maurice's sons Lloyd and Paul and his daughter Debbie have succeeded their father, who passed away in 2014.

There was even a brief revival of the original cafe up in Holly Hill that started the family empire. In 2006, Thomas Bessinger and his sons purchased the property that used to be Joe's Grill, and in 2010 they reopened the restaurant. Serving breakfast and lunch only, the menu included traditional diner specialties like eggs, grits, and toast along with the family's famous barbecue and hash and rice. It only lasted a few years before closing its doors, but for that brief period it was a working reminder of the roadside cafe that spawned a South Carolina barbecue dynasty.

meal. The same drive-in-style hamburgers and hot dogs are still on the menu, but over the years the barbecue has moved much more into the foreground.

Bessinger's today is two restaurants rolled into one. On the right side of the building is the sandwich shop, where you can order Big and Little Joe sandwich baskets and pork or rib platters from the counter. On the left side is the country-buffet room, which from Friday to Sunday offers an all-you-can-eat spread that includes all the barbecue items plus an array of classic Southern dishes and specials like shrimp and grits and pork tenderloin.

For my money, the real action is over in the sandwich shop. The Big Joe basket is excellent—a large chopped pork sandwich with fries, slaw, and a single massive onion ring. That onion ring has so much sweet, doughy batter that it eats almost like a doughnut. The pork has a pleasantly smoky flavor and comes topped with the sweet yellow-mustard-based sauce that's the signature of the Bessinger family—not enough to drown the barbecue flavor but a sufficient amount to give it a zip. You can get that same meat on a chopped pork platter, which includes either a dinner roll or a square of sweet, cakelike corn bread along with two sides. There are a dozen sides to choose from—all the usual barbecue suspects like coleslaw, collards and mac 'n' cheese along with more meat 'n' three fare like fried okra and cinnamon apples. Be sure to make hash and rice one of your selections, for Bessinger's has one of the best versions in the Lowcountry, minced fine and mixed with a lot of spices to make a thick, reddish gravy that's savory and slightly sweet.

In something of an anomaly for South Carolina barbecue, Bessinger's also serves brisket and St. Louis–style ribs. But the real ringer on the menu harkens back to the old drive-in days, for Bessinger's serves one of the best cheeseburgers in the city of Charleston. Wide and flat with a toasted bun and just the right combination of bread to cheese to meat, it's the perfect alternative for the spouse who can only eat barbecue a mere two or three times a week.

Big T Bar-B-Q

2520 Congaree Rd., Gadsden, SC 29052; (803) 353-0488; bigtbbq .com **Founded:** 1993 **Cooking Method:** Whole hog on closed metal pits **Serves:** Lunch and dinner Wed–Sat **Cards Accepted:** Yes **Other Locations:** 7535-C Garners Ferry Rd., Columbia, SC 29209; (803) 776-7132; lunch and dinner Mon–Sat; and 1061-G Sparkleberry Ln., Columbia, SC 29223; (803) 788-4295; lunch and dinner Mon–Sat
When I lived in Columbia, the Big T on Garners Ferry Road was my go-to barbecue source, since it was just down the road from my house, and its big steam table brimmed with excellent chopped pork and plenty of other

Southern delicacies. But it's worth a drive down to Gadsden to check out the "Mothership," where the pigs for all three Big T's locations are cooked. It's the original location and is now takeout only, but there's no better way to get barbecue straight from the pit and hash straight from the pot.

Big T is sort of a blend of a barbecue house and a soul food joint. The heaping Big T dinner includes chopped pork, hash and rice, and your choice of side (try the collards or mustard greens). But, the ribs are tender and juicy, too, and the sauce is a classic Midlands sweet mustard. Big T is the only place I know that serves barbecue over rice, which is just what it sounds like: chopped pork barbecue served atop a bed of rice. Other combo plates let you sample the chopped pork with ribs, fried chicken, fried pork chops, or even pigs' feet, and there's fried whiting and flounder, too. The sweet, tender collards and mustard greens are joined by mac 'n' cheese, green beans, coleslaw, and potato salad, and smoked turkey legs, chitlins, and hoppin' John show up from time to time.

Bluffton Barbecue

11 State of Mind St., Bluffton, SC 29910; (843) 757-7427; blufftonbbq .com **Founded:** 2008 **Cooking Method:** Pork shoulder over hickory, oak, and pecan on closed metal pits **Serves:** Lunch and dinner Wed– Sat **Cards Accepted:** Yes

"You're paying for the BBQ, not the service," the website for Bluffton BBQ declares, a clear warning that this is a barbecue joint that does things their own way and isn't shy about saying it. Ted Huffman, the restaurant's cigar-chomping owner and pitmaster, cooks Boston butts and ribs on a big torpedo-like smoker, using oak, hickory, and—whenever he can get it—pecan. The butts are transformed into true pulled pork, cooked 12 hours and pulled with tongs into long, thick shreds.

The meats might be familiar to South Carolinians, but Huffman's a Florida native and doesn't feel particularly constrained by any of the Palmetto State's barbecue conventions. They'll pile pulled pork on Texas toast and top it with, of all things, a slice of tomato, and they'll roll it inside a tortilla to create a "pig in a blanket," too. The meals are served in black plastic baskets lined with red-and-white checked waxed paper. There's no yellow mustard or spicy vinegar sauce to be found, just big squeeze bottles of a Ted's bright-red barbecue sauce. To drink, sweet tea and canned sodas are augmented by a big washtub filled with cans of fine brews like Pabst Blue Ribbon and Busch Lite on ice.

The location is as unique as the barbecue. Huffman got started selling barbecue out of a red caboose, but in 2008 he moved into a new building in Bluffton's Calhoun Street Promenade, a mix of businesses and homes in the Old

The Truth about South Carolina's "Truth in Barbecue" Law

In 1986, Representative J. J. "Bubber" Snow of Hemingway introduced South Carolina House Bill 3718, which became known as the "Truth in Barbecue" law. The bill required the Department of Agriculture to design and print "distinctive decals that may be displayed wherever barbecue is sold." Each decal would announce which type of barbecue the establishment sold, and there were four possible categories:

1. "Barbeque - Whole hog - Cooked with wood."
2. "Barbeque - Whole hog - Cooked from a heat source other than wood."
3. "Barbeque - Part of, but not whole hog - Cooked from any source of heat."
4. "Barbeque - Part of, but not whole hog - Cooked with wood."

Anyone displaying a decal that falsely stated the type of barbecue he or she was selling could be fined up to $200 or imprisoned for up to 30 days.

Snow predicted the law would benefit both farmers and consumers, bringing publicity to farmers so they could sell more pork and transparency for consumers so they could better choose their barbecue. "Let the connoisseur compare, and decide what they like best," Snow told the press. Governor Dick Riley signed the bill into law in May 1986, but there was one major shortcoming in the measure: It stated that restaurants *may* display the decals, but it didn't require them to. It's not clear whether any restaurants actually posted the decals at all, and there certainly was no effort at enforcing the rules.

These days, writers still cite the Truth in Barbecue law as evidence of how seriously people in the Palmetto State take their 'cue, and many seem to think that the law is still on the books. Alas, it did not remain in effect for very long. Representative Snow quietly introduced a bill repealing the truth in barbecue law in 1992, bringing to an end the first and, so far, the only effort in the country to regulate the definition of barbecue.

Town district. The restaurant has brown plank sides and a metal roof, and off to one side is a brick and screened-in pit room. The neat, yellow-walled dining room is adorned with a variety of pig statuary, and diners eat at metal-topped tables with low backless stools. Out back is a patio with round metal tables where guests can enjoy their barbecue outdoors. Huffman insists on selling meat that's fresh cooked each day, and once they sell out they close their doors, so it's worth calling ahead before you drive over to make sure there's still some left.

Cannon's BBQ

1903 Nursery Rd., Little Mountain, SC 29075; (803) 945-1080
Founded: 2004 **Cooking Method:** Hams and shoulders on closed pits over oak and hickory coals **Serves:** Lunch and dinner Thurs–Sat
Cards Accepted: Yes

Cannon's BBQ is not the kind of place you're just going to stumble upon. It's tucked back off a little side road that angles off of US 76 just outside of Little Mountain on the way to Chapin. The low white building is nondescript, and there's not even a sign that says "BBQ," just the word "Cannon's" stenciled in blue block letters over the front door (and even that is a recent addition). Barbecue lovers should make the effort to seek the place out, though. With just over a decade of operations under its belt, it is, chronologically speaking, a relative newcomer on the South Carolina barbecue scene. But, everything else about it is as old-school as it gets.

On Wednesday, Brice and Ray Cannon fire up a burn barrel fashioned from a 55-gallon drum with metal bars inserted through the bottom, reducing hickory and oak logs down to coals, which they use to fire their black metal pit. They cook hams and shoulders for 8 to 10 hours, misting them periodically with vinegar. When the meat is finished, they hand chop it with cleavers and dress it with a sweet mustard sauce. On Thursday, they put chicken quarters, beef briskets, and St. Louis–cut ribs on the pit, and they open for business at 11 a.m. They'll serve their barbecue straight through until Saturday evening, by which time the pork may well be all gone.

That finely chopped pork is a delight. The big scoop that arrives on your plate, pre-sauced a golden yellow, is tender and rich with a subtle touch of hickory smoke. The sauce is sweetened with honey and maple syrup, the gentleman refilling my ice tea told me on my first visit. "But the key," he said, "is that it's made with bran mustard. That's less tart than the regular yellow kind." The sauce goes quite nicely on Cannon's ribs, too, which are meaty and smoky and have a brick-red ring from hours of hardwood smoke. You can get any of the meats on a sandwich with fries and slaw or as a permutation of

dinners with one or two meat selections plus two sides and a slice of white bread. Those sides include some really tasty mac 'n' cheese and properly firm baked beans that are complemented by their sweet sauce instead of drowning in it. There are burgers, hot dogs, and fried chicken, too.

Cannon's hash is worth notice for a couple of reason. First, unlike the tan or reddish brown varieties found in most of the state, theirs has a decidedly yellow color because it's seasoned with the same sweet yellow sauce as the chopped pork. It's also cooked the old-fashioned way: in a big cast-iron kettle over a real wood fire. There are a few concessions to modernity: The Cannons abjure hog heads and organs in favor of pork shoulders and a little beef seasoned with onions and red pepper. They simmer the meat until it's falling off the bone, then run it through a grinder to chop it into ½-inch bits. The stew is finished back in the pot over the wood fire, with plenty of sweet mustard sauce added. The result is a thin, yellow hash, flecked through with a generous dose of black pepper. It's light and sweet but still quite filling, its savory juices merging perfectly with the plain white rice over which it's served.

The restaurant itself is quite modest: a green prefab metal building with a white-walled dining room tacked on the front. Inside there's a white linoleum floor and a battered metal ceiling with a few American flags hanging down from it. The tables are all the plastic-topped kind with folding metal legs. A couple of high-backed wooden benches make booths out of some of them, and the rest have folding chairs. You order at a window looking into the kitchen, and the friendly staff will bring the food out to you and refill your Styrofoam cup of sweet tea from a big plastic pitcher, too.

Cannon's doesn't need anything fancy—not even a real sign—to draw a steady stream of locals who know where to get top-notch barbecue cooked the right way. It's definitely one of South Carolina's most under-the-radar houses, but as word continues to get out, I expect that might begin to change.

Hash & Rice: South Carolina's Signature Side Dish

Like yellow mustard-based sauce, hash is one of the regional twists that baffles newcomers to South Carolina barbecue. A cross between a meat stew and a gravy, it's almost always served over a bed of white rice and is the state's signature barbecue side item. For those who grew up eating it, it's a sublime creation in which potentially unappealing ingredients are brought together, simmering and melding slowly over time, to create a flavorful and utterly delightful dish.

Many are suspicious about what goes into the hash pot, and if you are of the squeamish sort, you may not want to inquire too closely. It's true that the stew originated as an economical way to use up the various pig parts (especially the livers and the heads) that couldn't be put on the barbecue pit. In the early days, it was often called "liver and lights" hash, *lights* being a popular term for the lungs of a hog. A few places in South Carolina—these tend to be in the Pee Dee region—still make old-fashioned liver hash, but most cooks have switched over to using inexpensive cuts like pork shoulder and hams, and they'll often put chuck roast or other beef cuts in the pot, too. As you get up into the Upstate of South Carolina, you'll start finding hash that's made exclusively from beef.

Regardless of which cuts are used, hash making begins by simmering the meat in water with onions and spices for hours on end until the meat is falling off the bone. In an area running from Lexington County down to Georgia border, you can still find so-called string hash—meat that is pulled into shreds by hand. But, as the old generations pass on, newer cooks have tended to adopt the more convenient mechanical chopper. Once pulled or chopped, the deboned meat goes back into the hash pot until it merges into a thick, consistent substance that's savory and delicious. Some flavor it with tomatoes or ketchup, giving it a reddish hue, while others use mustard or their own mustard-based barbecue sauce to tinge it yellow.

Hash originated before the Civil War in the counties on either side of the Savannah River in South Carolina and Georgia. Estrella Jones, who was born into slavery on Powers Pond Place near Augusta, recalled that when she was a child, the men would sometimes steal hogs from other plantations and "cook hash and rice and serve barbecue." At the opening of the Civil War, a barbecue was held to honor the Edgefield Riflemen as they prepared to leave for battle. The menu included "barbecued meats and hash." By the 1880s, hash was being served as far north as Newberry, South Carolina, and as far south as Macon in central Georgia, which is much farther south than hash is found today.

At outdoor barbecues in the Midlands of South Carolina, it was standard near the pits to find a couple of big iron pots of hash bubbling over open wood fires. As barbecue transitioned into more of a commercial product, hash and rice became one of the regular side dishes that accompanied the meat. A few restaurateurs actually dispensed with cooking barbecue altogether and made hash the core of their business (see "The Hash House" sidebar, Free Spirits chapter).

These days, there are a handful of old-style barbecue houses, like Jackie Hite's in Leesville and Cannon's BBQ in Little Mountain, that still cook their hash in iron cauldrons over wood fires. Most restaurants, though, have moved their hash production indoors, where they use stainless steel pots on gas stoves. But, two things haven't changed a bit: the use of slow simmering to transform less-wanted ingredients into a succulent dish, and the love of South Carolinians for their favorite barbecue side dish.

ENJOY

Old Fashioned Restaurant

Carolina Bar-B-Que

109 Main St. South, New Ellenton, SC 29809; (803) 652-2919
Founded: 1969 **Cooking Method:** Shoulders and hams over charcoal on closed metal pits **Serves:** Lunch and dinner Thurs–Sun **Cards Accepted:** Yes

Many of the restaurants in the far-flung network associated with the Dukes family (see "The Dukes" sidebar, this chapter) are more notable for their down-home atmosphere and the variety of their buffets than they are for the actual barbecue they serve, for most switched to gas cookers long ago. Carolina Bar-B-Que in New Ellenton is a notable exception, and its splendid chopped pork is one of the state's real sleepers. Its small shreds have lots of pinkish-red outer bits mixed in, and from the very first bite, it bursts with the wonderful richness of hardwood smoke. It's a tempting suggestion of what the barbecue of Willie Baltzegar and Manuel Dukes must have tasted liked back in the early 20th century.

Carolina Bar-B-Que was founded in 1969 by Willie Mae Walker (née Baltzegar) and her son, Jess Walker Jr. It's been remodeled over the years, and there's a newish if modest feel to the two small dining rooms with their blue ceramic tile floors, green tablecloths, and paintings of flying ducks and country scenes that adorn the gray paneled walls. It's an all-you-can eat joint, and the small buffet is focused on the essentials. In addition to the chopped pork, there's barbecue chicken glazed in yellow sauce and a bright orange hash that's smooth and very peppery. The sides include coleslaw, big round hush puppies, tender greens with hint of vinegar, and baked beans with chunks of pork in a sweet orange sauce. Two of the more unusual items are the discs of yellow squash fried in a nice crisp batter and the fried sweet potato "tots" dusted with cinnamon sugar.

Next to the cash register are laid out white Styrofoam cups filled with ice and an urn of lemonade and another of unsweetened tea. The sweet tea, which is what almost everyone takes, awaits at the table in clear plastic pitchers along with two bottles of sauce. The bright orange version is a sweet, smooth, and sort of creamy mustard/ketchup blend—the signature sauce of the Dukes clan (see "'Orangeburg Sweet' or 'Rust Gravy'" sidebar, this chapter). There's a Midlands-style mustard sauce, too, that's laced with a generous dose of black pepper flakes, and it's very peppery on the tongue. Either one goes just fine with the pork, but to me the meat is so smoky and flavorful it really doesn't need anything else added to it.

The area behind the restaurant is enclosed by a high, white wood fence, and you can get a glimpse through the gaps in the gate of a tin-roofed smoke-house with screened walls with big clouds of smoke rolling out. That's the secret to Carolina Bar-B-Que: real pit cooking.

"Orangeburg Sweet" or "Rust Gravy": The Fifth Carolina Barbecue Sauce?

Almost everyone who has surveyed the different regional barbecue styles has pegged the Carolinas as having four distinct varieties of sauce: the spicy vinegar-pepper sauce of Eastern North Carolina and the Pee Dee, the vinegar-and-tomato of Piedmont North Carolina, the bright yellow mustard-based of the Midlands, and the sweet, heavy tomato sauce that is found in various parts of the Upstate and along the South Carolina–Georgia border. But, these culinary taxonomists may have missed an elusive fifth style of sauce: the orangish-red concoction that's the hallmark of the Dukes barbecue family from Orangeburg County (see "The Dukes" sidebar, page this chapter). The sauce is a blend of ketchup, mustard, sugar, and, in some incarnations, a little whipped salad dressing. Sweeter and milder than the more common Midlands mustard-based sauce, this fifth style can be found in both of the Dukes barbecue restaurants in Orangeburg as well as places that spun out of the Dukes empire over the years, like Antley's in Orangeburg and the Palmetto Pig in Columbia. Some call the sauce "Orangeburg sweet," but Tony Kittrell, who runs the Dukes Barbecue on Whitman Street in Orangeburg, has my favorite term for it: "rust gravy."

DENNY CULBERT

Dukes Barbecue

1298 Whitman St., Orangeburg, SC 29155; (803) 534-2916 **Founded:** 1972 **Cooking Method:** Hams and shoulders on closed gas-fired pits **Serves:** Lunch and dinner Thurs–Sat **Cards Accepted:** Yes

You'll find Dukes Barbecue restaurants all over the lower part of South Carolina, and though they are independent operations, each are connected one way or another to the Dukes family from Orangeburg County (see "The Dukes" sidebar, this chapter). The Dukes on Whitman Street in Orangeburg remains for me the archetypical example of the family's barbecue style (but don't tell that to diners who prefer the Chestnut Street location, for folks in Orangeburg can get quite passionate when it comes to which Dukes they prefer). The business was founded by Earl Dukes in the 1950s, and he ended up selling to a couple of partners in 1972, one of whom was Harold Kittrell, whose family still operates it today.

As is the case for most of Dukes restaurants, the hours are limited (lunch and dinner three days a week), and the setting modest. The low cinder-block building with a wood-lined front and gray wooden shingles contains a big, bare-bones dining room. It's all-you-can-eat, and the steam-table buffet offers chopped pork, barbecue chicken, and fried chicken along with a narrow slate of sides: hash and rice, green beans, baked beans, mac and cheese, slaw, and potato salad. To round things out, there are dill pickle chips and sliced white

The Dukes: First Family of South Carolina Barbecue

In the Midlands and Lowcountry of South Carolina, the kings of barbecue are actually Dukes—that is, members of the Dukes family. At least a dozen barbecue restaurants named "Dukes" are in operation today, covering a geographic area from Aiken all the way down to Charleston, and several more have some sort of loose connection to the family. And that's not counting a dozen more establishments that were once in existence but have since closed down.

Note that the restaurants names are properly spelled "Dukes," not "Duke's." Almost all of the Dukes joints can be traced back eventually to the children of a single patriarch, Emanuel (Manuel) Dukes, who was born in rural Orangeburg County around 1875. One of Dukes's children married into the family of Willie Baltzegar, a noted local pitmaster who cooked barbecue for dances and other events in the Rowesville community about 10 miles south of Orangeburg. The Dukes sons helped out at the events and learned Baltzegar's barbecue techniques and recipes. Starting in the 1950s, they put that learning to commercial use by opening a series of restaurants in and around Orangeburg County.

Earl Dukes pioneered the barbecue trade in the town of Orangeburg, opening a thriving downtown business, which he later sold, only to open another restaurant in Cameron. Brother Danny Dukes headed a little west, opening a restaurant in Aiken, while sister Cercie was involved in the Dukes Barbecues in Elloree and Smoaks (both long closed). Other family members and in-laws opened joints in Ridgeville, New Ellenton, and Blackville.

Before long, the Dukes family had quietly and steadily built a sprawling barbecue empire. With two separately owned Dukes barbecue restaurants, the town of Orangeburg remains the center of that kingdom. In Orangeburg today, you still identify your preferred Dukes not by which family members run it or by the street it's on but rather by what it's near. Thus, you must specify whether you mean the one "next to the fire station" (that is, on Chestnut Street) or the one "by the Pepsi plant" (on Whitman Street), an identification made a bit more difficult for outsiders a few years ago when the Pepsi bottler closed down. A third Orangeburg barbecue house, Antley's, spun out of the Whitman Street Dukes when four brothers who got their start working at Dukes decided to open their own place.

The Dukes family was among the first to bring Midlands-style barbecue to the Charleston area, too. In the 1950s, Harry Ott and his wife Elma (another Dukes sister) opened Dukes Bar-B-Q on Spruill Street in North Charleston, which was then booming thanks to postwar jobs at the Navy Yard. The Otts remained Orangeburg residents, cooking their barbecue at home and bringing it down to Charleston to sell on the weekends. That business is run today by Elma Ott's granddaughter Lisa Warner in the same modest, white-painted cinder-block building, and the barbecue is cooked up in Orangeburg at the Chestnut Street Dukes, which is owned by Warner's mother. Another member of the Orangeburg Dukes clan, Milton Jefferson Dukes, was not only a barbecue restaurateur but also one of the state's most colorful (if not most successful) political figures. A staunch anti-whiskey campaigner, his political career included runs for governor in 1962, 1970, and 1974, as well as assorted bids for the state legislature and for sheriff, all of which gained lots of attention in the press and all of which ended in defeat. "You know I've always been a good loser," he told the *Post and Courier* in 1974. "I don't know how to do anything but lose." That statement isn't exactly true, because he certainly knew how to cook barbecue. Like the Otts, Milton Dukes arrived in North Charleston just after World War II, and his business career included stints as a trailer salesman, used car dealer, and finance man. On the side he ran several barbecue stands in North Charleston before finally moving out to Summerville and opening a more permanent establishment.

So, as you travel through the lower half of South Carolina, don't be surprised if you pass by more than one restaurant with "Dukes Barbecue" on the sign out front. Stop in any one of them and you'll find a big buffet brimming with pulled pork, hash and rice, and the Dukes signature rust-colored sauce, a style whose roots run deep in the barbecue tradition of the Palmetto State.

loaf bread straight from the bag, and big pitchers of very sweet tea await at each of the tables, which are the long collapsible variety with folding metal chairs.

There's not much in the way of smoke flavor to the meat because, like almost all of the other Dukes restaurants, the Whitman Street one converted to gas cookers years ago. For outsiders, the fried chicken, which is tender and juicy beneath its crisp batter, is as much a draw as the pork. But for locals who grew up eating the stuff, the finely chopped pork dressed with Dukes's signature sauce is the essence of real barbecue. That sauce is either a variant of the Midland-style mustard-based barbecue sauce or a unique sauce category in and of itself, for it has both ketchup and mustard in it, which gives it an unusual orangish-red hue. Tony Kittrell, who runs the Whitman Street Dukes today, calls it "rust gravy." The recipe is said to have been originated by Earl Dukes himself, and it's kept warm in a big silver pan on the buffet so patrons can ladle as much as they like on the chopped pork. There's a spicy vinegar sauce available in squeeze bottles, too, but using that seems contrary to the spirit of the place. It's that rust gravy—plus the crispy fried chicken and savory red hash— that keeps the fans of the Whitman Street Dukes coming back for more.

Fiery Ron's Home Team BBQ

1205 Ashley River Rd., Charleston, SC 29407; (843) 225-7427; home teambbq.com **Founded:** 2006 **Cooking Method:** Boston butts in a Southern Pride smoker, plus ribs and chicken on closed metal pits over red oak, hickory, and pecan **Serves:** Lunch and dinner **Cards Accepted:** Yes

Charleston's Home Team BBQ represents a new generation of Carolina barbecue, one that's not connected to a long-standing family business nor ingrained local tradition. "I grew up in Atlanta," owner Aaron Siegel says. "I didn't have that much barbecue experience growing up."

What he did have was a passion for cooking, and that led him to the Culinary Institute of America (CIA) for a classical culinary education. "I was always planning on getting into fine dining," Siegel says. "But when I was at culinary school I got a little Brinkman dome smoker and started cooking turkeys at home. I started brining them, and then cooking chickens, too."

After graduation, Siegel found himself in Aspen, Colorado, where he worked in the kitchen of a high-end restaurant at night and at a quick-service burrito spot during the day. He started smoking ribs for parties with his friends, who were mostly fellow restaurant workers and ski bums. "I started thinking about this quick-service barbecue concept," he says, "and I decided to move back South with an idea of starting my own restaurant." While the

JONATHAN BONCEK

idea developed, Siegel served as the executive chef at Blossom, a fine dining restaurant in downtown Charleston, where he snuck a little smoked duck and other barbecued items onto the menu. Finally, in 2006 he traded in his chef's whites for a pitmaster's apron and opened Fiery Ron's Home Team BBQ.

Though he had been smoking meats on a small scale for years and had worked in plenty of high-volume kitchens, Siegel admits that his barbecue style has evolved considerably over the year. "Most of my experience has come since we opened the restaurant," Siegel says. Stylistically, Home Team's offering is literally all over the map, taking traditional recipes from across the South and delivering them with a few fine-dining twists. They serve pulled pork, ribs, chicken, turkey, and beef brisket in an array of combination platters. Home Team's Brunswick stew is modeled not after the North Carolina variety but the kind Siegel remembers eating as a kid at the now-defunct Sweat's Barbecue in Soperton, Georgia, where his family would stop off en route to vacation in Savannah. There are barbecue sliders and nachos, and you can get pulled pork, chicken, or brisket served on tacos or in quesadillas. I'm particularly partial to the smoked chicken wings, which are wonderfully smoky and delicious, especially when paired with Siegel's tangy Alabama-style white sauce

"Certainly no one has to have classical training to do barbecue," Siegel says. "But, man, does it help." Siegel recruited much of his team, including executive chef Taylor Garrigan and Madison Ruckel, from other high-end Charleston restaurants, and they put their training to good use when coming up with their original brisket. "It's a smoked-braised combo," Siegel explains. "We make a mirepoix with herbs, red and white wine, and tomatoes. We put the brisket in a pan and pour the liquid about halfway up it and put the whole thing in the smoker." Hours later, they remove the now-tender beef from the smoker, slice it thin, and put it back in the jus for service. Moist, tender, and exceptionally flavorful, it's really good beef.

The Home Team crew is still learning as they go, and they are dedicated to studying the traditional methods of the best barbecue cooks from all over the country. When the restaurant first opened, they used a Southern Pride cooker that's fired by gas and burns wood for flavor, and they still use that today for cooking Boston butts. A few years in, Siegel added a pair of black metal Lang pits in the back, where they cook ribs, chicken, and brisket over oak with a little hickory and pecan. They render that wood into coals in a burn barrel modeled after the ones created by Rodney Scott up in Hemingway, South Carolina (see Scott's Bar-B-Que listing). Two years ago, the whole cooking team took a road trip to Texas, where they sampled a mountain of beef and toured the pits at many of that state's most respected joints. They returned home with plenty of new ideas, including a fantastic Texas-style salt-and-pepper brisket that's been added to the menu alongside their original half-braised, half-smoked version.

No, Home Team BBQ doesn't traces its roots back through generations of pitmasters, and the content of its menu and the cross-region fusion and upscale flourishes may throw the traditionalists for a loop (white barbecue sauce? brisket braised in wine?). But, Aaron Siegel and his team are passionate about the art of barbecue cooking, and the pulled pork and smoked chicken wings are nothing if not delicious. Heck, even Carolinians need to enjoy some good Texas-style brisket every now and then.

Hite's Bar-B-Q

240 Dreher Rd., West Columbia, SC 29169; (803) 794-4120; hitesbbq
.com **Founded:** 1957 **Cooking Method:** Open pit, whole hogs and
hams over oak and hickory **Serves:** Takeout all day Fri and Sat (closing at 6 p.m.); also open July Fourth, Memorial Day, and Labor Day
Cards Accepted: Yes

If you have any doubt that Jerry and David Hite are cooking with wood, just
step through the front door of their small market on West Columbia's Dreher
Road. The moment you enter, your nostrils are filled with the beguiling aroma
of hardwood smoke drifting in from the big screened-in pit room that stretches
back behind the retail area. If you need further proof, just wander over to the
dirt area behind the pit room, where you'll find cord and cord of split hardwood
piled in two long haphazard rows. It's an impressive amount of wood, and it all
goes to fire the pits for an operation that is open just two days a week.

Hite's is a takeout-only joint, catering to folks who want to pick up a little
barbecue for lunch or dinner at home or whole lot of it for whatever big gathering they have planned for the weekend. It opens early at 8 a.m. on Fri and Sat
and closes before sundown, though they also keep alive an old tradition in the
Columbia area of selling barbecue on holidays like Memorial Day, the Fourth
of July, and Labor Day. They've been doing it since 1957, and, yes, Jerry Hite is
a cousin of Jackie Hite of Hite's Barbecue in Leesville.

Jerry Hite's son David has taken over managing the restaurant now, and
he aims to keep cooking the same way as his father did. That means whole
hog along with a few Boston butts over oak and hickory on the big pits in
the back. Hite's sells chopped pork, ribs, and ham by the pound and either
half or whole barbecue chickens. To go alongside, there are quart and pint
containers of hash and pint and half-pint containers of slaw. A glass case to
the left of the counter displays big mounds of sausage and fresh cuts of pork
for purchase, too.

Hite's skins are among the best in the state. As the hams for the barbecue
are cooking, they rest on the pit with their skin against the rectangular wire
mesh, which leaves perpendicular lines in the skin. The Hites trim that skin
off, cut it into big, oblong shards, and pack them in clear plastic bags. The very
first bite explodes with deep smoky flavor, and it grows with each jaw-tingling
crunch of the salty skin. How good are they? You need to call at least a day in
advance to find out, because Hite's takes reservations for bags and most weekends there aren't any left over to sell to walk-in customers.

What Do You Do with the Skin?

If you're cooking a whole hog, you want to make the most of the animal. And that leaves an interesting question for pitmasters: What do you do with the skins?

At the Skylight Inn in Ayden, they take a simple but effective route: They chop the skin right into the meat. Pitmaster Samuel Jones maintains that it adds extra flavor and lots of crispy texture, and it's one of the factors that makes Skylight's barbecue so different from everyone else's. At Scott's in Hemingway, they take a different approach. They let the skins crisp up on the pit, then chop them into pieces and dunk them in the deep fryer. Scott's actually has two kinds of skins: "off the hog" and "kettle fried." The latter, Rodney Scott says, aren't from the pigs they cook on the pits but are instead ordered precut from their hog supplier and deep-fried at the restaurant. The crisp-fried skins are an addictive treat, but the local customers seem to prize the pit-seared, off-the-hog variety even more.

At Jackie Hite's in Leesville, South Carolina, they rub the skin with salt water, put it on a sheet of chicken wire, and put it down on the pit with a lot of heat underneath. The result is what they call "meat skins," and they're charred and crisp. At Hite's Bar-B-Que in West Columbia, they make them a similar way (though they use square wire mesh instead of hexagonal chicken wire), and the smoke-infused skins are so popular that customers call in a day or more in advance to reserve themselves a bag to go along with their take-out barbecue and sausage.

Some people call them "cracklings," some "pork rinds," some just "skins." If you see some fluorescent pink or purple spots on them, don't worry. That's from the stamps USDA inspectors apply once the hogs have been examined, and it's just edible food dye. You'll see skins on occasion up in the Upstate of South Carolina and the Piedmont of North Carolina, but they don't seem to be nearly as popular as in the lower part of the two states. The reason, one can only assume, is pretty simple: They aren't cooking whole hog, so they didn't have a whole lot of leftover skin that they needed to figure out what to do with.

Jackie Hite's Bar-B-Q

460 E. Railroad Ave., Leesville, SC 29070; (803) 532-3354 **Founded:** 1979 **Cooking Method:** Whole hog over hickory on open cinder-block pits **Serves:** Lunch Wed–Sun **Cards Accepted:** Yes

The last time I ate at Jackie Hite's Bar-B-Q in Leesville, there were three fire trucks parked in the lot outside and what must have been the better portion of the local fire department eating lunch inside. That's not only a leading indicator of excellent barbecue but poetically appropriate, too, since Jackie Hite learned to cook barbecue from his father, who served as Leesville's fire chief

for a time and regularly cooked the barbecue for the annual Fireman's Ball fund-raiser. Jackie Hite opened a take-out stand in 1979, and, as the business flourished, he enclosed the stand and added table service.

Hite still cooks his barbecue the old fashioned way: burning hickory logs down to coals and using them to fire cinder-block pits. He cooks whole hogs, though he cuts them into six pieces to make them easier to handle on the pits. Hite makes his hash the old-fashioned way, too: in giant iron pots over a wood fire, and it's the increasingly hard-to-find string variety, where the meat is pulled rather than chopped. It may well be the best hash in the whole state: long shreds of superbly tender pork in a thin sauce with a sharp mustardy tang to it. The barbecue is pulled into long strands, too, and it has the smoky but not too smoky kiss that you can get only by cooking over real wood embers.

Inside the long white building is a front room with a big buffet and two additional rooms behind it, where diners sit community style at rows of folding tables with black-padded metal chairs. That buffet includes fried okra, greens, soft dinner rolls, and a wonderfully gooey mac and cheese. Waitresses bring your choice of tea or lemonade to your table and keep the Styrofoam cups filled while you eat. An array of sauce bottles rests next to the barbecue on the buffet station, including a thick tomatoey red sauce, a Pee Dee–style vinegar-and-pepper sauce, and a mustard-based sauce that's so sweet it's almost a honey mustard, but at each table is a squeeze bottle of Hite's original sauce, which is a tart and tangy concoction that, apart from liberal flecks of black pepper, seems almost pure mustard.

Jackie Hite's opens early for takeout around 9 a.m., and closes the doors by midafternoon, which is 2 p.m. Wed, Thurs, and Sun and 3 p.m. on Fri and Sat. If you can, visit for lunch on Friday so you can enjoy the weekly pig pickin', when they put out half a hog cut into piece and let diners pull their own pork from the various cuts. Hite's charred "meat skins" (think pork rinds, but not fried) are a rare barbecue delicacy, too.

JB's Smokeshack

3406 Maybank Hwy., Johns Island, SC 29455; (843) 557-0426; jbssmokeshack.com **Founded:** 2002 **Cooking Method:** Over hickory in closed metal pits **Serves:** Lunch and dinner Wed–Sat
Cards Accepted: Yes

Out on Johns Island south of Charleston is a low red building on the side of Maybank Highway, and it's where locals head when they're in the mood for some good Lowcountry barbecue. Beside the front door, a black pig on a big sign declares, "The flavor's in the meat, sauce is on the side," and that pig knows what he's talking about. Diners pay as they enter, pick up a Styrofoam plate, and help themselves to a well-appointed barbecue buffet. The offering includes some 30 items, and it's all you can eat, of course.

J. B. Quinn got started cooking barbecue in his backyard for gatherings of friends and family, and they kept telling him he needed to open his own restaurant. Finally, in 2002 he teamed up with his son Billy and did just that. There are two main draws in terms of the meat: the hickory-smoked pork and the juicy, pepper-tinged fried chicken. At dinnertime, they're joined by a carving station with a pretty good beef brisket, too. The side dishes cover all the South Carolina barbecue essentials, including hash and rice, collards, green beans, black-eyed peas, and sweet potatoes. The pork is tender and flavorful, but the real treat, available on Friday, is the applewood-smoked chicken, which is rich, juicy, and full of great smoky flavor. Smoked sausage, smoked pork chops, and even smoked meat loaf show up on the buffet from time to time, offering tasty novelties for barbecue lovers in the Charleston area.

Maurice's Piggie Park BBQ

1600 Charleston Hwy., West Columbia, SC 29169; (803) 796-0220; piggiepark.com **Founded:** 1953 **Cooking Method:** Hams on closed brick pit over hickory coals **Serves:** Lunch and dinner daily **Cards Accepted:** Yes

Maurice's has 14 locations scattered all around Richland and Lexington Counties, which makes it easy to swing through a drive-thru and pick up a Little Joe sandwich. But, the restaurant on Charleston Highway in West Columbia is the original spot where the empire was born, and it has more character than the newer and more fast-food-like branches.

Out front, the tall sign features a pig in a red shirt emblazoned "Little Joe." Beneath it, the word "Bar-B-Q" in bold capital letters lights up at night with hundreds of white bulbs. It would have fit in quite nicely on the Las Vegas strip during the Rat Pack era, and, indeed, its design was inspired by one of Maurice Bessinger's trips to Vegas. At the bottom, the sign also modestly declares, "World's Best Bar-B-Q."

The restaurant itself is a red wooden building with a tall sloping roof inscribed with the word "barbecue" in white letters tall enough to be seen by the jets taking off at the nearby Columbia airport. The parking lot is filled with old-style drive-in canopies with angling metal roofs, though now they're used just as covered parking spots since car service has long been discontinued. Inside, there's a blend of brick and wood paneled walls and red-backed booths with red-and-white checked tablecloths.

The South Carolina Barbeque Association

In 2004, Lake High and Walter Rolandi were driving back from judging a barbecue contest in Florence, South Carolina. "You know," Rolandi said, "South Carolina has the best barbecue in the whole nation and the worst judges." They were dismayed by the lack of knowledge of the volunteers recruited to judge as well as the inadequacy of the scoring system they were asked to use. High and Rolandi were equally annoyed by cable television shows that played up the characteristics of barbecue then popular on the national competition circuit—meats injected with flavorings and coated with thick, sweet sauces—and ignored the traditional regional styles of barbecue, like the four found in South Carolina. So, they decided to do something about it. The result was the South Carolina Barbeque Association (SCBA).

"We said what we are going to do," High recalls, "is come up with something that teaches people how to judge. And we immediately came up with the idea that we would bring every-one to Columbia . . . to show for the first time in South Carolina the four different kinds of barbecue that we have side by side and use it as an educational thing so South Carolinians can see the diversity of the barbecue we have." Sixty-seven people showed up for the first seminar and became certified SCBA judges. The organization held their inaugural Carolina Q Cup in October 2004, bringing 50 teams to the State Farmers Market for a competition that drew over 4,000 attendees to sample barbecue from all parts of the state. They then began spreading their judging system and philosophy to barbecue competitions across the state.

At the time he launched the SCBA, High was already certified as a judge by the country's major barbecue judging organizations, including the Kansas City Barbeque Society and by the Memphis Barbecue Network. But, he had been a certified wine judge for over 20 years, too, and felt that the existing barbecue judging systems had a lot of room for improvement. "We really, really do it differently from everyone else," High says. "It's so superior, and the reason is that when we sat down to do this we deliberately looked at everybody's system. We threw out the crap and kept the good stuff."

For starters, the SCBA puts in the time to properly train their judges. Aspiring jurists must attend a full-day training seminar, and then they serve a sort of apprenticeship at competitions. For their first four events, they are put at a special "newbie table," where they work with a master judge who mentors them through the process, and their scores are not counted in the official results. Finally, with a sufficient body of experience and a lot of pork under their belts, they are eligible to serve as official judges for future competitions.

The SCBA system also disposes of a lot of the foolishness rampant in barbecue competitions and focuses instead on the meat itself. Some judging systems, for instance, make a big deal about the kind of lettuce used as garnish in the box in which competitors submit their entries. A team lining its box with the wrong variety can be disqualified, as can anyone submitting a cup of sauce or slice of bread with their meat. Other systems combine blind judging, where the meat is sampled and scored from unmarked containers, with on-site judging, where judges visit with the cooking team and get flattered and buttered up and served barbecue on elaborately set tables with china and crystal. Byzantine scoring rules in some systems require judges to bestow a perfect score on at least one of the samples they taste, while others award points for presentation and showmanship, including the creativity of teams' costumes and how elaborately they decorate their barbecue rigs and booths.

In their system, the SCBA focuses on the barbecue itself, and they try to keep things positive, too. They rejected the whole concept of disqualifying entrants for small missteps. Teams submit just the meat (no garnish, no sauces) in their boxes, but if they slip up and put in something extra, they're simply told what's wrong and allowed to fix it and resubmit their box. Only a grievous error, like serving undercooked meat or not submitting your sample by the judging deadline, can get a team disqualified at an SCBA event. All entries are judged blind, too, using a grading system that considers only the properties of the meat: the appearance, aroma, texture, taste, and overall impression, with texture and taste weighted to account for 10 of the total 17 possible points.

In addition to bringing sanity to barbecue judging, we might just have the SCBA to thank for the migration of barbecue sauce styles across traditional regional lines. "Before the SCBA came along," High says, "you would go into a barbecue house and they would have just their sauce there. Now you go in and they have four and maybe five sauces. It's because the SCBA taught South Carolinians that there a four kinds of sauces and if you want to change the flavor profile, you can sample it and see if the barbecue is complemented by or is covered up by the barbecue sauce." The SCBA's membership now consists of around 800 passionate barbecue lovers. And, High notes, "Every year we grow. We add more festivals, and more cookers, and more judges. It's word of mouth now; we don't even advertise."

The SCBA plans to carry on its unique form of barbecue evangelism well into the future, spreading the word about the rich diversity of South Carolina barbecue and ensuring that the state's barbecue competitions keep their eyes on what matters the most: the meat.

At Maurice's, they still cook the barbecue the same way they have since 1953: long and slow and over real wood. And they cook an awful lot of it, perhaps more than any other restaurant in the Carolinas. The pits are essentially a row of tall closets with metal doors, a compartment at the top with a rack to hold the meat and a door at the bottom through which the tenders shovel glowing red coals all night long. They go through about two cords of wood per day to barbecue at least a ton of meat. And they do that every day of the week, cooking around the clock, 24 hours a day.

At Maurice's they cook hams, not shoulders, and the pork is chopped into generous chunks and coated in Maurice's signature Carolina Gold mustard-based sauce. Maurice's fans tend to go one of two ways: a sandwich basket or one of the numbered platters. The sandwiches come in two sizes (the 4-ounce Little Joe and the 6-ounce Big Joe) and include fries, coleslaw, and two golden brown hush puppies. The platters let you mix and match among all the permutations of pit products—chopped pork, pork ribs, barbecue chicken, and sliced beef brisket—along with hash and rice, coleslaw, hush puppies, and a soft dinner roll. Reflecting the restaurant's lineage as a drive-in, there are burger and hot dogs, too.

Maurice's dates its founding as 1939, which is when Joe Bessinger, Maurice's father and the patriarch of what became one of the Carolina's most notable barbecue families, opened Joe's Grill in Holly Hill. Maurice Bessinger learned to cook barbecue from his father and later worked with his brothers in a restaurant called Piggie Park in Charleston. In 1953, after serving for three years in the US Army in Korea, Maurice moved up to Columbia and opened his own Piggie Park, a take-out barbecue restaurant with curb service in an old Zesto Ice Cream stand.

Maurice's has long been a controversial restaurant thanks to the segregationist views and inflammatory rhetoric of its founder, who passed away in 2014. A half century ago, Bessinger and his refusal to serve African-American patrons was the subject of a key Supreme Court case upholding the 1964 Civil Rights Act (see "Barbecue & Civil Rights" sidebar, this chapter), and he remained a divisive figure for the rest of his life. In 2000, when the South Carolina state legislature voted to remove the Confederate flag from the statehouse dome, Bessinger protested by raising the Stars and Bars on the flagpoles in front of all of his restaurants. This act, along with the many tracts with states' rights and slavery-apologist rhetoric that were being sold in the lobby of Bessinger's restaurants, led many Midlands residents to boycott Maurice's. Wal-Mart and local grocery store chains pulled the bottles of Maurice's barbecue sauce from their shelves.

Barbecue & Civil Rights: Newman v. Piggie Park Enterprises, Inc.

Columbia's Maurice Bessinger was at the heart of a key test case of the Civil Rights Act of 1964. The act invoked the federal power to regulate interstate commerce to prohibit discrimination in any places of public accommodation, including restaurants. Just days after President Lyndon B. Johnson signed the Civil Rights Act into law, J. W. Mungin, an African-American minister, filed a complaint with the FBI after being refused service at Bessinger's Little Joe Sandwich Shop in downtown Columbia.

When the case went to trial in 1966, Bessinger insisted that the Civil Rights Act did not apply to his business because it was not involved in interstate commerce. A previous landmark Supreme Court case challenging the Civil Rights Act, *Katzenbach v. McClung* (1964), had forced Ollie McClung of Birmingham, Alabama, to integrate his barbecue restaurant after it was shown that 46 percent of its food had been purchased from a local wholesaler who had, in turn, bought most of it from out-of-state producers. At Maurice Bessinger's hearing, his bookkeeper testified that all the meat purchased by Piggie Park Enterprises came from South Carolina slaughterhouses. Furthermore, Bessinger argued, his food was "made exclusively for the taste of central South Carolinians" and that people from New York, North Carolina, and Georgia had completely different preferences when it came to barbecue. In his strangest argument, Bessinger maintained that the act "contravenes the will of God" and violated his constitutional right for exercising his religion.

The district court had no truck for Bessinger's religious arguments, and they ruled that Little Joe's Sandwich Shop, which was a traditional sit-down restaurant, was indeed engaged in interstate commerce and therefore was in violation of the Civil Rights Act when it refused to serve people of color. In an unusual twist, the court ruled that Bessinger's five drive-in restaurants, which were takeout only, were not covered by the act and could remain segregated. The Fourth Circuit Court of Appeals tossed out that part of the ruling, declaring that Congress had not meant the law to depend upon a head count of people eating on-site and that drive-ins had to be integrated, too. *Newman v.*

Piggie Park Enterprises, Inc. made it all the way to the Supreme Court in 1968 because of an issue in the appeal's court decision over attorney's fees. The Supreme Court overturned the lower court's decision that the losing party in civil rights cases could not be forced to pay the prevailing party's legal fees, arguing that allowing such fees to be awarded was a key way to ensure that people who had been discriminated against could seek redress in court without going broke in the process.

Maurice Bessinger remained a divisive figure in South Carolina for the rest of his life, but he was on the losing side of history. The court cases he lost helped ensure that barbecue restaurants across the Carolinas would be integrated and that white and black patrons could enjoy slow-cooked pork side by side in the same dining rooms.

As Maurice Bessinger approached his 80s, he eventually stepped back from the business, and operations passed to the next generation of the family, who have quietly but steadily distanced the business from its divisive past. In 2013, the last Confederate flags disappeared from in front of the restaurants. "Dad liked politics," Lloyd Bessinger told Columbia's *The State* newspaper at the time. "That's not something we're interested in doing. We want to serve great barbecue."

Po Pigs Bo-B-Q

2410 SC 174, Edisto Island, SC 29438; (843) 869-9003 **Founded:** 1999
Cooking Method: Shoulders and Boston Butt on gas cookers **Serves:**
Lunch and dinner Thurs–Sat **Cards Accepted:** Yes
Po Pigs doesn't serve "bar-b-q." It's "bo-b-q," taking its name from owner Robert "Bobo" Lee. The restaurant shares an abbreviated strip mall with a gas station on the side of SC 174 about 10 miles from Edisto Island, and it's a favorite stop for vacationers on their way to the beach for a week in the sun. A low wooden

picket fence forms a chute that funnels diners straight from the front door to the head of the buffet line, where a bounty of fine Southern cooking awaits. There are creamy limas, okra and tomatoes, and field peas laced with smoky pork. The tender slow-cooked greens are studded with chunks of turnip, and Po Pigs offers two different kind of hash, one an orangish version made with slow-simmered pork and the other an old-style, dark-brown concoction with the rich, husky flavor of pork liver. At the end of the buffet, two stainless steel urns offer plenty of ice tea, while a small glass-doored cooler holds soft drinks and, in a rarity for a South Carolina barbecue house, a couple of brands of bottled beer and wine.

And, of course, there's the barbecue itself. The tender, moist pulled pork has a nice touch of smoky flavor to it. Perhaps to accommodate the vacation crowds, which come from all over the state, each table offers four different bottles of sauce: a "Midlands mustard," a pale orange "Orangeburg sweet," a thin vinegar-and-ketchup "Carolina red," and a spicy, brick-red "Pee Dee vinegar," which looks like it would be a thick sauce but emerges from the bottle thin and fiery. All told, Po Pigs is a fine representation of the Midlands and Lowcountry style of buffet-centric barbecue, and it's a prized resource for the hungry beachgoers on Edisto.

The Southern Belly BBQ

1332 Rosewood Dr., Columbia, SC 29201; (803) 667-9533; southern bellybbq.com **Founded:** 2013 **Cooking Method:** Pork over oak on closed metal pit **Serves:** Lunch daily, dinner Mon–Sat **Cards Accepted:** Yes

Carolina traditionalists might be hard pressed to accept the fare served at The Southern Belly as real barbecue. It is made from pork that was slow cooked over wood, but that's where any resemblance to traditional Midlands-style barbecue ends. They serve only sandwiches—eight of them, in fact—and they put things on them that are downright heretical, like bacon, cheese, and pineapple. And, they serve them with a choice of seven (yes, seven!) sauces that include the restaurant's own versions of Kansas City–style tomato-and-molasses-based and Alabama white barbecue sauces as well as international fusions like a spicy South American–style asada vinaigrette. The massive sandwiches are piled on soft fresh-baked rolls and delivered to your table with a wooden-handled steak knife plunged straight through the top to hold it all together.

You could get a Traditional sandwich with just meat and the locally inspired Midas sweet mustard sauce, but that would be missing the whole point of The Southern Belly. Creative cultural fusions are the order of the day,

like the Castro with Carribean-style *barbacoa* loaded up with pickles, banana peppers, and melted swiss on a buttered french roll. The Wookie, lovingly dubbed the "Big Mac of barbecue sandwiches," is a triple-decker concoction with two layers of meat and two layers of bacon topped with three different cheeses and grilled onions piled among three buttery slices of bread. The King Kahuna ups the ante with a sweet Hawaiian roll topped with cheddar, pineapple, grilled onions, and bacon, plus a cup of Yum Yum sauce on the side—a sort of sweet, fruity pink remoulade that blends quite nicely with the sweet and savory toppings.

The barbecue that forms the foundation of these creative sandwiches is cooked over oak coals on a rather small closed metal pit that sits out front in the parking lot, and it's pulled into long strands glistening with melted fat. Combined with the melted cheese, the soft rolls, and the sauce, and the results are some exotically tasty but very messy sandwiches. (Fortunately, the waitress brings a big stack of extra napkins with the foil and red-and-white waxed-paper-lined trays, for you'll need them.)

Owner Jimmy Phillips got his start in the business not cooking barbecue but rather managing bar and music venues. He describes Southern Belly as a "barbecue restaurant and dive bar," and it lives up to the billing. It's located in an old building at the base of Rosewood Drive not far from the University of South Carolina's Williams-Brice Stadium. Inside is a rather cramped, irregularly-shaped room with a long bar serving a full slate of liquor and bottled beers. A few high tables offer seating on stools, and a set of low tables line the wall. The dark bar-like interior is brightened a bit during the day by the white glow of the square skylight in the ceiling, and there are lots of picnic tables outside on the tin-roofed porch for dining, too.

The sandwich concepts may be pretty far out there, but the side items are as bare bones as can be: just potato chips and a cup of coleslaw, which has long shreds of cabbage and carrot in a creamy, vinegar-laced dressing that's pleasantly tangy and cool. Are restaurants like Southern Belly—funky, iconoclastic joints that give at best a passing nod to regional traditions—the future of barbecue in the Carolinas? It definitely appeals to the university crowd and a new generation of barbecue eaters that want something more exotic than the mustard-based pork and hash rice found at the old-school buffets that dot the Midlands (and to those who don't mind a couple of beers or a stiff cocktail with their barbecue, too). I'm not taking bets either way, but Southern Belly is a fun step away from the ordinary South Carolina barbecue experience.

Sweatman's Bar-B-Que

1427 Eutaw Rd., Holly Hill, SC 29059; (803) 496-1227; sweatmansbbq .com **Founded:** 1977 **Cooking Method:** Whole hogs on open cinderblock pits over oak and hickory **Serves:** Lunch and dinner Fri–Sat **Cards Accepted:** Yes

Harold "Bub" Sweatman and his wife, Margie, opened their first barbecue restaurant in 1959, though they closed it down after a while and just cooked pigs for local gatherings and other special occasions. In 1977, the Sweatmans got back into the game when they bought an old farmhouse on the highway that leads from Holly Hill to Eutawville and transformed it into a restaurant. Ever since, it's been a popular weekend destination for fresh-cooked whole hog barbecue.

Margie Sweatman passed away in 2003, and Bub followed in 2005. Their daughters kept the place running for a few years, but in in 2011 they sold the restaurant to Mark and Lynn Behr. The Behrs implemented a controversial change at first, replacing the all-you-can-eat buffet with a single small plate or large plate. They've since relented, and you can now purchase a "regular plate" (one trip through the line) or all-you-can-eat for a few dollars more.

The Myth of Health Departments, Wood Cooking, and Grandfathering

When people talk about or write about barbecue restaurants, the concept of "grandfathering" wood-fired pits is often brought up. The basic idea is this: Barbecue restaurants that cook over real wood can't be opened any more. Sometimes, the obstacle is described as being an outright ban. "Due to health department regulations," one blogger wrote recently, "having fire pits in restaurants is not allowed now. Barbecue restaurants opened prior to the new rules are grandfathered in." In other tellings, there's an even more nuanced set of rules. The health department inspectors and building code authorities, the line goes, will allow an existing business to use wood-burning pits as long as the same family maintains ownership. If the restaurant is sold to someone else who is not in the family, the new owners can't keep cooking with wood.

These tales appeal to our nostalgia for the dying of old ways, and they weave in the notion of honest small businesspeople stymied by bureaucratic meddling. But, in reality, there's a lot more smoke than fire in these stories.

"People grouse about you can't cook with wood anymore," says Chip Stamey of Stamey's barbecue in Greensboro, North Carolina. "It's not true. I think it's just economic reasons, or laziness. It's not regulatory."

Indeed, more than one barbecue restaurateur in the Carolinas can put the lie to the notion that barbecue cooking is on an irreversible course from wood to gas. Aaron Siegel, for example, opened Fiery Ron's Home Team BBQ in Charleston, South Carolina, in 2006, and he ending up going in the opposite direction, starting off with a gas-fired Southern Pride smoker and later adding two wood-burning Lang cookers in an open area behind the restaurant. Siegel and his team did have to work with the South Carolina Department of Health and Environmental Control to get their new cooking area up to code, but none of the changes stemmed from their use of hardwood for cooking. "They have a lot of detail in their manuals about smokehouses," Siegel says, noting that they had to install a hand-washing sink in their new pit area. "I've never heard any issues with the wood."

In April 2014, John Shelton Reed and Dan Levine of the Campaign for Real Barbecue (see "Taking the True 'Cue Pledge" sidebar, Shoulders & Light Red Sauce chapter) published an editorial in the *Raleigh News & Observer* in which they issued the "True 'Cue Challenge," promising to give a free "No Faux 'Cue" apron to any one who could provide an actual citation or the name and title of any government official who had ever forbid a restaurant to cook with wood. No one came forward to claim the prize.

There are plenty of reasonable factors that might compel a barbecue restaurateur to switch from wood to gas or electric cookers: Oak and hickory are expensive; cooking with them is unpredictable and labor intensive. One can see why businesspeople might opt for a method that allows them to load a cooker with meat, set the thermostat, and then go home and get a good night's sleep instead of shoveling hot coals all night long. But, let's not blame the government for that decision.

Pricing matters aside, there's not much else different under the new regime. The same crew, led by 30-year-veteran Douglas Oliver, still works the pits in the cookhouse out back, producing classic old-fashioned South Carolina whole hog barbecue cooked over oak and hickory. They make the hash on Wednesday and cook hogs all night Thursday and all night Friday for Sweatman's two days of operations. They pull the ribs out of the whole hogs and cook them separately, slathering them at the end in yellow mustard sauce.

You eat that barbecue in one of several rooms of the old farmhouse, which have been filled with lots of tables topped with red-and-white checkered table-cloths. At the buffet, they helpfully separate the chopped pork into two bins, one the inner white meat the other the darker meat with the crisp outer bits in it. Usually, I'm a big fan of "outside brown," especially in the chopped pork you find up in the Piedmont of North Carolina. With Sweatman's, though, as much as I like the like the big smoke flavor from the darker meat, I end up gravitating toward the inner white meat, which is moist and tender and isn't soaked through with barbecue sauce like the brown stuff. Bub Sweatman's original sauce is a classic Midland's mustard base, and it's quite tasty and a

The Ellenton Agricultural Club

One Saturday a month in Barnwell County, South Carolina, a group of men gather in an old two-story clapboard building to carry on a barbecue tradition that dates back more than a century. The men of the club (and it's still an all-male group) assemble upstairs in the un-air-conditioned main room, where they sit in rows of wooden rocking chairs and listen while the minutes from the previous month's meeting are read, a few pieces of business are conducted, and a guest speaker delivers a short talk on anything from a historical topic to current issues affecting the community. Once the speaking's done, the members head downstairs, where a barbecue dinner awaits on white-painted tables with long wooden benches.

The Ellenton Agricultural Club is a remnant of a much earlier age in rural South Carolina. The pig is still cooked over a wood fire in a cinder-block building behind the clubhouse, and the hash is made in an old iron pot over a wood fire, too. The clubhouse was built in 1904, and from the creaking wooden floors to the old fading photographs of prominent clubmen from years past, little has changed since.

When the Ellenton Agricultural Club was founded in 1894, it was just one of many hundreds of similar organizations that flourished throughout the South. "Pitchfork Ben" Tillman, who had ridden to power on a platform of agricultural reform and farmer education, was the governor, and what would evolve into Clemson University—then known simply as Clemson Agricultural College—had just accepted its first class of students the year before. Agricultural clubs like Ellenton's filled an important need as a source of mutual education and improvement for area farmers.

Once a month, the members gathered at the clubhouse for their regular meeting. On June 26, 1920, the Ellenton Farmer's Club meeting was attended by 150 members and friends, and Ralph Wallis gave a talk on the topic "control of the boll weevil." Some of the other topics addressed in the early part of the 20th century included how to side dress cotton; the history of farm credit and how to borrow safely; and hog cholera, its prevention and treatment. From the very early days, each meeting concluded with a barbecue dinner, too. The club's 1924 constitution and bylaws dictated that the dinner "shall consist of cue, rice, hash, two kinds of bread, one salad, one pickle, coffee, and nothing more." This menu is very typical of barbecue dinners in the era before restaurants, and it's pretty much the same thing the club members eat at their gatherings today, though coleslaw has replaced the pickle and the coffee has been supplemented by glasses of ice tea.

Ellenton became New Ellenton in the 1950s, when the federal government acquired 300 square miles of land to build the Savannah River Site, a nuclear facility to refine weapons-grade material. The entire town was moved lock, stock, and barrel 14 miles north to a new location in Barnwell County, and the clubhouse for the Ellenton Agricultural Club was moved to its current location at the side of SC 64, a few miles outside of Barnwell.

Most of the new generations of members who join the Agricultural Club aren't farmers but rather the children of members who have chosen other lines of work. But, by gathering each month and sharing knowledge and fellowship—and by sitting down to eat barbecue with each other—they are maintaining a connection with the members of their local community and, in the process, keeping alive a unique century-old barbecue tradition.

little thinner than most. It's now joined on the table by two other varieties, one the sweet, tangy orange sauce you find at the Dukes places in Orangeburg (see "The Dukes" sidebar, this chapter) and the other a Pee Dee–style vinegar-and-hot pepper sauce.

Tasty as the barbecue is, the ribs are the prize at Sweatman's. Big, meaty, and coated in the tangy yellow mustard sauce, they've got just the right tender but chewy texture and a great smoke flavor to them. Even if you get the all-you-can-eat buffet option, the pleasant attendant doles out the ribs in judicious quantities so no one hogs them all. The great crisp pork skins are regulated, too. They're not fried but crisped on the pit, giving them a mild smoke flavor and a bite of char. It's all accompanied by such things as wide green beans with chunks of pork, a great creamy mac 'n' cheese, coleslaw, pickles, and baked beans. And, don't forget to pick up one of the little Styrofoam cups of banana pudding that wait at the end of the buffet.

The real whole hog barbecue and the excellent ribs are the core of Sweatman's offering, but the real appeal is in the unique setting of the century-old farmhouse at the curve in the road out in the farmland north of Holly Hill. When you walk up the creaky wooden steps of the front porch and step into the dining room, it's like stepping back decades to an earlier era of classic Carolina barbecue, and one can hope it continues just like that for many years to come.

True BBQ

1237 D Ave., West Columbia, SC 19269; (803) 791-9950; true-bbq.com
Founded: 2010 **Cooking Method:** Boston butts on closed metal pits
Serves: Lunch and dinner Wed–Sat **Cards Accepted:** Yes

Just a half block from the complicated intersection West Columbians know as Triangle City is True BBQ, a fairly recent arrival that didn't take long to earn the respect of barbecue fans in the Midlands. Brothers Ernest and Milton Zanders opened the restaurant in 2010, and they cook right out in the parking lot where customers can be tempted by the wafts of smoke from their big metal pits. Those pits are guarded by a collection of white-painted ceramic pigs and chickens, and an array of meats are cooked inside them, including the requisite pork shoulder and chickens but also smoked pork chops, turkey wings, and both baby back and spare ribs, which are wonderfully meaty and smoky.

The barbecue is chopped into generous-size chunks, and it's moist and quite smoky, too. The meat is served unsauced, and customers can add one of three choices: the Sexy Lady (a tomato base), the Pretty Lady (mustard base), and the more prosaically named Vinegar Red (a vinegar-pepper sauce). You can have the pork piled on a Little "Z" or Big "Z" BBQ sandwich, or get any of the meats as a dinner, which comes with True BBQ's thick, slightly reddish hash and rice and your choice of two other sides. Those sides include tender collard greens, baked beans, potato salad, and finely chopped coleslaw in a creamy white dressing. If you've been saving up your appetite, the Big Z Combo Platter is the way to go: It gives you a choice of three meats, two sides, plus hash and rice, too.

The setting is pretty unassuming: a small shop that's been converted into a restaurant with a brown tile floor, white-painted walls, and all-white tables

Hog Heaven: The Nation's First Barbecue Guide

South Carolina was, as best as I can tell, the first state in the Union to be the subject of a barbecue restaurant guide book. *Hog Heaven: A Guide to South Carolina Barbecue* was published in 1979 by Allie Patricia Wall and Ron L. Layne. Whereas most treatments (including this book) define three distinct barbecue regions in South Carolina, Wall and Layne came up with six, splitting up the Midlands and Lowcountry into the Central (Richland and Lexington Counties), the North Central (the counties between Richland and the North Carolina border), and the Southeast (the region stretching from Orangeburg and Calhoun Counties southeastward to the oceans).

Wall and Layne were writing well before the Internet made it easy to track down barbecue restaurants. "Some of the best places," they noted in their introduction, "seemed to be tucked away in remote areas that only local people knew." They logged over 5,000 miles of driving around the Palmetto State and visited 99 joints, recording not only their locations and hours of operation but also stylistic details like the type of cooker used and the sauce that was served. The book serves today as a historic snapshot of the state's barbecue landscape three decades ago, emphasizing the impermanence of the business (more than half the restaurants in the book are no longer in operation) and capturing the rise of electric and gas barbecue cookers, which by 1979 were already in use in well over half of the restaurants.

and chairs. The food is served on Styrofoam plates with plastic utensils. True BBQ's fans rave about one thing almost as much as they about do the quality of the barbecue itself: the exceptionally friendly and welcoming staff that serves it. Roll it all together, and you've got a winning recipe for a Midlands barbecue joint.

Wise's Bar-B-Q House

25548 US 76, Newberry, SC 29108; (803) 276-6699; wisesbbq.com
Founded: 1960s **Cooking Method:** Gas-fired pits **Serves:** Lunch and dinner Fri and Sat **Cards Accepted:** Yes

On the side of US 76 about 10 miles outside of Newberry, you'll find the iconic image of a Midlands barbecue house: a low white-painted cinder-block building with a metal roof set back in a gravel parking lot. High atop a rusted metal pole, a faded yellow sign with silhouettes of a pig and a chicken announces "Wise's Bar-B-Q, Fri. & Sat." You can buy takeout from a separate room in the front, and be sure to pick up one of the clear plastic bags of fried pork skins: They're light, crisp, and delicious. To the left, the main front door opens into a small, basic dining room populated with folding tables and folding chairs. The buffet inside includes pulled pork, ribs, and chicken along with a small selection of sides like green beans and white bread.

Extending off the back of the restaurant is a screened-in cookhouse with its metal roof stained black from decades of smoke rolling out of the vents at the top. It's a bit of a teaser, for after the original Wise passed away, his sons converted the wood pits to gas. The barbecue is now essentially roasted pork that's chopped into chunky strands and liberally coated with a bright yellow sauce that seems to be mostly mustard. That sauce seems to baffle a lot of outsiders, but locals from the Newberry area swear by Wise's as their favorite barbecue anywhere. The real draw for me is the soupy hash, which has shreds of pork swimming in a thin, mustard-laced sauce. Ladle it over a pile of white rice, and you've got a delicious example of a Midlands South Carolina barbecue delicacy.

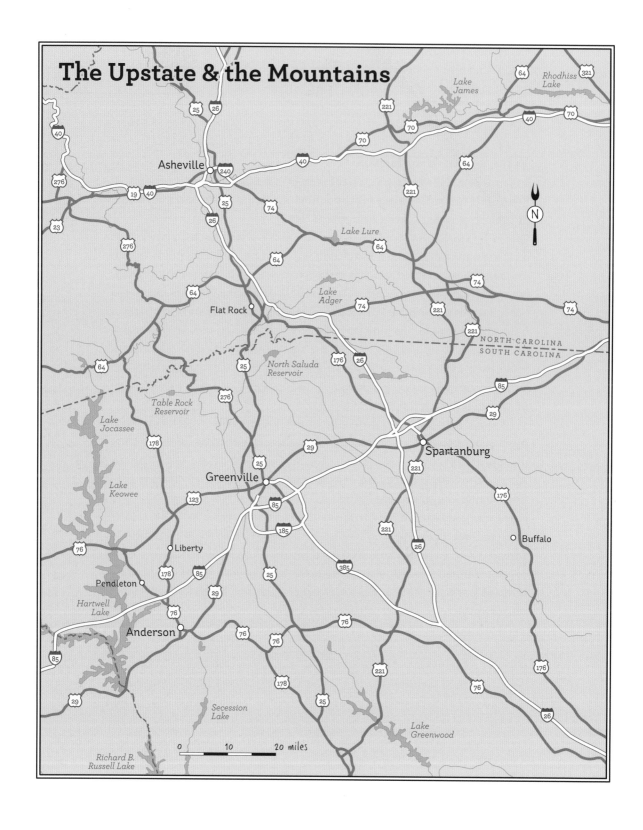

The Upstate & the Mountains

Free Spirits: The Upstate
& the Mountains

Once you get west of Newberry County in South Carolina, the barbecue changes, but it's difficult these days to categorize it as a particular style. You can visit a barbecue joint in Greenville and have ribs with hand-cut french fries for lunch, then drive over to Liberty for pulled whole hog with Brunswick stew. This isn't to say that there's not a long tradition of cooking barbecue in this part of the state; early 19th century newspapers are filled with accounts of barbecues in Oconee, Pickens, and Greenville Counties. Instead, it seems that there were many different influences felt in the area during the formative period of the early restaurant era, and no one of them took root firmly enough to evolve into a definitive style.

Up in North Carolina, the town of Lexington was the cradle of the Piedmont style, and as it moved outward it trickled down across the border into South Carolina, too. In the decades after World War II, many of the barbecue restaurants to be found in and around Greenville and Spartanburg cooked pork shoulders and dressed them with a thin vinegar-and-tomato sauce very similar to that found in Lexington and Shelby. The short-lived Little Pigs of America barbecue chain (see "The Short, Smoky Run . . ." sidebar, this chapter) seems to have left a competing legacy of a thick, somewhat spicy tomato-based sauce that's more akin to what one would find in Memphis (which is where Little Pigs was headquartered) than in the rest of the Carolinas. For whatever reason, the early restaurants in what South Carolinians call the Upstate didn't manage to stick around as long as their cousins in the Tar Heel State, so this area doesn't boast a parade of classic joints still cooking the way their founders did a half century or more ago. Of the 12 barbecue restaurants listed in the Northwest region in Allie Patricia Wall and Ron L. Layne's *Hog Heaven* guidebook (see "*Hog Heaven*" sidebar, Yellow Mustard & Hash chapter), only one, the Beacon Drive-In, is still in business today. Midway BBQ in Union County (which Wall and Layne put in their North Central region), founded in 1941, is by far the oldest to be found.

The Hash House: A South Carolina Tradition

Hash is an old South Carolina tradition, the essential accompaniment to a plate of barbecue from the Midlands down to the coast. It's easy to understand how hash became so closely connected with pit-cooked hogs. In the old days, cooks didn't order a fresh, fully dressed pig from the local meatpacker. If a family was going to have a barbecue, then odds were they were going to have a hog killing first, and making hash was how they put to use all of the leftover parts that couldn't go on the pit. Indeed, as far back as the 19th century, newspaper accounts capture big iron pots of hash being cooked alongside the pits at big community barbecues.

In what one might term the lower Piedmont of South Carolina—a ribbon of land running from Cherokee and York Counties on the North Carolina border down to Edgefield and McCormick on the Savannah River—hash making developed into an art of its own, and the thick, savory stew often stood alone as a meal by itself. These counties became the home of two related phenomena: the hash house and fund-raising hash sales. Both were linked to the transition of the region's economy from rural agriculture to textile manufacturing.

In the heyday of the textile industry in the Upstate of South Carolina, the practice of cooking hash migrated from the farms to the mill villages, and it took on a slightly different identity in the process. In the early days of the industry, most of the mill workers came from rural areas, so they had grown up making hash during hog killings and eating it at family and community gatherings. As families took up their new lives in the mill villages, they brought this tradition of hash making with them, though they no longer had their own hogs to kill and purchased the meat instead. Many started using beef alongside or in place of pork for the pots, and today hash in Greenwood, Newberry, and Union Counties is quite different from that found down around Columbia and farther east, since beef, not pork, is generally the primary ingredient.

Each mill had its own "hash house"—a wooden structure with a shingled roof and screened-in sides. Some hash houses were equipped with old syrup kilns that farmers once used to make molasses (sugar cane grows quite well in the middle part of South Carolina), while others used cast-iron washpots. The big kettles were placed in a sort of stand or enclosure made of brick with a cement top that had giant circular openings to hold the pots, which were heated by burning hardwood logs underneath. A hinged metal lid or just a loose sheet of metal was put over the top to cover the stew while it simmered. Whole families pitched in to peel potatoes and onions to feed the pot, and the hash maker and his helpers stirred the mixture continuously with long wooden paddles to keep it from sticking to the sides. The Fourth of July was the most popular day for cooking hash, and in one mill village after another in the lower Piedmont, the entire community came together to celebrate Independence Day by eating hash together.

A lot of hash masters in the region started cooking their specialty to sell on weekends and holidays like Labor Day and the Fourth of July, and some even opened permanent restaurants. From the 1950s to the 1970s, dozens of hash houses dotted the towns and countryside of the Lower Piedmont. For decades, Ruth Ivester Polattie, known by all her customers as "Miss Ruth," operated The Hash House in a tiny building on Cambridge Avenue in Greenwood, continuing a business opened by her mother in 1952. They served their dark-gray hash in white bowls on ceramic saucers. To the eye, it looked thin and souplike, but in reality it was thick and viscous enough to eat with a fork. Other hash houses were more casual businesses, selling takeout only and operating just one or two days a week. Around the same time, volunteer fire departments started cooking and selling hash as a way to raise funds for equipment. They used black iron washpots and wooden paddles just like the hash houses at the mills, slowly simmering the meat to break it down to a thick, gooey stew. Hungry citizens would come from miles around to buy the hash, and for many departments hash sales became an annual tradition, with pots, recipes, and technique passed from the older generation of firefighters to the newer ones.

This vibrant hash tradition was chronicled by Stan Woodward in *Carolina Hash* (2001, rereleased in 2008), an excellent documentary that captures images and voices of some of the last of the great Carolina hash masters. Since its release, the hash-house tradition has continued to fade so rapidly that it seems destined for extinction. The decline of the textile industry in South Carolina meant the end of many company-owned mill villages, and by the time Stan Woodward's cameras found them, their hash houses were long abandoned and overgrown with weeds, their old iron pots rusted or gone missing altogether. The commercial hash houses that once were fixtures of the downtowns of small Upstate communities have steadily closed their doors, too, as their owners pass away and the next generations elect not to continue on in the business.

The South Carolina Department of Health and Environmental Control (DHEC) played a role in the demise of hash houses, too, particularly those that were casual, irregular businesses. Bailey Riser's Hash House, which had been in operation since the early 1960s, used to sell hash on major holidays like Labor Day and the Fourth of July, but by 2001 Riser had slimmed back to being open a single day each year—the Fourth of July. He told Stan Woodward that he received a notice from DHEC informing him that that was the only day he could cook and sell hash. If he wanted to have more frequent operations, he would have to fully enclose his hash house and add a cement floor and running hot water. Another hash master told Woodward that DHEC had given him similar stipulations, though they allowed him to cook four days out of a year.

The single biggest group keeping this style of hash alive today are volunteer fire-fighters. The Northwest Volunteer Fire Department in Greenwood still has its annual hash sale on Memorial Day, and members of the department still cook it the old-fashioned way in big iron pots stirred with long wooden paddles. The nearby Coronaca Fire Department in Greenwood sells hash for $9 a quart on Memorial Day, too. Many other departments, like the CKC Fire Department in Blacksville and the Bethesda Volunteer Fire Department in Rock Hill, have annual fund-raisers where they sell barbecue and hash together. So, keep an eye on local newspapers or even Facebook (many of the departments have Facebook pages now) for announcements of a department's annual hash sale: It's the best way left to sample a unique food tradition from the Piedmont of South Carolina.

As you head northward from Greenville and Spartanburg up into the mountains of western North Carolina, the barbecue grows even more sparse. When people say "western North Carolina" barbecue, they are really referring to the Piedmont region and opposing its unique shoulder and vinegar-and-tomato style to the whole hog barbecue style of Eastern North Carolina. For years, North Carolina barbecue traditionalists sneered at the mountain 'cue found in places like Asheville and Cherokee for being some sort of western import brought in to feed the out-of-state tourists whose RVs clog the winding mountain highways during the summertime. And, indeed, there's a lot of truth in that depiction, and the barbecue stands and restaurants that have dotted the mountains over the years have tended to be rather transitory. Herb's Pit BBQ west of Murphy, founded in 1982, is perhaps the oldest barbecue to be found in the region.

Fortunately for barbecue lovers, a new generation of cooks have stepped up to fill in the gaps in both the Upstate and the mountains. They may not have quite the same tenure as Piedmont North Carolina classics like Lexington Barbecue or Red Bridges Barbecue Lodge, and they don't have the storied pedigrees of famous barbecue families like the Bessingers (see "The Bessinger Family" sidebar, Yellow Mustard & Hash chapter) and the Dukes (see "The Dukes" sidebar, Yellow Mustard & Hash chapter) in the Midlands of South Carolina. But they are just as passionate as their brethren to the north and east, and some of them turn out some pretty top-notch barbecue.

One of the side-effects of a region's not having a long barbecue tradition is that the new cooks who come along don't feel constrained by any particular local style. Pitmasters who've opened barbecue restaurants in the past few decades have tended to bring with them styles and techniques they learned somewhere else, and they've found a market that isn't overly constrained by preconceived notions of what "real barbecue" is. In recent years, the Upstate has also experienced a bit of sauce creep. The mustard-based version that is omnipresent around Columbia and Orangeburg would never have been seen in Greenville County two decades ago, but now you'll find bottles of the yellow stuff side by side with the light vinegar-and-tomato style. Pork-based hash and rice (and not the traditional beef hash of Union County) is inching its way into the region, too. The mountains are becoming something of a hot bed of nouveau 'cue, a nonconformist approach that seems right at home with the free spirits and artistic types that colonized the area around Asheville. The cooks are quite serious about doing some things the old-fashioned way, especially using real wood on custom-built pits, shoveling coals, and tending their fires for hours on end. At the same time, they bring a more contemporary and broad-ranging sensibility, throwing in a few fine-dining twists and culinary fusions. They aren't shy about concocting a blueberry-chipotle sauce to slather on ribs or serving jalapeño cheese grits alongside pulled pork, innovations that would leave the old-timers to the east scratching their heads.

The many diverse influences that have converged in the Upstate and in the mountains may one day coalesce into a distinctive style that barbecue lovers can tabulate and catalog. For now, though, diners can confidently hop from one joint to another, never quite knowing just what they'll find but with a high probability of coming across something delicious to eat.

The Beacon Drive-In

255 John B. White Sr. Blvd., Spartanburg, SC 29306; (864) 585-9387; beacondrivein.com **Founded:** 1946 **Serves:** Breakfast Mon–Sat; lunch and dinner daily **Cards Accepted:** Yes

The Beacon's pork sandwich made its way into this guide mostly because it's so much fun to order. The second largest drive-in in the United States, the Beacon serves over a million customers a year and, they believe, more sweet tea than any other restaurant in the world. For over 50 years J. C. Stroble, the iconic "call it" man, shouted out customers' orders to the line cooks, and he invented a special lingo for customers to use when ordering. Stoble passed away in 2013, but other callers continue the tradition, demanding that customers voice their orders ("call it!") and, once they have, prompting them to "move on down the line"—that is, to take their plastic tray and walk down the long stainless steel counter to the spot where their food will be delivered. A Sliced Pork A-Plenty will get you a sliced pork sandwich, the "a-plenty" meaning you'll get a mound of onion rings and french fries alongside. Calling "outside pork" will get you a chopped sandwich, while "a Lowcountry," for some reason, is how you ask for a pulled-pork plate.

Whether sliced, chopped, or pulled, the pork makes for a quite passable barbecue sandwich. There's a smoky bite to the meat, and it's served on the same broad toasted buns as the justly more famous Chili Cheeseburger A-Plenty. Be sure to ask for extra sauce when you pick up your order: It's a thick red tomato-based version, and the spicy variety adds a nice zip to the sandwich.

Circle M

345 Martin Sausage Rd., Liberty, SC 29657; (864) 375-9133 **Founded:** 1992 **Cooking Method:** Whole hog over hickory **Serves:** Dinner Fri and Sat **Cards Accepted:** Yes

Circle M is a bit of the oddity in the Upstate, since proprietor J. Marion Martin cooks whole hogs over real wood and serves them with a vinegar-and-pepper that's more akin to Pee Dee barbecue than what you find elsewhere in the Upstate. There's a simple reason for that, too: When Martin was a student at Clemson University, he started dating Mary Helen Coleman, whom he later married, and he learned to cook whole hog while attending her family's barbecues in the Kingstree area in the heart of the Pee Dee.

The restaurant occupies a long, low brown wood building about 8 miles south of Liberty on US 178, and it's open very limited hours—just Fri and Sat evenings. Inside, the dining room is all brown wood walls with a big rock-faced fireplace and spartan wooden tables with black metal chairs. They serve pulled pork barbecue, dry-rubbed ribs, and barbecued chicken. For sides, there's just slaw, Brunswick stew, beans, and white dinner rolls. The pork is pulled into long shreds, and the vinegar-and-pepper sauce is deep red in color. The excellent Brunswick stew is served in small Styrofoam cups, and it's filled with limas and potatoes.

Henry's Smokehouse

240 Wade Hampton Blvd., Greenville, SC 29607; (864) 232-7774; henryssmokehouse.com **Founded:** 1991 **Cooking Method:** Boston butt over hickory coals on a closed metal pit **Serves:** Lunch daily; dinner Mon–Sat **Cards Accepted:** Yes

There are now two satellite locations of Henry's Smokehouse, one on Woodruff Road in Greenville and another on Main Street in Simpsonville, but the small restaurant set back in a parking lot off of Wade Hampton Boulevard is the original. They serve hand-pulled Boston butt along with ribs and chicken, and they'll often run beef brisket as a weekend special.

Henry's is a small place with counter service and a wood-paneled dining room. There are only 30 seats, but they still serve an awful lot of barbecue: 64 butts and 40 racks of ribs each day. Through the doorway to the kitchen you can see the big double-door metal pit where they cook the Boston butts, while out behind the restaurant are two big metal drum smokers used for ribs and brisket. The pork is cooked 12 hours over hickory coals, then pulled by hand into long shreds, with extra care taken to remove any extra fat—the origin of the restaurant's slogan, "The Leanest Butt in Town." To finish it off, they pour over a little of the drippings that are left in the pans from the pit. The result is tender, juicy, and quite smoky pork. Piled onto a toasty warm bun with Henry's spicy red sauce, it makes for one of the best barbecue sandwiches in the Upstate.

Owner Bo Hammond grew up cooking whole hogs with his father for family and friends, and he started selling barbecue out of the back of a truck around 1991. A few years later, he transitioned that into a permanent restaurant, which he named after his father, Henry Hammond. Stylistically, Henry's straddles the Piedmont North Carolina region and the Midlands of South Carolina. They offer three sauces: a mild one with a tomato base, a spicy version of the tomato base, and a spicy mustard base. They serve both a South Carolina–style hash as well as a North Carolina–style Brunswick stew.

You can get the barbecue on a sandwich or on a plate, and the sides include old standards like beans, slaw, potato salad and mac and cheese. Henry's also

has the distinction of selling, hands down, the best french fries to be found in any barbecue restaurant in the Carolinas. They're the result of a laborious three-day process that starts with hand cutting potatoes and soaking them to achieve just the right balance of starch and sugar. Then they blanch the spuds in moderately hot oil, cool them down, and finally give them a second dip in higher-temperature oil. The finished fries are deep brown in color with a splendidly crisp exterior and nice chewy texture inside. And, unlike most fries, they are just as delicious as they cool (maybe even more delicious) than they are when hot from the fryer.

In addition to his two satellite locations, Bo Hammond recently launched Henry's Hog Hauler, a food truck that takes his barbecue on the road to local businesses and parks around Greenville. It might just be an Upstate barbecue empire in the making.

Hubba Hubba Smokehouse

2724 Greenville Hwy., Flat Rock, NC 28731; (828) 694-3551; hubba hubbasmokehouse.com **Founded:** 2007 **Cooking Method:** Boston butts over oak and hickory on closed brick and metal pits **Serves:** Lunch Mon–Sat; dinner Thurs–Sat **Cards Accepted:** No

A tin rooster perches atop the chimney at Hubba Hubba Smokehouse, and he gets a smoke bath pretty much constantly throughout the year. Owner Starr Teel keeps his pits fired around the clock seven days a week, steadily adding wood to keep it at a constant 200°F. He's the only pitmaster in the Carolinas that I'm aware of who is a graduate of Le Cordon Bleu in Paris, but he gave up the whisks and saucepans in favor of tall custom-built brick pits with huge black metal doors, where he cooks hand-rubbed Boston butts, beef brisket, ribs, and chicken over a blend of red and white oak and hickory wood.

A selection of sandwiches mound pulled pork, pulled chicken, or sliced brisket atop toasted Kaiser rolls with a little slaw and sliced pickles. You can also get the meat on a plate with two sides and either cheddar biscuits or corn bread, which is slightly sweet and more like cake than what an eastern North Carolinian would call corn bread. The sides include deviled eggs, greens seasoned with chunks of pork, and a blend of black-eyed peas, okra, smoked cherry tomatoes, and andouille sausage. Hubba Hubba's menu has plenty of unique twists, like the barbecue bowls, which deliver cheese grits topped with a layer of collards then pulled pork and fried onions. On weekends, they wrap brisket, pork, and even fish inside corn tortillas to make tacos. Taking a cue from barbecue joints in Mississippi, they sell tamales on Thursday. Hubba Hubba makes their own sauces, and they borrow styles from all over the place: There's an Eastern North Carolina vinegar sauce, a Piedmont tomato, a Carolina sweet mustard, and even a Southwest tomatillo sauce and a cherry-chipotle concoction.

Though decidedly casual, the location is still quite impressive, suggesting a world of possibility for mountain barbecue joints. It's tucked away behind a row of folk art and gift shops on the Greenville Highway in downtown Flat Rock. There's a brown wood-sided, tin-roofed building where you order at a window from a menu that's handwritten on a chalkboard and pick up your food when your name is called. The main seating is outdoors on a large brick-paved courtyard decorated with folk art pieces. Leafy trees and picnic tables topped with red umbrellas provide shade and seating, though there is an enclosed dining room for cold or rainy days. In the mountains, they don't feel constrained by the traditions of the lowlanders, and if you give some of Starr Teel's creative new 'cue a shot, you might want to shout "Hubba Hubba" yourself.

Midway BBQ

811 Main St., Buffalo, SC 29321; (864) 427-4047 **Founded:** 1941 **Cooking Method:** Shoulders & Hams on combo gas/wood smoker with hickory and oak **Serves:** Lunch and early dinner Mon–Sat **Cards Accepted:** Yes

Every day at 11:05 a.m., Mike Stevens of WBCU radio calls Jay Allen at Midway BBQ, and Allen reads out the day's menu live on air. The specials might feature chicken 'n' dumplings and country fried steak, and the sides may include black-eyed peas, broccoli casserole, or even their famous macaroni-and-cheese pie. There are at least three things that don't need announcing, for they will always be available: hash, chicken stew, and barbecue.

Midway BBQ sits in the fork of two roads in Buffalo, a small town (well, technically, a "census designated place") of about 1,200 residents located 2 miles west of Union. The red pig-shaped sign outside says "BBQ," but diners are just as likely to stop in for the hash and the chicken stew. In fact, the restaurant's three white catering vans announce that Midway BBQ is the "hash and chicken stew capital of the world." The restaurant was founded in 1941 by Jack O'Dell, the "hash king" of Union County, who made a name for himself as a skilled cattle and hog buyer before he left the business to devote himself full time to cooking. When Midway first opened, it was a known as a "hash house," a restaurant style unique to the area (see "The Hash House" sidebar,

The Short, Smoky Run of Little Pigs of America

If you look around the Carolinas today, you might notice a lot of barbecue restaurants named Little Pigs, and it might occur to you that it's a predictable coincidence. Everyone knows the story of the Three Little Pigs, and pig imagery is omnipresent in barbecue restaurant decor, so it would be only natural that more than one entrepreneur might independently choose to name their joint "Little Pigs." In actuality, though, it's more than just a happy coincidence. A great many of the Little Pigs do share common roots in a short-lived barbecue-franchise empire that originated outside the Carolinas.

In the early 1960s, two businessmen named Bill Newman and Ben Burch teamed up with Frank O. Howell Jr., who was running a small chain of barbecue restaurants in Memphis, to create Little Pigs of America (LPOA) and take the concept nationwide through franchising. In return for a $6,000 upfront investment, Little Pigs promised franchisees a net income between $15,000 and $20,000 per year. No prior barbecue experience was necessary, since the company trained recruits at its Memphis headquarters and supplied them with detailed blueprints for constructing a wood-burning pit made out of brick.

This was in the early years of fast-food franchising, with the McDonald's Corporation and a young upstart called Burger King trying to mass-produce the hamburger and a nascent chain called Kentucky Fried Chicken starting to do the same for fried chicken. So why not pit-cooked barbecue? A typical Little Pigs of America outlet sold a pork basket for 59 cents, a pork plate for 69 cents, and a rib platter for $1.59. By 1965, the budding chain had some 200 restaurants in operation in the US and Canada, and the company announced bold plans to exceed 1,000 locations in just a few years. (McDonald's, by way of comparison, had just opened unit number 800.)

But a nationwide barbecue empire wasn't in the cards. The company grew rapidly but never managed to become profitable. In 1967, its founders threw in the towel and filed for bankruptcy, ending the brief run of what was, at the time, America's largest barbecue chain. Most of the Little Pigs outlets closed their doors not long after their parent company folded, but a few stayed in business as independent operators and retained the Little Pigs name. The Little Pigs in Columbia got its start as an LPOA franchise. It was once housed in a shopping plaza off of Rosewood Drive, but in 1978 owner Lawrence Britton left his original location in favor of a larger stand-alone building off Alpine Road, ditching the counter-service format of the old chain in favor of the now-dominant all-you-can-eat buffet. The Little Pigs on McDowell Street in Asheville, North Carolina, and the one on North Main in Anderson, South Carolina, also got their starts as franchises of the Memphis-based company. Each has evolved and taken on more of an individual identity over the almost half century since the parent company folded, but in their names, at least, they echo back to the fledgling barbecue empire that never quite came to be.

this chapter). Union, Newberry, and Greenwood Counties were once dotted with such businesses, but now Midway is one of the last of the breed remaining. It's run today by Amy Allen, Jack O'Dell's daughter, and her husband, Jay.

A recent renovation gave the building new brick and wooden sides and a shiny red metal roof, but there's still sawdust on the floor beneath the wooden tables with red-and-white checkered tablecloths. Part restaurant, part meat market, Midway still buys cows and hogs, butchers them, and displays them for sale in two big glass counters. The selection ranges from bright red steaks and center-cut chops to house-cured bacon and liver mush, and they'll hand cut meats to order, too.

Those who want meals order from a long counter in the back corner, and the daily offering of meats and sides is hand printed on sheets of white paper hung over the counter. The barbecue is chopped into long, thin chunks, and you can order it with the house's original sauce or with no sauce at all. The meat is from shoulders and hams, and the smoke flavor is pretty mild. (After a pit fire in 2010 almost wiped them out, Jay Allen installed a new Southern Pride smoker, which heats with gas and burns a little hickory and oak for smoke.) It's nicely complemented by the house's original sauce, a fairly unique thick tomato-based concoction that was formulated by Jack O'Dell and has a touch of heat to it. Bottles of a vinegar-pepper sauce and a thin mustard-based sauce have been added in recent years, too.

Midway sells a barbecue plate, a hash plate, or a mixed plate, and the mixed plate is definitely the way to go, for you don't want to miss sampling the famous hash. Jay Allen reports that they sell at least three times as much of it as they do barbecue. It's made in three 100-gallon hash pots, and it's classic Union County–style beef hash, something quite unlike the pork and mustard stuff you'll find farther south and east in the Midlands. The cooks start with a front quarter of beef cut into pieces, which they simmer for 12 to 16 hours in the big iron pots along with butter, onions, salt, and pepper, plus a few secret seasonings. Once the meat is done, they remove it from the pot and strip out the bones, fat, and gristle, then return it to the pot to finish. The result is a fantastically thick, salty, and savory mass of tender beef shreds with an unusual savory flavor from whatever those secret ingredients are.

Then there's Midway's signature chicken stew, a smooth, milky, and buttery mixture with fine shreds of chicken, quite salty and studded with black pepper. It's served in a paper tray with half a sleeve of saltine crackers and a little cup of sweet cucumber and cauliflower pickles. That stew was the creation of founder Jack O'Dell, who needed something to sell in the fall and winter when barbecue demand dipped. Though it's popular now year-round (I recently ate a tray on a 95-degree June day, and it went down quite nicely), winter is still the prime season, and Midway can sell as many as 150 gallons on a cold day. Like the hash, it's made in 100-gallon cast iron pots, slow cooked till the chicken is tender enough to almost melt in your mouth. Barbecue, beef hash, and chicken stew: It's a trio that seems guaranteed to keep the parking lot at Midway BBQ filled for many more years to come.

Mike & Jeff's BBQ

2401 Old Buncombe Rd., Greenville SC 29609; (864) 271-5225; mike andjeffsbbq.com **Founded:** 1996 **Cooking Method:** Hickory and oak **Serves:** Lunch Tues–Sat; dinner Tues–Fri **Cards Accepted:** Yes

Mike & Jeff's occupies a modest building off Old Buncombe Road in the Sans Souci neighborhood just northwest of downtown Greenville. There are only a handful of tables inside the small dining room, and its menu is correspondingly slim: pulled pork, pork ribs, and chopped chicken. You can order any of the three (or a combination) on a regular or large plate with a choice of two side items from a slate that includes coleslaw, potato salad, baked beans, sweet potato soufflé, and hush puppies. The pork, which is pulled into fine shreds and is quite smoky, comes on two sizes of sandwich, too. There are three plastic bottles of sauce: a sweet tomato-based sauce, a spicier version, plus a mustard-based one that's a nod to the Midlands.

A few other special items crop up from time to time, like a thick-cut fried bologna sandwich. Mike and Jeff's is also home to its own unique delicacy called the BBQ Hot Dog, which is pretty much just what it sounds like: pulled pork piled atop a hot dog in a warm bun. Why no one else has thought to serve this combination is beyond me.

12 Bones Smokehouse

5 Riverside Dr., Asheville, NC 28801; (828) 253-4499; 12bones.com
Founded: 2005 **Cooking Method:** Closed metal pit over hardwood coals **Serves:** Lunch Mon–Fri **Accepts Cards:** Yes

In December 2005, Tom Montgomery and Sabra Kelley, a husband and wife team, opened 12 Bones Smokehouse in Asheville's River Arts District along the banks of the French Broad River. Alums of the New England Culinary Institute, they left careers in fine dining in favor of the barbecue pit, and they brought to the business a sense of creativity and daring. What they created is far removed from traditional North Carolina barbecue, but 12 Bones' lunch-only offering quickly struck a chord with local diners, and you'll usually find a long line that snakes out the door into the parking lot.

What they are lining up for is a prime example of nouveau 'cue, in which new restaurateurs are serious about the barbecue but don't feel bound by any regional traditions or conventions. At 12 Bones, you can get a standard sandwich topped with pulled pork, pulled chicken, and chopped or sliced beef brisket or the same range of meats on platters with your choice of two sides. A rotation of sauces can include traditional varieties from all parts of the Carolinas along with more unique creations like jalapeño, blueberry-chipotle, and even butterscotch. The barbecue is served on round metal trays, and the selection of sides includes canonical items like mac 'n' cheese, baked beans, and coleslaw plus more novel dishes like sweet-potato salad and jalapeño cheese grits. With nouveau 'cue , beer is the beverage of choice, and in addition to ice tea and RC Cola, 12 Bones has beers from local breweries on tap.

The restaurant's more inventive items include sandwiches like the smoked turkey with bacon, brie, and pesto mayo on Texas toast, and the Hog-zilla, a monstrosity that layers a split bratwurst link with pulled pork, thick strips of sugar-cured bacon, and melted Pepper Jack cheese and piles it on a toasted hoagie roll with a sweet reddish-brown sauce. But 12 Bones has earned the most recognition for their baby back ribs, which are served in three or four different flavors that rotate each day. There's always a "nekkid" version with just salt and pepper and another with the standard brown-sugar-rub, but the more unusual flavors are what tend to get the attention—things like sweet honey onion, Cheerwine (see "Cheerwine" sidebar, Shoulders & Light Red Sauce chapter), or spicy Thai. In 2007, 12 Bones' blueberry-chipotle ribs won the "Best Bites Challenge" on ABC's *Good Morning America*, and its popularity has been further cemented by not one but two visits from President Barack Obama.

The parking lot at the Riverside Drive location, known as the "River Store," stretches almost to the banks of the French Broad River. To the left of the main building is a big metal shed with open sides covering about a dozen wooden picnic tables for al fresco dining. Inside, bumper stickers of all sorts plaster the walls. There's now another location, the "South Store," about 10 miles south in Arden, which has slightly different hours (closed Mon and open for lunch on Sat). 12 Bones changed hands in 2013, when Bryan King and Angela Koh, who had been managers working for Montgomery and Kelley, purchased the business, but so far the winning combination of fast service and creative flavors has remained the same. And don't worry, that line may look long, but with 12 Bones' well-oiled operation, it moves pretty darn fast.

If You're Just Passing Through: Barbecue Side Trips

Some barbecue lovers will gladly drive a hundred miles or more for the sole purpose of visiting a legendary joint and sampling the pig that made it famous. The most passionate may undertake full weekend tours and dine at a half dozen or more restaurants in a single trip. But, family and work and other obligations often get in the way of such pork-centric adventures, and it pays to be opportunistic. You may only be passing through the Carolinas on a road trip to somewhere else, but that doesn't mean you can't sample a little of the unique barbecue styles that the two states have to offer.

This chapter aims to make it a little easier to plan out such diversions. It takes each of the most common thoroughfares through the Carolinas and indicates the most promising locations to make a barbecue pit stop during your trip. The rule of thumb used is that you shouldn't have to drive more than 10 miles or so off the highway, a distance that has been scientifically determined to be the limit of what non-barbecue-obsessed spouses and young children will tolerate, especially when they are antsy to get wherever it is you are really going. Here's how to quickly find some good Carolina barbecue the next time you are just passing through.

Important: As with any time you visit barbecue restaurants in the Carolinas, call ahead before making your detour! Hours are prone to change, and some joints close their doors arbitrarily when the owners decide it's time for a vacation or they run out of barbecue for the day. We've included the regular days of operation here for your convenience and also the restaurant's phone number. *Call ahead.*

I-95 from the North Carolina–Virginia Border to the South Carolina–Georgia Border

I-95 is the great migratory route for Yankees heading from the Northeast down to Florida, and even snowbirds owe it to themselves to sample Carolina barbecue when they get a chance. If you've got a few hours to spare, you can swing down US 64 to take in B's Barbecue in Greenville, then head over to Skylight Inn and Bum's in Ayden, and finally circle around to Grady's in Dudley and Wilber's in Goldsboro before making your way back to the interstate via US 70—a 150-mile circuit that will take you a good 3 hours, not counting eating time, and lets you experience five legendary barbecue houses. But, if you're in a hurry, there are several good options just a few miles off of I-95, all of them serving classic barbecue in the Eastern North Carolina, Pee Dee South Carolina, or Midlands South Carolina styles.

I-95 exit 119A in North Carolina, 7-mile detour

Parker's Barbecue. 2514 US 301, Wilson, NC 27893; (252) 237-0972; lunch and dinner daily

Take exit 119A onto US 264 South (which is also I-795 South) toward Wilson. Drive 4½ miles and continue on US 264 when it splits from I-795. One mile later, take exit 43A onto US 301 North. Parker's Barbecue will be on your left in about 1½ miles.

I-95 exit 181A in South Carolina, 4-mile detour

Shuler's Bar-B-Que. 419 SC 38 West, Latta, SC 29592; (843) 752-4700; lunch and dinner Thurs–Sat

Take exit 181A onto SC 38 east toward Latta. Shuler's will be on the right in 4 miles.

I-95 exit 122 in South Carolina, 3-mile detour

McCabe's Bar-B-Que. 480 N. Brooks St., Manning SC 29102; (803) 435-2833; lunch only Thurs–Sat

Take exit 122 onto US 221 toward Manning, which will become Brooks Street as you enter town. McCabe's will be on the left in approximately 3 miles.

I-95 exit 98 in South Carolina, 13-mile detour

(**Note:** We're pushing the 10-mile rule a little here, but this one's worth it.)
Sweatman's Bar-B-Que. 1427 Eutaw Rd., Holly Hill, SC 29059; (803) 496-1227; lunch and dinner Fri–Sat

Take exit 98 on SC 6 south toward Eutawville. Drive 9 miles. As you approach Eutawville, bear right onto Galliard Street. In ⅓ mile, turn right onto Factory Road. Drive another ⅓ mile and turn right at the stop sign onto Eutaw Road / SC 453. Drive 3 miles; Sweatman's will be on your left.

I-77 from the North Carolina–Virginia Border, then I-20 to the South Carolina–Georgia Border, or I-26 and I-95 to the South Carolina–Georgia Border

If you're heading down I-77 from, let's say, Ohio (and a lot of Ohioans do, generally en route to Florida), you'll be passing about 30 miles west of the great barbecue corridor that stretches from Winston-Salem through Lexington to Salisbury. But you can still sample some classic Piedmont North Carolina barbecue with a quick detour to Carolina Bar-B-Q in Statesville and then, no matter which way you fork when you hit Columbia, explore the yellow mustard-style of the Midlands of South Carolina.

I-77 exit 50 in North Carolina, 1-mile detour

Carolina Bar-B-Q of Statesville. 213 Salisbury Rd., Statesville, NC 28677; (704) 873-5585; lunch and dinner Mon–Sat

Take exit 50 and turn right onto East Broad Street. Drive 1 mile and take a left onto Salisbury Road. Carolina Bar-B-Q will be on your left at the end of the block.

I-20 to the South Carolina–Georgia Border

I-20 exit 44 in South Carolina, 10-mile detour

Jackie Hite's Bar-B-Q. 460 E. Railroad Ave., Leesville, SC 29070; (803) 532-3354; lunch only Wed–Sun

Take exit 44 onto Pond Branch Road. In about 8 miles, Pond Branch Road will become East Avenue as you enter Leesville. Jackie Hite's is about 1 mile ahead on the left, where East Avenue meets Railroad Avenue.

I-26 and I-95 to the South Carolina–Georgia Border

I-26 exit 111B in South Carolina, 1-mile detour

Hite's Bar-B-Q. 240 Dreher Rd., West Columbia, SC 29169; (803) 794-4120; takeout only, lunch to early evening Fri and Sat

Take exit 111B onto US 1 north. Drive ¾ mile and take a right onto Dreher Road. Hite's will be on the right in ½ mile.

I-26 exit 113 in South Carolina, 2-mile detour

Maurice's Piggie Park BBQ. 1600 Charleston Hwy., West Columbia, SC 29169; (803) 796-0220; lunch and dinner daily

Take exit 113 onto Airport Boulevard toward Columbia. Maurice's is in the triangle of the intersection of Airport Boulevard and US 321 about 1½ miles from the interstate. It's easier to get in the parking lot if you drive 1 mile down Airport Boulevard from I-26, turn right onto Glenn Street, and then turn left onto US 321. Maurice's will be on your right as you approach the big intersection.

I-26 exit 145A in South Carolina, 6-mile detour

Dukes Barbecue. 1298 Whitman St., Orangeburg, SC 29155; (803) 534-2916; lunch and dinner Thurs–Sat

Take exit 145A and merge right onto US 601 south toward Orangeburg. Drive 5 miles on US 601 into downtown Orangeburg. Pass the South Carolina State University campus, then turn left on Whitman Street. Dukes Barbecue will be on your right in ¾ mile.

I-85 from the North Carolina–Virginia Border through Charlotte to the South Carolina–Georgia Border

Okay, now you're talking. This route is the pinnacle of barbecue side trips, since it takes you through the heart of Piedmont North Carolina–style barbecue country, including the town of Lexington, where the region's style was born. Once you cross the border into South Carolina, I-85 takes you past some of the better examples of Upstate barbecue, too.

I-85 exit 170 in North Carolina, 6-mile detour

Allen & Son Barbeque. 6203 Millhouse Rd., Chapel Hill, NC 27516; (919) 942-7576; lunch Tues–Sat; dinner Thurs–Sat

Take exit 170 onto US 70 West. In 1 mile, turn left onto University Station Road. Drive 3½ miles on University Station. Turn right onto Mount Sinai Road. Drive 1½ miles. Allen & Son will be on your right at the intersection of Mount Sinai and Millhouse Roads.

I-40 exit 217 in North Carolina, 6-mile detour

Stamey's. 2206 High Point Rd., Greensboro, NC 27403; (336) 299-9888; lunch and dinner Mon–Sat

If you're heading south/west on I-85 and I-40 (the two are combined between Durham and Greensboro), stay on I-40 when it splits from I-85 just east of Greensboro. Continue 9 miles, take exit 217, and turn right onto High Point Road. Drive 1 mile to the Greensboro Coliseum area. Stamey's will be on your left, and you'll have to make a U-turn to get into the parking lot.

If you're heading north on I-85, take exit 120 onto I-85 Business North. In 2½ miles, take exit 35B onto US 220 North / Freeman Mill Road toward the Greensboro Coliseum area. Drive 2 miles and take a left onto Coliseum Boulevard. Drive 1½ miles and turn left on W. Lee Street, which becomes High Point Road. Stamey's will be on your right in a 1/10 mile.

Lexington: The Barbecue Capital of the Piedmont (and Maybe the World)

I-85 exit 96 in North Carolina, 4-mile detour

This is the place. A short 4-mile drive from I-85 will put you in Lexington, North Carolina, the capital of Piedmont-style barbecue, which is frequently called "Lexington style" after the city where it was born. There are at least a dozen good barbecue restaurants in Lexington, so you have your pick. First, though, you have to get to town. Take exit 96 and head west on US 64. The directions to each of the joints below assume you are approaching town from the east on US 64.

Barbecue Center. 900 N. Main St., Lexington, NC 27292; (336) 248-4633; breakfast, lunch, and dinner Mon–Sat

Head west on US 64. In 3½ miles, at the junction with US 70 and US 29, take the exit on your left toward downtown Lexington. Drive ¼ mile; Barbecue Center will be on your right.

Lexington Barbecue. 100 Smokehouse Ln., Lexington, NC 27295; (336) 249-9814; lunch and dinner Mon–Sat

Head west on US 64 about 3½ miles. Continue straight on US 64 as it merges into US 70. In just under 1 mile you should see Lexington Barbecue on the hill to your right. Turn right onto Service Road and left onto Lookout Avenue to reach the parking lot.

Smiley's Lexington BBQ. 917 Winston Rd., Lexington, NC 27295; (336) 248-4528; breakfast, lunch, and dinner Tues–Sun

Head west on US 64 about 3½ miles. Continue straight on US 64 as it merges into US 70. In ½ mile, take the NC 8 exit and head north (to the right) on NC 8 / Winston Road. Drive 2 blocks and Smiley's will be on your right on the corner of 10th and Winston Road.

I-85 exit 76 in North Carolina, 1-mile detour

Wink's King of Barbecue. 509 Faith Rd., Salisbury, NC 28146; (704) 637-2410; breakfast, lunch, and dinner Mon–Sat

Take exit 76 and turn left onto US 52 South. Drive ¼ mile and turn right onto Faith Road. Wink's will be on the right in ½ mile.

Richard's Bar-B-Que. 522 N. Main St., Salisbury, NC 28144; (704) 636-9561; breakfast, lunch, and dinner Mon–Sat

Take exit 76 and turn right on East Innes Street. Drive just under 1 mile and turn right onto North Main Street. Richard's will be on the left in ½ mile.

I-85 exit 51C in South Carolina, 7-mile detour

Henry's Smokehouse. 240 Wade Hampton Blvd., Greenville, SC 29607; (864) 232-7774; lunch daily and dinner Mon–Sat

Take exit 51C onto I-385 North toward downtown Greenville. Drive 6 miles until I-385 ends and becomes East North Street. In ¼ mile, turn right onto North Academy Street. Drive ¼ mile and turn right onto North Church Street. In just under 1 mile, bear right onto Wade Hampton Boulevard; Henry's Smokehouse will be on your right in 100 yards.

I-40 from North Carolina–Tennessee Border through Asheville, then West toward Raleigh-Durham

I-40 is a very promising barbecue route, at least once you get past the mountains, for it takes you along the top of the great Piedmont barbecue region. If you time it right, you can whet your appetite by sampling some excellent nouveau 'cue in Asheville, too.

I-40 exit 46B in North Carolina, 4-mile detour

12 Bones Smokehouse. 5 Riverside Dr., Asheville, NC 28801; (828) 253-4499; lunch only, Mon–Fri

Take exit 46B and merge onto I-240 East toward Asheville. Drive 3 miles and take exit 3B toward Westgate. Midway down the exit ramp, take a right on the Craven Connector, then take a hard left onto Hazel Mill Road. Drive to the bottom of the hill and take a left at the stop sign onto Craven Street. Drive ¼ mile on Craven Street, crossing the French Broad River, and turn right onto Riverside Drive. 12 Bones will be on the right in about ½ mile, where Riverside dead ends into Lyman Street.

I-40 exit 150 in North Carolina, 2-mile detour

Carolina Bar-B-Q of Statesville. 213 Salisbury Rd., Statesville, NC 28677; (704) 873-5585; lunch and dinner Mon–Sat

Take exit 150 and turn right onto Center Street. Drive 1½ miles and take a left on Broad Street. Drive ½ mile and take a right on Salisbury Road. Carolina Bar-B-Q is on your left at the end of the block.

I-40 exit 184 in North Carolina, 5-mile detour

Little Richard's. 4885 Country Club Rd., Winston-Salem, NC 27104; (336) 760-3457; lunch and dinner Mon–Sat

Take exit 184 and turn left onto Lewisville Clemmons Road. Drive ½ mile and turn right onto South Peace Haven Road. Drive 4 miles and turn right onto Country Club Road. Drive ⅓ mile; Little Richard's will be on your left.

I-40 exit 263 in North Carolina, 3-mile detour

Allen & Son Barbeque. 6203 Millhouse Rd., Chapel Hill, NC 27516; (919) 942-7576; lunch Tues–Sat, dinner Thurs–Sat

Take exit 263 and turn left onto New Hope Church Road. Drive ¾ mile and take a right on NC 86 South. Drive 2 miles, and Allen & Son will be on your right at the intersection with Millhouse Road.

I-40 exit 298B in North Carolina, 2-mile detour

The Pit. 328 W. Davie St. Raleigh, NC 27601; (919) 890-4500; lunch and dinner daily

Take exit 298B onto Saunders Street. In ¾ mile, bear right onto McDowell Street toward downtown. Drive 1 mile and take a left onto West Davie Street. Drive 2 blocks; The Pit is on the right.

I-40 from North Carolina–Tennessee Border through Asheville, Then I-26 Toward Columbia and I-95

If you're heading east on I-40 and take I-26 into South Carolina, you can sample a different flavor of mountain nouveau 'cue at Hubba Hubba Smokehouse, then make your way southeastward into the hotbed of mustard-based barbecue style in the Midlands.

I-26 exit 53 in North Carolina, 3-mile detour

Hubba Hubba Smokehouse. 2724 Greenville Hwy., Flat Rock, NC 28731; (828) 694-3551; lunch Mon–Sat, dinner Thurs–Sat

Take exit 53 and turn right onto Upward Road. Drive 2½ miles on Upward Road, which becomes North Highland Lake Road when you cross US 178. When North Highland Lake Road comes to a dead end at a traffic light, take a left onto Greenville Highway. Drive 1 mile, and Hubba Hubba Smokehouse will be on the left, just past the Wrinkled Egg gift shop.

I-26 exit 66 in South Carolina, 4-mile detour

Wise's Bar-B-Q House. 25548 US 76 Newberry, SC 29108; (803) 276-6699; lunch and dinner Fri and Sat

Take exit 66 and turn right onto Jalapa Road. Drive 2¼ miles and turn right onto Pete Harris Road. In ¼ mile, turn right onto US 76 West (Wilson Road). Drive 1¾ miles, and Wise Bar-B-Q House will be on your left.

I-26 exit 85 in South Carolina, 4-mile detour

Cannon's BBQ. 1903 Nursery Rd., Little Mountain, SC 29075; (803) 945-1080; lunch and dinner Thurs–Sat

Take exit 85 and turn right onto SC 202 toward Little Mountain. Drive 1¾ miles and turn left onto Main Street / US 76 East. Drive 1 mile on US 76; Cannon's BBQ will be on the right where Nursery Road forks off from the highway.

From here, as you head to Columbia, you can visit Hite's, Maurice's, and Dukes, as detailed in the I-77 to I-26 tour.

RECEIPES

In the Kitchen & Around the Pit: Recipes & Techniques

This chapter lays out the essential techniques and recipes for preparing a genuine Carolina-style barbecue feast. Of course, what constitute genuine barbecue varies greatly from one part of the Carolinas to another, so I've included versions of each of the essentials to capture particular barbecue regions.

The recipes presented here are pretty simple, and that's by design. Barbecue in the Carolinas tends to be a very straightforward food, but a lot of people writing recipes don't seem to be content with leaving things simple. They insist upon adding chopped garlic to Eastern North Carolina barbecue sauce and doctoring up hash with Worcestershire sauce and Kitchen Bouquet. I feel it's far better to stick to the fundamentals. Once you get them down you can begin to add your own twists and secret ingredients to create your own signature versions.

Cooking Butts & Shoulders

This section presents an indirect heat method of cooking barbecue, which is what most of the nouveau 'cue guys cooking on metal offset smokers do. It assumes you will be using one of the relatively inexpensive barrel-style combo grill/smokers with a side firebox, but you can cook shoulders quite well using banked coals in a kettle or barrel grill without a side box (see "Alternate Equipment" sidebar for a few tips). If you want to take it up a notch, you can cook shoulders or butts on an old-school cinder-block pit as outlined in the section on whole hog cookery later in this chapter. To my mind, though, if you're going through the trouble of building a pit and burning logs down to coals, you might as well go whole hog.

For those who are just learning to cook barbecue, starting off with a pork shoulder is a wise move. The shoulder is a fatty cut, so it's pretty forgiving when it comes to temperature. You have three options for the type of shoulder to buy. Whole shoulders, which generally weigh between 12 and 18 pounds, come from the front leg of a pig (versus the hams, which come from the back). They are often cut into two portions that are sold separately: the butt from the upper part of the shoulder (often called a Boston butt) and the so-called picnic shoulder, which is the lower part of the shoulder and usually includes the bone and skin from the lower leg. Competition barbecuers seem to favor butts over picnics, and you do get more yield per pound since there's less bone, skin, and connective tissue in the butt. But, I've generally found that I get better results with the picnic shoulders. Whichever cut you select, be sure to get it bone-in, which greatly improves the flavor.

Probably the hardest thing for a novice barbecuer to learn is how to maintain a constant temperature, but fortunately it's not rocket science. You just have to learn a few basic things: how to gauge when the fire is starting to cool and needs more wood, how much wood to add so that you keep the heat steady and don't spike the pit temperature to 500°F, and the right way to open and close whatever vents you have on your pit to bring in more oxygen or to restrict it. These are all things you learn with experience, and you just have to get a feel for the rhythm of the fire. When it comes to cooking shoulder, you don't need to overthink it. The odds are it will turn out pretty good even the first time you tackle it.

When Time Is Not on Your Side

Ideally, you'll cook your pork shoulder start to finish on the grill or pit. But, if you get a late start and it doesn't look like the barbecue is going to get to its final temperature before the guests arrive, there are a few tricks you can use to goose things along. The simplest thing to do is to bump the heat up to between 250°F and 270°F after the first 3 hours or so (you want to keep it right around that magic 225°F range before that). The pork won't have quite the character and texture as if you let it go fully low and slow the whole time, but it will still be pretty good.

Another option is a technique that's often called "the Texas crutch," and it's exactly the kind of trickery you would expect a bunch of beef eaters to pull. Remove the meat from the pit after about 3 hours of cooking, wrap it tightly in foil, and return it to the pit. The foil will prevent the moisture in the meat from evaporating, overcoming the thermodynamics that create the stall and helping you get to the finish line an hour or two faster.

If all else fails, you can remove the meat from the pit altogether, wrap it tightly in foil, and finish it in a 300°F oven. As long as it's gotten at least a good 6 hours on the pit, it will have great smoke flavor and the foil will keep it from drying out. Remember: You need an internal temperature of at least 170°F for good chopped or sliced barbecue, but if you are going to pull it you really need to get it up to 190°F.

Equipment

Large barrel-style grill with side firebox

Two 20-pound bags lump charcoal

Charcoal chimney

3 or 4 sheets of newspaper

Grill lighter or matches

Two 5-pound bags hickory chunks

Meat thermometer

Oven or instant-read digital thermometer (for the pit)

Clean pair of heavy work gloves

Tray

Aluminum foil

Metal or foil drip pan

Tongs or pair of forks (for pulling pork; optional)

Cloth towel for your hands

A word of advice when it comes to slow cooking pork shoulder: Allow yourself plenty of time. You're looking at a good 12 hours or more, and that means cooking overnight if you're planning on an afternoon gathering or starting before

---

A Word on Thermometers

If you've been barbecuing for decades, you probably use the palm of your hand to tell whether the pit is at the right temperature, and your eyes and nose to know when the meat is done. And you probably don't need to be reading this. For everyone else, an investment in two thermometers—one for the pit and one for the meat—will save lots of anguish and subpar barbecue.

A lot of cookers come with a little dial thermometer in the lid. These are notoriously inaccurate (the one on my side-box smoker is off by 50°F compared to a good digital probe thermometer). In part this is because they're cheaply made, but also they are measuring the temperature at the top of the cooking chamber, not down on the grill where the meat is. You're much better off using either an old-fashioned oven thermometer placed inside the cooking chamber next to the meat or a fancy digital probe thermometer that connects to an electronic display outside the pit. The latter has the advantage of letting you read the temperature without having to open the cooking chamber, which is something you generally want to avoid. Another option is to insert a standard instant-read digital thermometer through a hole in the side of the cooker right near the level of the grill that holds the meat. (Some pits come with holes predrilled in the right spot.)

To monitor the meat, a digital probe thermometer is invaluable, since when it comes to getting pulled pork right, cooking the meat to the proper temperature is key.

Alternate Equipment

Having a barrel cooker with a side firebox makes things a lot easier, since you don't have to lift the lid to the cooking chamber to add charcoal or wood. But you can barbecue a pork shoulder just fine in a large Weber-style kettle smoker. Simply bank your coals to one side of the grill and put the pork on the other. (Some cooks bank coals to either side and put the meat in the middle.) Place an aluminum-foil pan under the spot where you plan to place the meat so that it can catch the fat and other drippings and keep you from having flare-ups. It's a good idea to have a squirt bottle of water handy, too, to bat down any grease flares as they occur.

dawn if you're serving guests at dinnertime. The last thing you want is to take the meat off the pit before it hits the optimal temperature, since just 10°F can make all the difference in the texture of the final product. (There are a few tricks for speeding things up if you need to; see "A Word on Thermometers" sidebar.)

If you want to be really serious about things, you can use split oak or hickory wood instead of the lump charcoal and hickory chunks listed above, but I would still recommend having a bag of lump charcoal around for starting the fire. It's also nice to be able to toss on a couple of handfuls if your temperature dips and you want to get the fire going again quickly.

Before you get started with the pit, go ahead and pull whatever meat you're going to be cooking out of the refrigerator or cooler. You want it to start coming up to room temperature, which will reduce your overall cooking time.

Next, clean out your grill, removing all the old ash and excess drippings from previous adventures. Take a wide metal pan (I usually use one of the disposable varieties made from stiff aluminum foil), fill it with about an inch of water, and place it beneath the grates where you will put the meat. This is to catch the drippings from the meat as it cooks, and with a pork shoulder there will be quite a lot of those.

Light a load of charcoal in your chimney. (To do so, stuff three sheets of wadded newspapers in the bottom, fill the top with charcoal, and light the newspaper in several spots with a match or grill lighter.) Once charcoal has burned down to coals, pour the coals into the side firebox and toss on 3 or 4 hickory chunks. Open the vents all the way on the top of the grill and the side of the firebox. This maximizes the airflow and lets the fire burn hot until you get the cooking chamber up to temperature. I usually let it get up to at least 250°F, since it will cool off some when you open the lid to add the meat.

Ah, Where's the Rub?

Some people slather the pork shoulders with mustard or other condiments, and most hard-core barbecue guys have Byzantine rub recipes with 20 or more spices in them. But, if you talk to classic Carolina pitmasters who cook whole shoulders for a living, you'll find that most of them don't use any fancy rubs or spices. All they do is salt the meat and put it on the pits. Feel free to use a rub if you want to get all highfalutin (there are plenty of recipes in Texas barbecue cookbooks), but don't think a teaspoon of celery salt or a couple of tablespoons of paprika is going to make much of a difference in the flavor of your finished product: Smoke and time are the real flavorings here.

While the pit is heating, prepare the meat. Place the shoulders on a sheet tray or baking pan and sprinkle liberally with plain table salt on all sides.

Once the pit is up to temperature (around 250°F), open the lid and place the meat on the grate. Close the lid and monitor the temperature with your pit thermometer (see "A Word on Thermometers" sidebar). If it's dropped below 225°F, keep the vents open and add a few chunks of hickory if needed to bring the temperature back up. Once the fire gets back to 225°F, close the vents down to restrict oxygen. From here, you'll open those vents when you need more heat and close them when you need to cool it.

In fact, for the rest of the cooking, pretty much all you'll be doing is monitoring and maintaining that temperature. Don't open the lid to the cooking chamber unless you really need to: Each time you do, you'll lose 50°F or more of heat, and that will wreak havoc on keeping things "low and slow." The real art of barbecuing is learning how to maintain the steady, constant heat right in the 215°F to 235°F sweet spot, adding a little more charcoal and wood as needed to keep a good layer of embers and adjusting the vents on the top and side of the cooker.

Depending upon your cooker, even a small change in the vents can make a big difference in temperature. Start by opening each about a quarter of the way and give it a few minutes. If that doesn't move the thermometer enough, open them another quarter of the way. Be patient with the vents: The temperature of the cooker will rise or fall gradually with the adjustments in oxygen flow, and it can take several minutes before you see the effects of the adjustment. If your temperature drops sharply—down to, say, 175°F—open the vents wide and toss on a few lumps of charcoal and a few chunks of hickory to bring it back up.

Once the internal temperature of your pork gets up to around 155°F, you'll enter what many cooks call "the stall." This is an odd period when your meat holds at basically the same temperature or maybe just creeps up a few degrees for hours on end—often 6 hours or more. There's no need to worry: It's still cooking. As long as you hold your cooker at 225°F, everything will come out fine on the other end.

The stall is caused by evaporative cooling. As the temperature of the meat rises, the evaporation rate of its moisture increases until it reaches an equilibrium point where the cooling effect of evaporation balances out the heat input from the pit. It stays at that point until every bit of moisture is evaporated, and then the meat starts heating again. So check that meat thermometer regularly. As soon as you get past the stall, you've got just a couple of hours left.

It's essential that you get it all the way up to the right temperature for the way you plan on serving it. If you're going to chop or slice the pork, you need it to be at least 170°F to be done. For pulling pork (and, to my mind, if you are going to go through all this trouble it really is best served pulled), you'll need to get it all the way up to 190°F. Once it's gotten there, remove the meat from the grill (a clean pair of heavy work gloves is really handy for these steps), place it on a tray, and cover it with a tent of aluminum foil. Allow the meat to rest half an hour before cutting or pulling. To pull, use tongs, a pair of forks, or just your bare hands to pull the meat into long strands, discarding any excess fat or gristle. If you've invited guests over, you'll probably have plenty of volunteers to help with this final step. Try to keep them from eating more than they put on the serving platter.

Going Whole Hog

When it comes to Carolina barbecue, the pinnacle achievement is cooking a whole hog (or maybe two). When it comes to learning how, there really is no better way than to find someone who is already an experienced hog cooker and stay up overnight with them a couple of times helping to tend the pit. But, if you want to set out on your own, here are instructions for how to get it done. It follows the style developed by some of the masters of whole hog cookery in the Pee Dee region and, as such, is a little different than the way folks in other parts of the Carolinas (not to mention other parts of the country) might cook a whole hog. Any such instructions have to be a little bit vague, because cooking whole hog is as much an art as a science. After you've cooked a few, you start to pick up on the rhythm and feel of the process. In my experience, though, if you can just hold the pit at a good steady temperature—never letting it get too hot or drop too cool—your pig will turn out pretty darn well.

Be sure to allot yourself plenty of time. The pig will need to be on the pit a minimum of 12 hours, and you may want to allow 14 or more just to be sure. It's always easier to hold a pig at a warm temperature than to try to race one to the finish when you've got dozens of hungry guests waiting. Assembling the materials, building the pit, and acquiring and prepping the pig will take plenty of time, too. If you're starting from scratch, it can be a multiday project, plus at least a day to recover.

Part 1: Building the Pit

There are lots of ways you can go when you want to cook a whole hog. You can rent a metal cooker that is fired by liquid propane from companies specializing in such things. Or, if you want to dive right in, you can buy your own fancy wood-burning offset smoker like the kind sold by Lang BBQ Smokers down in Nahunta, Georgia. But, if you really want to do it right, you need to go old-school and construct your own impromptu pit. It won't cost but a few hundred dollars to do it, either. Here's how.

Materials

70 cinder blocks for a single-pig pit (standard 16 x 8 x 6 inches) or 90 for a
two-pigger, plus a few extra in case of breakage or for utility purpose

Pit Options

The pit design in this chapter is what you might call a semiclosed style of pit, and it emulates the ones used by legendary whole hog cooks like the Jones family of the Skylight Inn in Ayden, North Carolina, and Roosevelt and Rodney Scott of Scott's Bar-B-Que in Hemingway, South Carolina. There are, of course, many ways to construct a cinder-block barbecue pit. Here are a few options to the version outlined in this section:

Lower pit: Instead of a pit five blocks high, you can always make do with just four courses. This will bring the meat 6 inches closer to the coals and will change the circulation and cooking time, but you'll save a few bucks on materials.

Used expanded metal grating: Instead of a grate fashioned from rebar, you can shell out a little more for a big sheet of expanded metal grating cut to the exact size of the pit (96 x 64 inches for a one-pig pit, or 96 x 96 inches for a two-pigger). Instead of cutting notches in the cinder blocks, you use two pieces of angle iron cut to fit across the pit as support, lay the expanded metal grating atop the third course of blocks, and put the fourth course of blocks atop it to hold it in place (or between the second and third course of blocks if you are cooking on a four-block-high pit). This grating will allow you to use the pit for meats other than whole hog, too.

Open pit: To use even fewer cinder blocks and create a little more of a true open pit, build your structure just two cinder blocks high and place your metal grate or flat metal slats on top so the pig is essentially sitting at the top of the pit. You'll still want to cover the pig while it cooks, though, using either sheets of roofing metal or flattened cardboard boxes. A lot more heat is going to escape the pit during the cook, so you'll probably need more wood to keep it fired.

In the ground: If you want to go *really* old-school, dispense with the cinder blocks altogether and dig a trench in the ground about 4 feet wide, 2 feet deep, and as long as it needs to be to hold however many pigs you plan on cooking. In the old days, these literal pits weren't even covered with anything while the meat cooked.

Sand

Hacksaw (for cutting the rebar)

Rebar, about 55 feet for a single-pig pit and 70 for a two-pigger

One 32 x 24-inch piece of sheet metal or roofing panel

8-foot x 32-inch rib steel roof panels, 2 for a single-pig pit, 3 for a two-pigger

Drill

Wooden frames for roofing (optional)

Handles for roofing (optional)

Wire-mesh fencing, cut into pieces large enough to fully cover the pigs (about 5 x 2 feet), 2 pieces if cooking one pig, 4 pieces if cooking two

Choose the spot for your pit carefully, for the heat is going to kill the grass and leave you with a greasy patch of ground when you're done. You may want to line the bottom of your pit with a 2-inch layer of sand to make the cleanup easier, and make sure there's no brush and trees nearby that might catch fire from stray embers.

To create the pit, start by building a square enclosure out of the cinder blocks. How big you make the pit depends upon how many pigs you want to cook. If you're just cooking one, you'll need a pit that's five blocks long, two blocks wide, and five blocks high. For two pigs, it needs to be four blocks wide. (**Note:** You'll be overlapping the blocks, so the first course on a double pit will be five blocks by four blocks, the second will be four blocks by five blocks, etc.) Just stack the blocks one on top of another: No mortar or bracing is needed unless you want this to be a permanent installation.

As you lay out the first course of blocks, leave out two blocks on one side of the pit to create an opening. This will become the door you'll use to fire the pit with coals. On the second course, leave out one block directly above the two-block gap in the first course, and on the third course, fully block over the whole side. Go ahead and pour your sand into the frame at this point and spread it to an inch or two in depth.

Once you get the fourth course of blocks laid out, cut six notches in the inner edge of the cinder blocks along the long edge of the pit, each about 8 inches apart. The notches should be about 2 inches deep and wide enough to hold your rebar. If you're building a two-pig pit, cut two similar notches toward the center of the other walls, too, since you'll need to run two pieces of rebar lengthwise to support the grid. Using a hacksaw, cut the rebar in pieces long enough to stretch across the pit (this will be about 5 feet in length for a single-pig pit, 7½ feet for a double) and place each piece in the notches cut in the cinder blocks to create the grate that will hold the pig(s). Finish off the pit with one more course of cinder blocks.

Cut a piece of sheet metal a little larger than the opening, and use it as a door to cover the fire hole. You can hold it in place with two spare cinder blocks and slide the sheet to the left or right when you need to fire the pit.

Once your pit is constructed, place the sheets of metal roofing over the top and make sure they cover it completely. Drill a hole in the sheets about 6 inches in from each corner as well as one or two out toward the middle of the pit. You'll use these for checking the temperature with your instant-read thermometer. If you want to put in the effort, you can build a wooden frame and nail the roofing to it to allow the cover to be slid on and off in a single piece, or you could affix a handle in the middle of each sheet to allow them to be lifted from the pit more easily. But, it's simpler to just wear some heavy work gloves and slide the sheets off as necessary when you're cooking.

Part 2: Acquiring a Pig & Making the Mop Sauce

For cooking barbecue, what you need is a cleaned, butterflied whole hog with the skin on, the backbone split down the middle, and the spinal cord removed. This isn't exactly like picking up a gallon of milk and some sandwich bread. Most supermarkets carry Boston butts and sometimes even whole shoulders in their regular stock, but you're not going to be able to just waltz into your neighbor grocery store and pick up a whole hog. Some independent meat markets and full-service butchers can special order a whole hog for you with enough advance notice (allow two weeks to be safe). Most of the national grocery chains can't, since they buy only precut meat from their distributors. Here are a few retailers in the Carolinas who specialize in selling whole hogs for barbecue.

Larry's Super Market
2041 Milburnie Rd., Raleigh, NC 27610
(919) 834-0152
larryssupermarketraleigh.com

Marvin's Meats
5314 SC 162
Hollywood, SC 29449
(843) 889-2225

Nahunta Pork Center
200 Bertie Pierce Rd.
Pikeville, NC 27863
(919) 242-4735
nahuntapork.com

How big your pig needs to be depends on how many people you will be serving. A fully dressed pig, once cooked, will yield about 40 percent of its original weight in edible meat. So, if you buy a 70-pound pig, you can expect about 28 pounds of cooked pork once you pull or chop it; a 125-pound pig will yield 50 pounds, and so on. Few cooks will use anything smaller than 70 pounds or larger than 125, and one around 100 pounds is ideal. At that size, it yields plenty of meat (40 pounds) to feed a crowd but isn't too onerous for two people to lift and flip. You will need at least ½ pound of cooked barbecue per guest, or a pound per person if your friends are as hungry and carnivorous as mine. So, the rough math is that a 100-pound pig will serve between 40 and 80 people.

To prep the pig, remove the membrane from the inside of the rib cage and trim away any excess fat and other gristle-like material. Save a few big hunks of fat for later in the process (the belly fat is ideal), when you'll use them to polish the pig. If the butcher left the spinal cord inside the split backbone, be sure to remove it (use your fingers or a knife to do so). Put the pig in a large cooler and cover with unopened bags of ice, keeping it below 45°F until about an hour before cooking, when you'll want to remove it from ice and let it begin to come to room temperature.

You'll probably want to make your mop sauce in advance, too, to get that out of the way and allow the flavors to meld. This is whole hog cookery, so you should use a standard Pee Dee vinegar-and-pepper-based sauce (see recipe for Eastern North Carolina Vinegar Sauce), and you'll need lots of it—scale the recipe up to start with 2 gallons of vinegar and go from there. Put it in a large pot or clean food-grade bucket, cover it, and put it aside until the end of the cooking process.

Part 3: The Wood

For cooking a whole hog, use hardwoods native to the Carolinas, like oak, hickory, and pecan, split into firewood. Like any firewood, it shouldn't be green but needs to have dried for a few months. The amount you need will depend on the pig. For a 70 pounder, you'll need at least a third of a cord; for 125 pounds, you'll need at least half a cord. A cord is a stack that's 4 feet wide, 4 feet high, and 8 feet long. So, for a 125-pound pig with typically sized split logs, you'll need a pile consisting of two rows of neatly stacked wood that's 4 feet high and 4 feet long. (Yes, that's a lot of wood.) You won't need twice that for cooking two pigs, but you will need probably 50 percent more.

It's also a good idea to have a couple of big bags of lump charcoal on hand, too. They're useful if you run low on coals and need to make some more quickly.

Part 4: Other Things You'll Need

Large cooler for keeping the pig (1 per pig)
Bags of ice for keeping the pig cool (3 10-pound bags per pig)
Newspaper and kindling for starting the fire
2 bags lump charcoal
Long-handled shovel (a transfer shovel with a flat blade, not a pointed digging shovel)
Short-handled shovel
Instant-read thermometer
Roll of paper towels
Several pairs of heavy work gloves
2 long pairs of tongs
Large metal spoon
Squirt bottle of water
Fire extinguisher (just in case)
Salt and spices for the hog (optional)
New white cotton mop
Big pot or food-grade bucket for the sauce
Tray for serving
At least one friend (and preferably more) to assist with the heavy lifting and provide company
A cooler of beer

Part 5: Firing the Pit

About an hour before you want to start cooking, you need to get a fire started in a side pit and prepare the coals to fire the main pit. You can do this the same way you would start a campfire or your home wood fireplace using newspaper and kindling, though some old hands I've cooked with take a shortcut and set the wood ablaze with the sort of liquid propane torch that's used to burn weeds. However you start the fire, you need to get six to eight logs burning well and let them burn till they are reduced to coals. You can add in a couple of shovelfuls of charcoal, too, to help expedite the process. The important thing to remember is that what goes into your main pit are shovelfuls of glowing embers, not flaming logs.

Once you have a sufficient supply of coals, fire the pit by taking a long-handled shovel, filling it with coals, and carrying them to the pit. Insert the shovel into the opening at the bottom of the pit, sliding it until the blade is where you want to the coals to go, then dump them with a quick twist of the handle. To get things going, you'll want to put at least two shovelfuls in each of the corners of the pit and one shovelful along each of the side walls. Most Carolina whole-hog cookers keep their coals along the sides of the pits and not directly beneath the hogs for most of the cooking. You'll want to put coals directly beneath the pigs only when finishing them at the end and, perhaps, periodically during the cook beneath the shoulders and hams if they are cooking slow and need a little heat to move them along.

Leave the main pit covered, throw a couple more logs on your side fire pit to get them working, and check the main pit's temperature with your instant-read thermometer inserted through the holes in the cover. Once it's reading 250°F, it's time to put the pigs on.

Part 6: Loading the Pig

Place one of the pieces of wire fencing atop the rebar grate and then, with a friend to help you, lift the pig and lay it atop the wire, skin side up. (**Note:** That's skin side *up*. This part is very important.) In the Carolinas, whole-hog cooks don't do anything fancy with the meat once it hits the pit. When I talked to Samuel Jones of the Skylight Inn, he told me, "The only thing we do once we get them on the pit is sprinkle some water on the skin and salt it moderately. That helps draw the water out, and when we flip it, that helps it to parch up." Rodney Scott of Scott's Barbecue doesn't even bother with that. He just puts them on fresh and doesn't add anything in the way of seasoning until the very end.

Part 7: And Now You Wait

The key for the next 12 hours or more is patience and tending the pit. Keep a few logs burning in your side pit at any one time to ensure you have a steady supply of coals. Watch that instant read thermometer and make sure you keep the pit in the 225°–250°F range. When it starts to drop below that, add a shovelful of coals into each corner.

Most whole-hog cooks use some form of banking their coals; that is, they shovel embers into each corner of the pit (or in a line along the sides) so that the embers aren't directly beneath the pig but instead keep the pit heated while burning slowly to last through the night. If you need a little nap, you can bank a generous amount of coals in each corner, close the pit door, and catch a few hours of sleep. You want to keep the pit between 225°F and 250°F during the whole cook, and ideally keeping it down around 225°F for the first 2 hours. After a while, you'll probably get the hang of using your palm to feel when the temperature is right. You simply lay your palm on top of the sheet metal cover, not too far from the corner. You should be able to hold it there for a fraction of a second before the heat makes you yank it away. While you're getting the hang of it, though, use your thermometer (inserted through the holes drilled in the cover) to be sure you're on track.

Part 8: Polishing, Flipping, and Mopping

Once the pig has been going a good 10 hours or so, start checking its progress by pulling back the cover and inserting an instant-read thermometer into the thickest part of the shoulder and into the hams. Once the shoulder is getting close to 190°F and the hams 175°F, it's time to finish things off. If you're closing in on 12 hours and those parts aren't up to temperature yet, spread a few shovelfuls of coals directly under the shoulders and the hams; they're thicker than the rest of the pig and often need a little more heat to get them finished.

Before you flip the pig, it's time to polish him up and get him looking presentable. First, using damp paper towels, rub the skin all over to remove the ash and soot that has settled on it during cooking. Next, take a big piece of the belly fat that you reserved when preparing the pig the night before (you did remember to do that, right?) and rub it all over the skin, letting the fat melt and coat the skin in an oily sheen. Using more paper towels, buff the skin until it's shiny.

Now it's time to flip the pig. You'll need a helper to pull this off, you at one end of the pit and your helper at the other. Remove the cover from the pit and put it aside. The pig should already be resting on a sheet of wire mesh. Lay a second sheet of wire over the top of the pig. Both you and your helper should have heavy work gloves on for this process. With each hand, grip the ends of both the top and bottom sheets of wire and squeeze them together. Then, perhaps with a count of three to make sure you are in sync, grasp the wire tight, lift the hog up, twist it over to one side, and lay it right back down on the grate with the skin side downward toward the coals. Take a swig of beer to celebrate.

Polishing the pigs and preparing to flip.

Remember, that pig has been cooking on the first piece wire mesh (the one that was on the bottom and now is on top) for about half a day, and odds are the meat has stuck to it and cooked around it in places. Don't try to lift the wire off the pig—you'll just rip the meat out. Instead, with your tongs or fingers, push the meat downward between the square of wire to free it. Once you've freed all the pork, peel away the top piece of wire mesh and put it to the side. With your tongs or the end of a long metal spoon, prep the meat by breaking it into large chunks and creating openings in it so it's ready to receive the mopping sauce. Be very careful, though, that you don't pierce the skin beneath the meat. Doing so would release a shower of hot grease directly onto the fire below, which can cause an instant pit fire. (Remember: Always have that fire extinguisher handy.)

Season the meat by sprinkling it liberally with a mixture of table salt and whatever other spices or seasonings strike your fancy. (There are a few secret ingredients that South Carolina pitmasters use in their seasoning, but I've sworn not to reveal them.) Before continuing, scoop several shovelfuls of coals directly under the pigs—you want to get the heat up now so that you are crisping the skins. Get your clean mop and the pot or bucket of sauce you prepared earlier. Dip the mop in the sauce, then bring it over to the pig, and pat the mop all over the meat. Use a long set of tongs to break the meat up within the cavity of the hog to let the sauce work its way down into the meat, then dip and mop again. The heat from the extra coals in the pit should be radiating up through the skin now, and you want to bring the mop liquid inside the cavity of the pig to a simmer—you should see tiny bubbles actually appearing in the liquid. If it's not simmering, add several more shovelfuls of coals under the shoulders and the hams.

Once the pig is well mopped and the sauce is simmering, use your tongs to break up the meat and start pulling it first into chunks and then into long strands, removing the loose bones and any big pieces of fat or gristle as you go and mopping it with more sauce as needed to keep everything moist and

Rodney Scott and Jeff Allen remove a pig from the pit at the Charleston Brown Water Society's SC-TX Invitational, July 2014. JONATHAN BONCEK

dressed. Effectively, you are pulling and dressing the pork right inside the bowl formed by its skin, and you want to get the meat to the point where it's ready for guests to serve themselves straight from the pig.

For serving, there are two options. If you have a wooden or metal tray large enough to hold the pig, you can serve the whole pig to your guests directly. Put the tray on a table next to the pit, then with a helper lift the pig on its wire base straight out of the pit and slide it onto the tray. Then lift up one side of the wire and slide it out from under the pig, leaving your whole hog in the tray and ready to bear triumphantly to your guests.

Alternatively, you can use your tongs to pull the meat from the pig and load it into serving trays to your guests. It doesn't make for nearly as impressive an entry as bearing aloft a whole pig on a giant platter, but the barbecue will taste just as good.

How to Cook Beef Brisket

Don't. Buy a plane ticket to Texas.

EASTERN NORTH CAROLINA VINEGAR SAUCE

You don't really need a recipe to make Eastern North Carolina–style vinegar-and-pepper sauce. Just put a bunch of salt, black pepper, and red pepper in a jar with vinegar. It's simple to make and requires no cooking or refrigeration. Some people use cider vinegar in their sauce, and others like a touch of sweetness and mix in a quarter cup or so of brown sugar, but for me a more basic formula does just fine.
Yield: 32 servings (2 tablespoons each)

Combine all ingredients in a jar or jug. Shake to mix and let stand at least 4 hours before using (overnight is better).

1 quart distilled white vinegar
3 tablespoons salt
1 tablespoon red pepper flakes (or more to taste)
1 tablespoon black pepper

STAMEY'S DIP

Recipe courtesy Chip Stamey

The ingredients in the barbecue sauce used in the Piedmont—and that sauce is almost always called "dip"—are pretty much the same from one restaurant to another. They typically include vinegar and water as their base with a fair quantity of ketchup, then salt, black and red peppers, and a little sugar, too. What varies most from one variety to another is the proportions of those ingredients, especially the amount of ketchup used. Here is the version used at a legendary barbecue joint, Stamey's in Greensboro. **Yield: 50 servings (2 tablespoons each)**

Combine all ingredients in a large pot and bring to a boil, stirring occasionally. Serve warm with cooked barbecue.

1 quart water
1 cup ketchup (preferably Heinz)
1 cup apple cider vinegar
¼ cup plus 1 tablespoon granulated sugar
2 tablespoons salt
1 tablespoon ground black pepper
¾ teaspoon crushed red pepper flakes
Pinch of ground red pepper

MIDLANDS-STYLE MUSTARD-BASED BARBECUE SAUCE

The kings of the Midlands South Carolina mustard-based sauces, like the Bessinger family, are pretty tight-lipped about their recipes, which they consider a form of trade secret and refuse to share even with their own brothers. The real difference from one restaurant's version to the next seems to be primarily in the proportion of mustard, vinegar, and sugar in the concoction. This recipe, which has served me well for many years, strikes a nice balance between tanginess and sweetness, and it's a great accompaniment for pulled pork. **Yield: 12 servings (2 ounces each)**

1 cup prepared yellow
   mustard
¼ cup cider vinegar
¼ cup honey
¼ cup light brown sugar
Dash of ground red cayenne
   pepper
Black pepper to taste
Salt to taste

Combine mustard, vinegar, honey, and brown sugar in a saucepan. Cook over medium heat just long enough for the honey and brown sugar to dissolve and mixture to bubble and simmer. Stir in cayenne, black pepper, and salt. Remove from heat and allow to cool to room temperature. Pour into bottle or plastic container and refrigerate before using.

Pick Up a Bottle: Commercial Barbecue Sauces

These days, it's pretty easy for fans of Carolina barbecue to get their hands on their favorite sauce. Plenty of barbecue pitmasters now bottle and sell theirs at their restaurants and market theirs through local retailers and specialty shops, too. An increasing number are starting to make deals with the big grocery chains and retailers like Wal-Mart to put the bottles on shelves throughout the Carolinas and even outside the two states. Here's a roundup of just a few of the traditional styles of Carolina barbecue sauce that you can now buy in stores.

Eastern North Carolina / Pee Dee Sauce
Carolina Treet (Wilmington)
George's Original Barbecue Sauce (Nashville, NC)
Scott's Carolina Barbecue Sauce (Goldsboro)
Wells Hog Heaven BBQ Sauce (Burgaw)

Piedmont-Style Vinegar-and-Tomato Sauce
Sam Dillard's Barbecue Sauce (Durham)

Midlands-Style Mustard-Based Sauce
Barry's Soon-to-Be-Famous South Carolina Style Barbeque Sauce (North Charleston)
Bear Branch Barbecue Sauce (Springdale)
Big T's Barbecue Sauce (Gadsden/Columbia)
Johnny Harris Carolina Style Bar-B-Cue Sauce (Savannah, Georgia)
Maurice's Southern Gold BBQ Sauce (Columbia)
Melvin's Original "1933" Golden Secret (Charleston)
Shealy's Bar-B-Q Sauce (Leesville)
Sticky Fingers Smokehouse Carolina Classic (Charleston)
Thomas Bessinger's Spicy Golden Recipe Bar-Be-Que Sauce (Charleston)
Wise's BBQ Sauce (Newberry)

Upstate South Carolina–Style Heavy Tomato Sauce
Dad's Recipe (Greenville)
Rick Fowler's Hogback Mountain Bar-B-Q Sauce (Inman)

BRUNSWICK STEW

It's pretty safe to say that there's no single standard Brunswick stew recipe that's used in North Carolina. Each cook varies theirs in one way or another, from the meats used—chicken, pork, and sometimes even beef or game—to the vegetables, which typically include onions, potatoes, corn, and limas, and also may incorporate green peas, carrots, green beans, and just about anything else from the vegetable garden (or from the canned veggie aisle of the supermarket). In the Carolinas, at least, Brunswick stew is generally pretty heavy on the tomato, ranging from a generous number of chunks of tomato incorporated into the stew to a full tomato soup-like base.

This version is sort of a middle ground that captures most common elements of North Carolina Brunswick stew. I am partial to slow-cooked and well-blended Brunswick stew, since the dish descends from a long line of outdoor stews that are cooked until the ingredients break down and merge together. If you prefer a stew with more distinct chunks of chicken, potatoes, and limas, hold off adding them until the last 30 minutes of cooking. **Yield: 8 servings**

2 quarts water

1 whole chicken, about 3 pounds, cut into pieces

4 cups fresh tomatoes, peeled and diced (or one 28-ounce can whole tomatoes, diced, with juice reserved)

1 large onion, diced

1 pound potatoes, peeled and diced

1 pound fresh lima beans (or frozen if out of season)

6 ears fresh corn, kernels sliced from the cob (or 1 pound frozen corn kernels if out of season)

4 tablespoons (½ stick) unsalted butter

2 tablespoons sugar

1 tablespoon salt

Ground black pepper to taste

Hot sauce to taste

In a large stew pot or dutch oven, bring water to a boil, add chicken, and adjust heat until it is slowly simmering. Stew chicken uncovered for 1 hour. Remove chicken from pot and set aside to cool. Strain broth from pot into a large bowl and reserve.

Return 3 cups of reserved broth to pot. Add tomatoes and onions and bring to a boil. Lower heat to a simmer and cook 30 minutes. While the broth is simmering, remove the chicken meat from the bones, discarding the skin, and pull it into shreds with your fingers. Put the shredded chicken back in the pot along with the potatoes and lima beans and cook for 2 hours, stirring regularly.

Add the remaining ingredients and cook another 30 minutes. Adjust seasoning to taste and serve.

HASH

South Carolina hash is pretty basic stuff: Meat slowly simmered in a broth, then chopped or pulled, and added back to the broth along with fillers and seasoning. The original way to make it is in a cast-iron pot over a real wood fire. A lot of recipes online and in cookbooks call for crazy things like corn and carrots in hash, but you'll never see such things in the hash on the steam table at a Midlands South Carolina barbecue joint. This version is inspired by the mustard-laced hash served in Lexington County. If you want to make more of an Orangeburg County–style red hash, use ketchup instead of the mustard. **Yield: 32 servings**

Cut the meat into 2- to 3-inch cubes. Put water, meat, onions, and salt in a large pot and bring to a boil over high heat. Reduce heat until liquid is just simmering. Cook for 4 hours, stirring regularly and adding water as necessary if the level drops.

After 4 hours, remove pot from the heat. Strain the meat and onions from the liquid, pouring the liquid into another container to reserve it for later. Allow meat to cool on a cutting board or sheet pan. Wash the pot, pour the strained, reserved liquid into it, and put in refrigerator to cool while you pull the meat.

Once meat is cool enough to handle, remove all bones, gristle, and fat and pull meat into shreds by hand (or, if you want to take the easy way out, run it through a food grinder).

Remove pot with reserved liquid from the refrigerator and skim away any congealed fat from the surface. Return pot with reserved liquid to stove. Put the shredded meat and onions back into the pot, then add the mustard, black pepper, and, if you choose to use them, the potatoes. Bring the pot to a boil, then reduce heat to a simmer. Cook for another 6 hours or as long as needed to get the texture right. Don't add any more water during this stage: You're reducing the mixture down to a thick stew. The meat should be broken down to fine, tender shreds, and the whole mixture should be thick and soupy. Adjust salt to taste.

To serve, scoop over a bed of cooked white rice.

A note on potatoes and other ingredients: The recipe presented here is a minimalist one meant to provide a solid foundation, so feel free to experiment and add your own spices or other secret ingredients. Many hash makers include potatoes in their recipes, which add a little extra body and give a smoother texture to the finished stew. But don't go crazy and start adding corn and limas and stuff like that. That's getting into Brunswick stew territory.

3 pounds pork shoulder / Boston butt

3 pounds chuck beef roast

1½ gallons water

1½ pounds yellow onions (about 3 medium-size onions), peeled and quartered

1 tablespoon salt

½ cup yellow mustard

1 tablespoon black pepper

1 pound potatoes, peeled and diced (optional; see note below)

Cooked white rice for serving

The hash pot at Jackie Hite's Bar-B-Q, Leesville, SC.
DENNY CULBERT

Corn bread, corn pone, corn muffins, corn sticks, hush puppies: You'll find at least one of these as a side item in most barbecue restaurants across the Carolinas. At some restaurants, you can even find two or three of them sharing the same menu. But what's the difference among them?

First, let's start with what they have in common. All are quick breads made with a cornmeal batter. A quick bread is simply any bread that is leavened with something other than yeast, and in the South that leavening agent is typically baking soda and/or baking powder. For centuries, ground cornmeal was a staple of the diet in most of the Carolinas; in the Lowcountry of South Carolina, rice was the staple grain, but cornmeal was still used quite regularly.

Though some folks use the term *corn pone* to refer to corn bread, that's not strictly accurate. Corn pone was the original form of bread made from ground maize, and in the 18th century it was a simple batter made from ground cornmeal, flour, salt, and water, and cooked in a cast-iron skillet or dutch oven placed in the coals of a fire.

CORN STICKS

To make corn sticks, you'll need a well-seasoned corn stick pan. That's a cast-iron pan with six or seven long impressions in it. Some are shaped like ears of corn, which are cute, but one with long rectangular indentations will make your corn sticks look more like the ones found in most of Eastern North Carolina. **Yield: 14 sticks**

2 cups cornmeal

1 teaspoon sugar

2 teaspoons baking powder

½ teaspoon salt

1 large egg

1 cup milk

1 tablespoon melted lard or
    unsalted butter

Put two empty well-seasoned corn stick pans in a cold oven and preheat to 450°F while you prepare the batter. In a mixing bowl, combine cornmeal, sugar, baking powder, and salt. Beat the egg in a separate bowl and combine it with the milk. Pour egg and milk into mixing bowl and stir well. Add in the melted lard or butter and stir it in. Remove the hot corn stick pans from the oven and pour the batter into each indentation. Return pans to oven and bake for 15–20 minutes until the corn sticks are golden brown. Remove from oven and invert over a cooling rack to dump sticks from the pans. If they stick (which they shouldn't if your pans are properly seasoned), use the blade of a butter knife to gently pry them free.

GRANDMOTHER MOSS'S CORN BREAD

This recipe is my paternal grandmother's, which she wrote down and gave to my mother not long after she and my father got married. My mother, in turn, wrote it down for me (on a 3 x 5-inch index card) when I got interested in cooking in my early 20s. It still holds up, and you'll see that I come from a family that's firmly in the corn-bread-shouldn't-have-sugar-in-it camp.

For the bread to turn out properly, you need to cook it in a cast-iron skillet. I have an 8-inch one that's just the right size for making corn bread for a family meal (the recipe here is for an 8-inch pan), but I use a 10½-inch skillet when making for a larger crowd (double the recipe when using the larger skillet). You can make this same recipe in a regular glass or metal baking pan, but you will miss out on the very best feature of corn bread: that crisp, firm quarter inch of dark-brown crust that's created from the heat of the iron pan. **Yield: 8 servings**

To begin, place an empty 8-inch cast-iron skillet in a cold oven. Turn the heat to 400°F and allow the oven to preheat with the skillet inside while you mix the batter.

Put all the dry ingredients in a mixing bowl and stir together. Crack the egg into a separate container (I use a large glass measuring cup) and beat it with a fork. Add the buttermilk and the vegetable oil to the container with the egg and stir to blend. Pour the liquid into the mixing bowl with the dry ingredients and stir until the liquid is mixed in and of a smooth consistency, but don't over mix it. If you are using any optional enhancements (see below) stir them into the batter now, too.

Once the oven is heated and the iron pan is good and smoking hot, move it from the oven to the stovetop (you'll need a good thick oven-mitt or kitchen towel to do so). Toss the butter in the pan and stir it around with a spoon till it's totally melted and coating the pan. This will both flavor the corn-bread crust and help it crisp up and not stick to the pan. Pour the batter into the skillet, return the skillet to the oven, and bake for 25 minutes or until the top is golden brown.

Some folks find getting the finished corn bread out of the skillet to be tricky, but it shouldn't be. The key is to not let it cool in the pan. Put a dinner plate on the counter, remove the skillet from the oven (again using a thick oven mitt), and invert it over the plate. If your skillet is well seasoned, the corn bread should drop right out onto the plate and you're done. If you turn the skillet upside down and the corn bread doesn't move, simply put the pan down on the stovetop, get a butter knife, and run it around the inside of the pan to loosen the crust from sides of the pan. Then invert it over the pan again and it should pop right out. Once it's on the dinner plate, let it cool at least 10 minutes before serving.

1 cup stone-ground cornmeal
½ teaspoon baking soda
1 teaspoon baking powder
½ teaspoon salt
1 egg
1 cup buttermilk
3 tablespoons vegetable oil
1 tablespoon unsalted butter

Note on potential enhancements: I often augment my grandmother's recipe with ¼ cup chopped onions and/or about 12 pickled jalapeño rings diced small. I think they add extra moistness and flavor to the bread, and lest you're worried about the heat factor, as long as you use the pickled variety from a jar and chop them finely, the jalapeños don't make things too spicy (using chopped fresh jalapeños is a different story).

HUSH PUPPIES

Yield: 8 servings (about 32 hush puppies)

2 cups cornmeal

1 cup flour

2 tablespoons sugar

1 tablespoon salt

4 teaspoons baking powder

2 eggs

1 cup buttermilk

Oil for frying

Mix cornmeal, flour, sugar, salt, and baking powder in a large mixing bowl. In a separate bowl or measuring cup, beat eggs, then add buttermilk and stir to combine. Pour liquid into mixing bowl with dry ingredients and stir well.

Put 2 inches of oil in a dutch oven. Heat over medium high heat to 375°F (use a deep-fry thermometer to check). Using two spoons, scoop out a heaping dollop of batter with the first spoon and use the back of the second spoon to push it into the hot oil. Repeat until the hush puppies fill the bottom of the dutch oven, leaving generous room between each. Fry till golden brown (1–2 minutes), then remove from the hot oil with tongs or a strainer and place on paper towels to drain. Repeat process till all the batter is fried.

Note: If you prefer more uniformly shaped hush puppies, put the batter into a frosting bag and pipe it in 2- to 3-inch long cylinders into the oil.

You'll find potato salad in lots of barbecue restaurants, especially those in South Carolina with buffets, but there's really no predominant type or style. Boiled potatoes dressed with mayonnaise are the foundation, but from there everyone puts in different ingredients. Here are two varieties. The first one is a standard, middle-of-the-road potato salad like you'll find in the Midlands of South Carolina, while the second is a funky version goosed up with sour cream and bacon.

STANDARD POTATO SALAD

Yield: 8 servings

Bring pot of salted water to a boil. Cut potatoes into 1-inch chunks. Once water is boiling, add potatoes to pot and lower heat to medium high. Cook 20 minutes or until potatoes are tender. Strain potatoes and set aside to cool.

In a large mixing bowl, combine onion, mayonnaise, vinegar, mustard, and salt. Add potatoes and eggs and toss lightly till they are well coated. Put potato salad in a storage container and refrigerate till fully chilled, at least 6 hours.

Note: People are very particular about whether they like crunchy elements like celery or green pepper in their potato salad. If you like the crunchy stuff, chop 2 stalks of celery and/or 1 bell pepper and stir them in alongside the onion.

2 pounds medium potatoes
⅓ cup chopped onion
1¼ cups mayonnaise (people in the Carolinas tend to be partial to Duke's, which has no sugar and was first launched to market in Greenville, South Carolina)
1 tablespoon white vinegar
2 teaspoons yellow mustard
1 teaspoon salt
6 hard-boiled eggs, peeled and chopped

POTATO SALAD WITH BACON & SOUR CREAM

Yield: 8 servings

1 strip good smoky bacon
Salt to taste
2 pounds red potatoes
⅓ cup mayonnaise
⅓ cup sour cream
2 teaspoons Dijon mustard
1 teaspoon vinegar
Pepper to taste
1 tablespoon chopped parsley

Cut bacon into ½-inch squares. Add to cold frying pan and put on stove. Turn heat to medium and cook until bacon is brown and crispy. Remove bacon from pan and allow to cool on paper towels.

Bring pot of salted water to a boil. Cut potatoes into 1-inch chunks. Once water is boiling, add potatoes to pot and lower heat to medium high. Cook 20 minutes or until potatoes are tender. Strain potatoes set aside to cool.

In a mixing bowl, combine mayonnaise, sour cream, mustard, and vinegar. Stir in bacon and season with salt and pepper to taste. Once potatoes are cool enough to handle, add them to the mixing bowl with the dressing and the chopped fresh parsley and toss lightly till they are well coated. Put potato salad in a storage container and refrigerate till fully chilled, at least 6 hours.

Folks elsewhere may call it by its full name, coleslaw (which is derived from the Dutch koolsla), but in the Carolinas we tend to just call it "slaw," and it's a side item that's found almost universally in barbecue restaurants. Cabbage is plentiful and inexpensive in the Carolinas, and when it's shredded and dressed with a generous amount of vinegar, it creates a side dish that isn't very perishable—an important feature in the early days of restaurants. Plus, the crunch of coleslaw and the tanginess of its dressing offer a pleasing contrast to a bite of tender, smoky barbecue, especially when the two are piled on a hamburger bun to make a barbecue sandwich.

There are endless variants of slaw to be found in the Carolinas. In the Piedmont of North Carolina, "red" or "barbecue slaw" is predominant; it's given its distinctive color, like the region's barbecue sauce, by a dose of ketchup added to the dressing. In the eastern part of the state, slaw is usually dressed with mayonnaise, and in many places it gets a yellow tinge, too, from prepared mustard. In South Carolina, the recipes vary a lot more, but you'll never find ketchup or tomato in it. A cool mayonnaise base is the norm, and lots of places add shreds of carrot and even purple cabbage for a little color.

EASTERN-STYLE WHITE SLAW

Yield: 16 servings

Combine cabbage and onion in a large bowl. In a separate bowl, stir together mayonnaise, sugar, vinegar, celery seed, and salt. Pour mayonnaise over cabbage in large bowl and toss lightly until it is well dressed. Refrigerate several hours before serving.

1 head cabbage, finely shredded

1 medium onion, peeled and diced

1 cup mayonnaise

2 tablespoons sugar

2 tablespoons vinegar

1 teaspoon celery seed

1 teaspoon salt

DENNY CULBERT

STAMEY'S BARBECUE SLAW

This recipe was provided by Chip Stamey of Stamey's in Greensboro, and it's a canonical example of the Piedmont style barbecue slaw (aka "red slaw"). Stamey's recipe starts with eight heads of cabbage, which is fine if you are expecting a big crowd, but I've altered the proportions to use a single head of cabbage, which produces almost 2 quarts of slaw. **Yield: 16 servings**

1 head cabbage, coarsely chopped
⅓ cup sugar
1 tablespoon salt
⅔ teaspoon ground black pepper
Dash of ground red pepper
⅔ cup ketchup
2 tablespoons apple cider vinegar

Mix together cabbage, sugar, salt, and black and red peppers. Add the ketchup and vinegar and stir well. Refrigerate at least 1 hour before serving.

Glossary: Carolina Barbecue Terms

Baby back ribs: A term for the cut of ribs that connect to a pig's spine beneath the loin muscle. The leanest and most tender of the ribs, they're called "baby back" because they are shorter than spare ribs, and they taper from 6 inches long on one end of the rack to just 3 inches on the other.

Banking: The technique of moving hot coals to the sides of a barbecue pit, which produces a low, long-lasting heat and will allow a pig to cook slowly, unattended, overnight. In the morning, the pitmaster will spread the coals back out and finish the pig at higher heat.

Barbecue: When used alone as a noun, Carolinians are referring to one thing and one thing only: pork that has been slow cooked over wood coals and then pulled, chopped, or sliced for serving. You can ask for "barbecue chicken" or "barbecue brisket," meaning chicken or brisket prepared in the style of barbecue, but without any modifiers attached, the word *barbecue* means pork in the Carolinas.

Barbecue salad: Dan Levine (aka Porky Le Swine of the BBQ Jew website) calls the Piedmont North Carolina barbecue salad "a strange creature that inhabits this part of the state." The ingredients vary from restaurant to restaurant, but it's usually your garden variety salad—lettuce, tomato, cucumbers, perhaps some cheese or onion—topped by a generous portion of chopped pork barbecue. Ranch appears to be the dressing most Piedmonters choose to top their barbecue salads.

Barbecue slaw: Another term for red slaw (see below).

Bark: The bits of outer meat that are exposed to the most heat and smoke. Another name for outside brown (see below).

Blocked: Another term for coarse chopped barbecue (see below).

Cabbage collards: An heirloom variety of collard greens found almost exclusively in Eastern North Carolina. Cabbage collards are a greenish yellow rather than dark green in color, and they are more tender than regular collards. You can find this unusual variant in barbecue restaurants like Bum's and the Skylight Inn in Ayden, the heart of cabbage collard country.

Coarse chopped: One of the three standard way you can order your barbecue in the Piedmont region of North Carolina (chopped and sliced being the other two). Rather than minced into fine bits like regular chopped pork, the coarse chopped version is cut into irregular, inch-long chunks.

Coleslaw: What you're trying to say is "slaw" (see below).

Corn sticks: Sort of a cross between corn bread and hush puppies (see below), corn sticks are long fingers of bread made from a cornmeal batter that are baked in a pan and, in many cases, also deep fried to give them a crisp exterior. They're found almost exclusively in Eastern North Carolina.

Cracklings: Small cooked pieces of fat and meat leftover after lard has been rendered out of pork, often eaten by themselves or incorporated into corn bread. Some folks use the term *cracklings* when they really mean rinds or skins (see below), but technically cracklings are made as part of lard rendering and not barbecuing.

Dip: At one Piedmont North Carolina joint, when I asked for some extra sauce on the side, my waitress replied, "Do you mean *dip*?" Don't make the same mistake when you're visiting the Piedmont.

Dry rub: A blend of salt, sugar, and spices shaken or spread on the surface of cuts of meats before they are put on the pit. Traditionally, Carolina pitmasters have seasoned their meats with just salt, but more complex spice blends are starting to become more common, especially in nouveau 'cue (see below) joints.

Hash: The classic Midlands South Carolina barbecue stew.

Hush puppies: Cornmeal batter deep-fried in hot oil till crisp and golden brown on the outside. The shape of a hush puppy is determined largely by how its batter is portioned and introduced to the oil. Some do it the old-fashioned way, scooping up a dollop of batter in a spoon or on a spatula and using another spoon or spatula to scrape the batter into the oil. Others use mechanical devices that carve off uniformly sized dollops, creating hush puppies that are perfectly spherical or oblong in shape. At Fuzzy's in Madison, they squeeze out the batter from a pastry bag, creating long, squiggly pups that look almost like funnel cake.

Inside white: Sometimes just "white," this is the leaner, softer white meat from the inner portion of a shoulder or ham which has been less transformed by direct heat and smoke. It's the opposite of outside brown (see below).

Meat 'n' three: A restaurant whose menu offers your choice of meat along with three vegetables on the side. (And, yes, in the Carolinas, macaroni and cheese is classified as a vegetable.) These days, it's becoming more common for the side selection to be limited to just two items, but meat 'n' two hasn't really taken off as a term of art.

Nouveau 'cue: My own term (though I'm hoping it spreads into popular usage) for newer barbecue joints whose pitmasters take their craft seriously but aren't particularly bound by traditional styles and conventions. They put fruit and habaneros in their sauces, whip up elaborate fine-dining sides, and serve their sandwiches on artisan-baked buns, but it can still be good eating nonetheless.

Outside brown: Sometimes just "brown," this is what folks in the Piedmont region call the outer bits of pork, turned brown and crisp from cooking. Many people prefer getting a little outside brown mixed into their barbecue because it adds a pleasantly chewy texture and extra smoky flavor to the meat, while some will even ask for an entire plate of outside brown. (Also see "Outside Brown" sidebar, Shoulders & Light Red Sauce chapter.)

Pig pickin': A rather recent term for a party or event where a barbecued pig is served whole and the guests pull the meat directly from the pig, generally using tongs (but as the night goes on, things can get more primitive).

Pitmaster: A pitmaster is a relatively new term for the person who manages the pits at a barbecue restaurant or a barbecue event; in the old days, they were just called "barbecue cooks" or "barbecue men." Implied in the name is a mastery of the art of cooking barbecue, and the pitmaster at a restaurant may be the owner or may just be an experienced employee who oversees the cooking on a daily basis.

Plate: In the Piedmont of North Carolina, a "plate" gives you the same contents as a tray (see below)—that is, pork, slaw, and hush puppies—plus french fries, too.

Pulled pork: Meat pulled from cooked pork shoulder or a whole hog by hand or tongs into long, thick shreds.

Red slaw: Sometime called "barbecue slaw," it's the style of coleslaw most typically found in the Piedmont of North Carolina. It's called red slaw because it's dressed either with ketchup or with the same reddish vinegar-and-tomato sauce that goes on the chopped pork.

Rinds: Often used interchangeably with "skins" (see below).

Rolls: On a lot of Piedmont, North Carolina, barbecue menus, you're offered a choice of hush puppies (see above) or rolls with your tray or plate. If you order rolls expecting a couple of Parker House–style dinner rolls, you might be disappointed: At most places, you'll get a hamburger bun that's been warmed or steamed.

Slaw: In the rest of the country, coleslaw is a salad of chopped or minced cabbage mixed with a creamy or tangy dressing and often shreds of carrot and bits of onion, too. In most of the Carolinas, it's just called "slaw." In the Piedmont it's often called "red slaw" (see above) and is made with a lot of vinegar and a touch of ketchup or barbecue sauce, while in Eastern North Carolina you often find it shaded bright yellow from mustard.

Skins: The skin of a whole hog, which is removed after barbecuing, cut into pieces, and either roasted or deep-fried until crisp. They make a delightful snack. Often called "rinds" and sometimes "cracklings" (see above).

Sliced pork: Pork from the ham or shoulder sliced about ¼ inch thick.

Spare ribs: Spare ribs are cut from the belly side of the rib cage, below the baby back ribs (see above), which connect to the spine. They are thinner and have more fat and connective tissue than baby backs, but cooked properly can have a better, meatier flavor.

St. Louis–cut ribs: A way of trimming a rack of spare ribs, removing the tips of the ribs along with the cartilage to create uniform-length ribs with less gristle than a full rack of spare ribs.

String hash: Most hash these days is made with a mechanical grinder, which chops the meat into tiny, uniform bits. Old-style string hash, like the kind served at Jackie Hite's in Leesville, South Carolina, is pulled by hand into long, thin strands, giving the finished stew a much different texture.

Tea: Like the term *barbecue* itself (see above), there are a lot of details that are merely implied in the word *tea* when you utter it in a Carolina barbecue house. You can order "unsweet tea" or "hot tea," and some places may even be able to accommodate such requests. But, if you simply ask for "tea," it's going to be served in a cup over ice and it's going to be tooth-rattlingly sweet.

Tray: In the Piedmont of North Carolina, a tray is typically a generous helping of chopped pork next to a pile of red slaw (see above) in a small cardboard tray. In most places, you get a basket of hush puppies or rolls (see above) alongside.

Appendix: Websites & Blogs

BBQ Jew

bbqjew.com

A website created by Porky LeSwine and the Rib Rabbi, two Jewish North Carolinians who love barbecue (no, they don't keep kosher). It offers restaurant reviews, news, and plenty of opinions and rants and raves on anything and everything related to North Carolina barbecue.

Discover South Carolina BBQ

South Carolina Department of Parks, Recreation & Tourism

bbq.discoversouthcarolina.com

A collection of web resources designed to promote South Carolina barbecue and attract visitors to the state. The site presents videos and articles outlining all aspects of barbecue in the Palmetto State plus the South Carolina BBQ Trail, a comprehensive map to virtually every barbecue restaurant in the state.

North Carolina Barbecue Society

ncbbqsociety.com

In addition to society news and information, this website presents recipes, a schedule of barbecue competitions, and the NCBS Historic Barbecue Trail, an interactive map and guide to 24 of North Carolina's classic wood-burning barbecue restaurants.

South Carolina Barbeque Association

scbarbeque.com

The website of the South Carolina Barbecue Association offers rules, schedules, and other information for barbecue competitions sanctioned by the association, along with a guide to the top 100 barbecue restaurants in the Palmetto State.

Southern Barbecue Trail

Southern Foodways Alliance

southernfoodways.org/oral-history/southern-bbq-trail

A program of the Southern Foodways Alliance, this site provides a splendid online oral history archive that includes two dozen in-depth interviews with barbecue restaurateurs and cooks in North and South Carolina.

Bibliography

Books

Early, Jim. *The Best Tar Heel Barbecue: Manteo to Murphy*. Winston-Salem, NC: The Best Tar Heel Barbecue Manteo to Murphy, Inc., 2002.

Elie, Lolis Eric. *Smokestack Lightning: Adventures in the Heart of Barbecue Country*. New York: Farrar, Straus and Giroux, 1996.

Garner, Bob. *North Carolina Barbecue: Flavored by Time*. Winston-Salem, NC: John F. Blair, 1996.

——. *Bob Garner's Guide to North Carolina Barbecue*. Winston-Salem, NC: John F. Blair, 2002.

High, Lake E. *A History of South Carolina Barbeque*. Charleston, SC: History Press, 2013.

Moss, Robert F. *Barbecue: the History of an American Institution*. Tuscaloosa: University of Alabama Press, 2010.

Reed, John Shelton, and Dale Volberg Reed. *Holy Smoke: The Big Book of North Carolina Barbecue*. With contributions by William McKinney. Chapel Hill: University of North Carolina Press, 2008.

Stogner, Johnny. *Barbecue, Lexington Style*. Lexington, NC: Stogner Publishing, 1996.

Wall, Allie Patricia, and Ron L. Layne. *Hog Heaven: A Guide to South Carolina Barbecue*. Orangeburg, SC: Sandlapper, 1979.

Articles

Hitt, Jack Hitt. "A Confederacy of Sauces." *New York Times Magazine*, August 26, 2001.

Taylor, Saddler. "By the Light of the Moon: The Hash Pot Runneth Over." In *Corn Bread Nation 2: The United States of Barbecue*, edited by Lolis Eric Elie, 104–7. Chapel Hill: University of North Carolina Press, 2004.

Thompson, Michael D. "'Everything but the Squeal': Pork as Culture in Eastern North Carolina." *North Carolina Historical Review* 82, no. 2 (2005): 464–98.

Films & Documentaries

Barbecue Is a Noun. Produced and directed by Hawes Bostic and Austin McKenna. 2005. Post-South Productions, film.

Carolina Hash. Produced and directed by Stan Woodward. 2008. Woodward Studio, DVD.

Cut. Chop. Cook. Produced and directed by Joe York. 2010. Available online at southernfoodways.org/film/cut-chop-cook.

Index